TUMULT!

TUMULT!

The Incredible Life and Music of Tina Turner

Donald Brackett

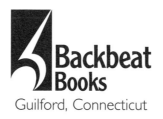

Backbeat
Books

Guilford, Connecticut

Published by Backbeat Books
An imprint of The Rowman & Littlefield Publishing Group, Inc.
4501 Forbes Blvd., Ste. 200
Lanham, MD 20706
www.rowman.com

Distributed by NATIONAL BOOK NETWORK

British Library Cataloguing in Publication Information available

Library of Congress Cataloging-in-Publication Data
Names: Brackett, Donald, 1951- author.
Title: Tumult! : the incredible life and music of Tina Turner / Donald Brackett.
Description: Lanham : Backbeat Books, 2020. | Includes bibliographical references and index. | Summary: "The narrative of Tumult! The Incredible Life and Music of Tina Turner is an extended exploration of the magical transformation of shy country girl Anna Mae Bullock into the boisterous force of nature we know today as Tina Turner"— Provided by publisher.
Identifiers: LCCN 2020010514 (print) | LCCN 2020010515 (ebook) | ISBN 9781493055067 (paperback) | ISBN 9781493055074 (epub)
Subjects: LCSH: Turner, Tina. | Singers—United States—Biography. | Rhythm and blues musicians—United States—Biography. | Rock musicians—United States—Biography.
Classification: LCC ML420.T95 B73 2020 (print) | LCC ML420.T95 (ebook) | DDC 782.42166092 [B]—dc23
LC record available at https://lccn.loc.gov/2020010514
LC ebook record available at https://lccn.loc.gov/2020010515

This book is dedicated to all those women who were strong enough to leave and also to all those who weren't.

"Being righteous is a full time job."

—Erikah Badu, *Wayback*, 1997

CONTENTS

ACKNOWLEDGMENTS

The author wishes to thank the many people who helped make this book possible and to express his appreciation to Aaron Cohen, John Corcelli, and James Porter for sharing their insights into Tina and her music. Thanks also to my musical friends, Gerry Watson and Kevin Courrier, for ongoing and fruitful discussions over the years. And to my partner, Dr. Mimi Gellman, for allowing me to spend so much time with amazing women like Tina.

INTRODUCTION

No North or South in Dreams: Turning into Turner

> "My legacy is that I stayed on course, from the beginning to the end, because I believed in something inside of me."
>
> —Tina, Minerva Lee interview, *World Tribune*, 2018

How often do you get a chance to paraphrase the French Enlightenment philosopher Voltaire in the context of rock and pop music? Here goes. If Tina Turner had not existed, it would have been necessary to invent her. And, strangely enough, that's exactly what did happen in reality.

This towering talent started out life as a little giant, Anna Mae Bullock, born November 26, 1939, to a tempestuous family in rural Nutbush, Tennessee, and grew up throughout the southeastern United States. Like many other future soul music queens, she first experienced the joys of singing in the heated reverence of local Baptist church choirs. Also, like many other future funk divas, such as Aretha Franklin and Sharon Jones, among others, Anna Mae didn't linger for too long in the pews of prayer. She preferred instead a different kind of soul-stirring rhythm, and she found it throbbing in the secular swagger of rhythm and blues–infused soul and bluesy rock music.

Designations of geography on maps, however, are only mere pieces of paper, and it was quickly obvious to young Miss Bullock that dreams have no north or south, a fact that allowed her to gravitate, like so many others before her, into the large northern urban centers of America, to places that seemed to always be waiting for a storm to happen. East St. Louis, Illinois, was just such a place beyond all maps, and she was indeed, though still in her early teen days, a secret storm waiting to be unleashed. And it was to be there, sixteen years after being born as Anna Mae, that she was reinvented by an aspiring bandleader with a penchant for capitalizing on valuable natural resources.

The most basic and salient fact about Tina Turner is that she is a master (or mistress) of pure, unalloyed transformation. What that *something* inside of her to which she refers might actually *be* is perhaps somewhat difficult to define in concrete terms, but it can certainly be amply described. Yes, this central fact of her life, one of perpetual change, growth, and evolution, is quite simple of course, yet it also helps to guide us through the twisting labyrinth of a very complex, sometimes even contradictory and many-layered woman and artist.

By believing in that *something* inside her, even without fully knowing what to call it, she would eventually transform herself from a hot and heavy rhythm-and-blues–oriented soul singer into a rock star, a movie star, and a global feminine celebrity of goddess-like proportions. Her mystique is partially embedded of course in her humble beginnings, her nightmarish domestic relationship, and especially her supersonic abilities as an evocative singer, entertainer, and dancer.

But what made her into an icon of female survival and human triumph was almost as indefinable as her raspy voice and as breathtaking as her endless legs. If I had to identify what she called that *something* she believed in, I'd have to resort to the rhapsodic and maybe even ambiguous: the idea of *no limits* and the ability to live one's dreams on a daily basis. In that respect, she's also a radical dichotomy: a figure serving as an enigmatic emblem of victimhood yet also a personification of triumph over physical and psychological adversity and poverty of affection as well as triumph over posttraumatic stress.

A magnificent sex symbol of fiercely unbridled sensuality who is also a devout and ardent practitioner of gentle Nichiren Buddhism, while it's true that she morphed herself several times over the course of her full-spectrum life, she also got some unexpected help from what we might call karma along the way. But it was from a surprising source since she didn't mutate herself from Anna Mae to Tina either overnight or certainly not all on her own. Not by any means.

The glowering presence of Ike Turner actually bestowed both her name itself and the opportunity to make it as well known as the weather, and heavy weather it was indeed. That's what makes embodying a paradox the heart of her story, both her life story and her love story: the fact that her menace was also her mentor, a sinister Svengali figure of Phil Spector–scaled lunacy. It was a chance teenage encounter with Ike that changed not only the course of her own life but also the course of musical history. Chance, it turns out, is the fool's name for fate.

There are three things about the notorious name of Ike Turner and three reasons why he is still important even after living a long life of self-destructive disgrace through both drug abuse and domestic violence. One, he recorded probably the very first rock-and-roll song in history, "Rocket 88," in 1951. Mr. Turner was back then the twenty-year-old leader of the Kings of Rhythm, and their rendition, with Jackie Brenston doing lead vocals, of a speeded-up basic twelve-bar blues song hit number one in the charts while also kick-starting an entire musical revolution.

This of course also long predated Elvis Presley, the white genius who borrowed the raunchy black vibe of Chuck Berry, popularized it immensely, and led us directly into the waiting arms of the Beatles. It's totally true that Ike heard the future coming, loud and clear. Besides, both Little Richard and Johnny Otis said he did. And Ike flagged it down to jump on board.

Two, he was definitely a tormented talent on a huge scale himself: musician, bandleader, arranger, songwriter, talent scout, and record producer of considerable skill, especially as the commanding leader of the Kings, until meeting a certain young tornado from Tennessee and forming his famed co-named Revue. You didn't have to like him—and few did—to appreciate his abilities.

But we could surmise that it is indeed number three that makes us still utter his name at all today: he invented Tina Turner. While watching his band play one night in 1957 at Club Manhattan in St. Louis, the diminutive teen Anna Mae Bullock approached the stage during an intermission and audaciously asked to sing with them after claiming that the bandleader's music "put her into a trance." Soon enough, she'd be putting all the rest of us in a trance, something we can only call that special jittery Tina Trance.

Together, as a boisterous but brilliant structural unit, Ike and Tina Turner pretty much started out their careers at the top of the pop game. This early acclaim was followed by a series of hits on a variety of small labels and also by one of the most grueling live concert touring schedules in music history.

Ever the swift cat when it came to seeing his main chance at success, Ike quickly invented a group of backup singers for Tina, called the Ikettes, while he remained as the puppet king mastermind playing balefully in the background.

The group acquired a solid reputation that audience members soon embraced as one of the hottest and potentially most explosive of all rock/pop ensembles with a show that rivaled that of the James Brown revue in terms of sheer sweaty spectacle. With a raunchy female screamer assuming the Brown sizzling star role, between 1963 and 1966, the band toured constantly throughout the country even in the absence of a hit single, a major accomplishment on its own, as they were fueled by sheer word of mouth and ear power.

In something like that era's equivalent of going viral, Tina's profile rapidly elevated as a result of public appearances on *American Bandstand* and *Shindig!*, while the whole Revue spotlit her on *Hollywood a Go Go* and the *Andy Williams Show* as well as the *Big TNT Show* in 1965. This brought her to the attention of not only a large white audience but also a huge pop mainstream public awareness in general. She was ready for her close-up.

To finally cement their worldwide acclaim, they appeared on the *Ed Sullivan Show* in 1970, which was probably the first real mass encounter with Ike and Tina by music lovers with pale complexions like my own. They had marked a huge turning-point stage in their careers not just by being commercially anointed by Sullivan but also by switching from their prior rhythm-and-blues and soul music vibe to certified rock and roll and then to rock music proper. To some extent, they may even have personally helped evolve rock and roll into *rock* per se. At the very least, they certainly inaugurated pop rock.

In a series of interview exchanges with musicians, music critics, journalists, and broadcasters, I have greatly benefited from their shared insights into what makes Tina tick. My exchanges with Aaron Cohen, Chicago-based author of *Move On Up: Soul Music and Black Cultural Power*; James Porter, broadcaster/author of *Wild in the Streets*, a history of the black origins of rock and roll and the evolution of black rock; and John Corcelli, a Toronto-based music journalist and author of *Frank Zappa FAQ* who also kindly wrote the foreword to my book on the soul music of Sharon Jones, have all proven very fruitful in terms of exploring and unearthing the staggering range of Turner's musical achievements in the context of a broader cultural milieu. Their input into what made Tina so special proved very helpful in navigating the rough waters before, during, and after the Ike storm.

Ike Turner finally passed away in 2007 (truth be told, he'd already been dead inside for years), and at Ike's funeral oration, the great but totally loopy master producer Phil Spector started his eulogy by declaring that Ike had turned Tina into a jewel. So far so good, and quite true. But then the psychopathic Phil (currently an imprisoned murder felon) began to explain that *any* five other singers could have done what she did under his masterful tutelage, especially, he also intimated, if they had been under his own Spectorized production sway, even though he had produced only a single song for her (although it was admittedly a very important song).

This may have been the first moment when the world at large realized the full depth of Spector's mental illness since by then everyone on the planet also knew well what Tina was not only creatively capable of but also had already accomplished on her own in the thirty years *after* escaping from Ike's paranoid and coke-addled clutches. And this was Ike's third paradoxical contribution to musical history: the ironic fact that his own pathological possessiveness eventually drove née Bullock *away* from him and into the welcoming arms of a grateful global audience, into our welcoming arms.

But first they had a shared and well-deserved stardom together as a creative team albeit something of a tortured partnership on her part. With a new stylistic persona and a much higher profile for Tina, they turned another corner professionally when they recorded an up-tempo version of the Creedence Clearwater Revival song "Proud Mary," which forever altered the Turner landscape and made it obvious who was really leading the charge forward musically. It sold more than a million copies and won a Grammy for best duo/group rhythm-and-blues performance. She was obviously branching out both creatively and professionally and clearly moving way, way beyond Ike.

Not surprisingly, many younger listeners and readers who were captivated by her stellar solo career may be far less familiar with their earlier work as a collaboration. By the mid-1970s, a combination of forces were driving the pair toward a decline of the duo format that had served them so well for more than ten years. Tina was of course coming into her own confident persona, and Ike had descended into a disastrous dependence on Bolivian nasal remedies, not to mention his cascading violence toward the blossoming Tina. Shows started to be missed, and contracts went unsigned.

In 1976, Tina filed for divorce and fled his company, both personally and professionally, stating that about this time her embrace of Buddhist meditation and chanting practices helped her survive the ravages of their suffocating relationship. To her chagrin, she discovered that by walking out on Ike during the middle of a concert tour, she was then liable to tour promoters for the canceled shows. Their divorce was finally settled in 1978, and she was completely liberated from the overbearing impresario, who had nonetheless contributed to making her a household name, a name that she ironically retained as part of the court settlement.

Tina made a triumphant return to the stage in 1978, funded by United Artists management and directed by a new manager, Roger Davies, who advised her to drop the revue-format band and remodel herself as a much grittier rock-and-roll performer. She flung herself into a whirlwind of appearances to solidify her newfound identity, opening shows for the Rolling Stones and Rod Stewart (a sure way to rock royalty), and then signed a new lucrative solo deal with Capitol Records. A world tour commenced in support of her new comeback album and image.

Naturally enough, Hollywood also beckoned once again. The new and improved Tina Turner had arrived. The rest is herstory: an incredible life and even more incredible music, both of which are equally mesmerizing. The narrative of *Tumult!* is an extended exploration of the quite magical metamorphosis of shy Anna Mae Bullock into the force of nature we know as Tina Turner today. Turning into Turner: it is actually of course really the tale of someone who was already just patiently waiting to emerge, not a Svengali-guided Pygmalion creature at all but a fully formed if vulnerable young lady who was inevitably going to burst out of the claustrophobic shell imposed on her one way or the other. And, Lordy, burst out she did.

As of this writing, Turner is calmly simmering on the back burner of mortality's stove, having been struggling with intestinal cancer (the same ailment that took away two other soul goddesses: Sharon Jones in 2016 and Aretha Franklin in 2018) and having undergone a kidney transplant that was rejected and followed by numerous seizures and strokes. Her mighty voice and fantastically athletic form may have been stilled by this condition, but her true legacy is only now beginning to come fully into focus: that personal belief in her interior gift that could never be extinguished.

Even if mortality takes her away, as it appears it must, her spirit has been only quieted down some, not really silenced at all. And the sonic artifacts, records, concerts, videos, and films she left behind still convey that spirit loud and clear. Like my earlier books on two brilliant female musicians (*Back to Black: Amy Winehouse's Only Masterpiece* and *Long Slow Train: The Soul Music of Sharon Jones and the Dap-Kings*, both from Backbeat Books in 2016 and 2018, respectively), in *Tumult!* I tend to pass over the soap opera struggles as much as possible, except where essential to the narrative, in favor of a deep dive into the core of her creative sources and her lofty achievements in musical artistry.

But even the details of her harrowing early pre-solo years do still inform the inspiration and production of that impressive later work. *Exult!*—that could also be a fitting subtitle to her story as well. *Tumult!* just feels right, though, given her early and middle beginnings. In the main, it suggests the loud noise of an excited crowd, linking it to adoring rock stadiums for me, as well as a state of change, turmoil, upheaval, ferment, uproar, commotion, ruckus, frenzy, and turbulence, often associated with convulsions, tempests, storms, and maelstroms. Indeed, all these terms are easily identifiable with what happens when Tina Turner starts working her magic on a crowd.

Yet *exult* is perhaps equally applicable to her as well, especially in the long post-Ike tumult era we now most associate with her name: to feel or show triumphant elation or jubilation, to rejoice, to be joyful, to be ecstatic, to revel in, to be enraptured, and, maybe most important, to be proud. And just like one of the songs most often connected to her career, Proud Tina keeps on rolling.

In the example of this uniquely global superstar, we have a case study in sheer creative willpower, and her achievements were lofty indeed by any and all standards, both artistic and commercial. Singer, songwriter, dancer, actress, icon: she had risen to international prominence already as the featured singer in the Ike and Tina Turner Revue but then went on to far eclipse that fame with a new astronomically visible solo career entirely of her own making. Fate would even apologize to her later on for the mistake it made with her the first time and bring a new and vastly improved love interest, Erwin Bach, into her life, almost as if to make amends.

Becoming one of the best-selling recording artists of all time (no exaggeration) and often referred to as the Queen of Rock and Roll, she has sold more than 200 million records; has received a total of eight Grammy Awards from twenty-five nominations, three Hall of Fame Awards, and a Grammy Lifetime Achievement Award; was inducted into the Rock and Roll Hall of Fame in 1991; and also received Kennedy Center Honors in 2005.

It is definitely as a rock star and pop music goddess, rather than solely as a soul, funk, or rhythm-and-blues artist, that my book begins its appreciation of her truly transcendent popular appeal. I maintain—and always have—that pop music is a serious creative and cultural artifact, one reflecting our planetary cultures in a way often overlooked merely due to the sheer scale and volume of the vast commercial success levels in question among the upper echelons of pop performers.

A figure like Tina is often taken less seriously as an artist simply because she has also, according to the *Guinness World Records*, sold more live concert tickets than any other solo performer in music history. But more important for me, in addition to what caused her songs to be expressed so forcefully, is *how* they were recorded so effectively. The studio, band, and production levels on her albums are all supernaturally fine in their support of her craft.

In many ways, she was what the early feminist author Anais Nin described as "a spy in the house of love." She sent back dispatches from the front lines of the heart depicting the dynamics of personal relationships, usually the kind involving copious heartbreak merged with inevitable triumph. It was a signature style she had developed from living as a survivor.

Being Tina Turner day in and day out required having acres of stamina, and as the consummate spy for love, she shared a certain obscure skill with other experts in emotional espionage. Hers is an outsized talent for survival I can best paraphrase from an apt description I recently encountered in Ben Macintyre's book *A Spy among Friends*. In body, she was fragile, but her soul was made of some tensile, almost impossibly resilient material that never broke or even bent in its certainty.

So, in *Tumult!*, we try to take her seriously as an artist and unearth what uncanny skills enabled her to connect with so many of her fellow mortals at such a deep heart-to-heart level. She is, in fact, a beating human heart in high heels.

1

I COULD HAVE BEEN ANYONE ANYWHERE

The Origin Myth

"Physical strength in a woman, that's what I am. If you're unhappy with anything, get rid of it. When you're free, then your true creativity and true self comes out."

—Tina Turner, in *I Tina*, 1986

One of Tina Turner's lesser-known records is also one of her most important and revealing. "Nutbush City Limits" is a song released in 1973 as a single and on an album of the same name while she was still working with her partner and producer, Ike Turner. It's not her most beloved record or even her most popular song. It was, however, a crucial turning point, one we could even call a Turner Point since it was the first song she wrote by herself, for herself, and about herself. It was one that became quite a big hit for the prolific pair, who by that time had already been successful and revered for more than a decade but who were still only three years away from her divorce and hard-won independence.

It was also a song of deep intimacy, sentiment, and personal nostalgia in which she celebrated her rural roots in a frank and honest manner so meaningful for her that she would release different updated versions of it again and again over the years, notably a live recording in 1988 and several dance remixes in 1991 and yet another rerecording in 1993, long after she had become a stellar solo performer and a megastar in her own right. This raucously danceable ditty clearly had special meaning for her. The hidden truth behind the song was also of course the simple fact that it was always *her* who made the couple's music special right from the beginning, a fact that must have grated severely on her insecure and volatile husband.

This relatively elementary little tune was almost a private kind of national anthem for the sleepy town of Nutbush, Tennessee, a place hardly anyone knew existed apart from the roughly 258 other souls besides Anna Mae Bullock, the future Tina, who lived there. But the song is also elemental in the way it situates her origins and embeds them in a manner that would never quite leave her, no matter how much fame or wealth tumbled her way. Distant from Interstate 40, dropped by an obviously ironic creator in the middle of nowhere between Jackson and Memphis, it was close enough to Highway 19 to make that the escape route for every bored citizen wanting out in search of wider and freer horizons.

This humble song extols and elevates, even mythologizes, a space and time forever lodged in the heart of a southern girl like Miss Bullock. And though basic in its fondly recalled message of home and hearth, "Go to the store on Fridays, go to the church on Sundays . . . ," it is nevertheless propelled along in a full-charging way as fueled by Ike's admittedly swift arrangements and his own powerful throbbing electric organ and twanging guitar playing, both coupled with their Kings of Rhythm's customary swaying swagger.

As Nick Hasted effectively characterized it in *Classic Rock*, the 1973 song was clearly ironic, maybe even schizoid, considering the lifestyle she was trapped in during the period of her writing it: being forced onstage each night despite health issues such as bronchitis leading to tuberculosis, a collapsed right lung and infected legs, and a permanently bruised jaw from Ike's abuse. She called it "living in hell's domain," and Hasted mournfully referenced her claim that she was "brainwashed" during that period.

Indeed, it must have felt something like being stuck in a cult: "Her nightmare parody of suburban domestic bliss required her to treat Ike like a king while looking after their four children, and the musical life which once inspired her wasn't much better. On stage, the once blisteringly inspiring Ike and Tina Turner Revue could now be a sad, exhausted spectacle." So, perhaps it was natural enough, in the midst of the Ike cult, for her lonely imagination to return to her idealized country memories of the quiet hamlet where she first saw the light of day.

Now of course, though she was clearly utilizing her hometown motif as a survival mechanism until the effects of her own personal Stockholm syndrome could be evaded, neither Nutbush itself nor her childhood in general was anything remotely idyllic. It probably just seemed that way compared to Ike. Nutbush is an unincorporated rural community in Haywood County in the western part of the state of Tennessee. It was established in the early nineteenth century by European American settlers who brought along enslaved African Americans as workers to develop the area's plantations. Those African American forced migrants built houses and churches there that still stand to this day.

Historically, the town had been devoted to the cultivation and harvesting of cotton, a commodity crop since the antebellum years, when its processing and transport depended on institutionalized enslavement. Other notable musicians also emerged from this unlikely area, among them some prominent blues recording artists, including Hambone Willie Newbern, Noah Lewis, and the great Sleepy John Estes. There's even a famous line dance named the Nutbush, which survives still and was performed in an episode of the television show *Glee* of all places. Nutbush was basically the blues incarnate.

Her immediate family consisted of her mother Zelma Priscilla and father Floyd Richard Bullock, two mismatched souls with the misfortune to be married to each other, and two older sisters, Evelyn Juanita and Ruby Alline. After her birth in nearby Brownsville (where her actual delivery took place, at the Haywood Memorial Hospital, a tiny municipal building whose basement was set aside for the care of black patients), Anna Mae's extended family of maternal and paternal grandparents raised her in Nutbush and also in neighboring Ripley.

That larger clan also included a strong and distinct heritage from Anna Mae's maternal side. Her mother Zelma's parents—Josephus, a sharecropper, and Georgiana Currie—were from different dispossessed cultures that both formed a sad but crucial part of American history. He was three-quarters Navajo, while his wife, Anna Mae's grandmother, was three-quarters Cherokee, the first nation whose ancestral lands had been seized in the forging of Tennessee itself. Both of them were one-quarter black.

This might account for some of the exotically alluring features that always struck me as most appealing about the future Tina: a sharply defined Native bloodline as strong as her own impressive cheekbones. I've always enjoyed Kurt Loder's description of her when he helped her write the first of her two memoirs. He described her sisters and cousin as wearing their hair in the tight plaits customary for young black daughters, whereas Anna Mae, perhaps already genetically inclined toward rebellion, has "undone her mother's patient braidwork and gathered her full reddish hair into a rough ponytail at the back, revealing an exotic facial geography of elegant broad bones, richly sculpted lips, honey-toned skin, smooth as a breezeless sea, and eyes like tiny brown beacons."

And it was into this mixture of transported African migrants forced into slavery and the remnants of a once grand nation of Native dwellers that Anna Mae would be merged. She would be born into a world of conflict and trauma, both in her personal domestic family life of perpetually fighting parents at war with each other for unknown reasons as well as on a grand scale in the world at large, a world at war for equally questionable motives.

Two months before her birth on November 26, 1939, England and France declared war on Nazi Germany, which had invaded Poland with Soviet acquiescence if not outright assistance. Tumult was already latently active in the world outside her, just waiting to fully erupt within. Welcome to your childhood.

Unfortunately for Anna Mae, though she felt some warmth in her grandparents' home, there was zero in her own since her parents Richard and Zelma seemed to have no time or energy left over after their constant battles to ever care for their youngest daughter. She clearly felt like an unwanted child, and she evidently was, for her sister Alline had been lucky enough to be born into a marriage that had yet to deteriorate into open domestic warfare.

This left Anna Mae with much solitary time on her hands, often wandering through the natural backcountry domain outside the home, if only to escape the violent storms inside its unhappy walls. Equally impressive, along with her general psychic survival of potential parental harm at any moment, whether from violence or neglect, was her personal claim on that obscure force within her that permitted an out-sized optimism and hopefulness.

She didn't remember being poor exactly (perhaps a basic and simple life would be more accurate) largely due to her father's standing on Poindexter farm as the leader or manager (officially designated as over-seer) of the other sharecroppers. The rigid southern social strata did impact on her from a segregation aspect of course, but that was appar-ently just the way of the world to a young girl, incapable of understand-ing why her kind of folks were accepted as long they knew and kept in their place.

The only pleasure she occasionally had, apart from roaming the fields and streams, was attending large barbecue picnics at which live music would be played. Not even blues really, it was what she thought to call country music at the time, but it thrilled her to witness a live band of revelers whooping it up and making a joyful noise, at least until the pic-nic was over. That was regrettable, the music's ending, because it meant she had to return indoors to a mother who didn't communicate with her at all and a father who she felt sure just didn't want her around at all. The music was her only friend.

The trouble might have been, she used to surmise, because she heard her mother had stolen her father way from another girl, not because she loved him but just out of spite. So it was clear and obvious, even to a lit-tle girl, that the reason they didn't get along was simply that they didn't even like each other, let alone love each other. It's hard not to imagine, even at this early life stage, the faint echo of a future long-distant song, "what's love but a second hand emotion, who needs a heart when a heart can be broken?"

She also had to contend with growing up amid rumors that, aside from being unwanted because they were unhappy, she was also not really even her father's child at all and that, prior to her arrival, her fa-ther's sister Martha Mae and her husband had been living with her par-ents. The whispers went that Martha was playing around with another man and that Anna Mae was actually that man's child, not Richard's. Then, when she arrived, looking quite different from her very dark-skinned sister Alline (her self-description in memory was of a "red kid," fair skinned and fair-haired), the surrounding community, who were "church people," never cared much for her either.

The only thing she could really count on growing up was the love of her older sister, even though she was so different temperamentally from Anna Mae, Alline being more quiet and deliberate, while Anna Mae was wild to the core, right from the start. In the end, she was always left to her own solitary devices, always busy, running, moving, and doing things: tempestuous from the word go, feeling somewhat like a complete outsider (which she definitely was spirit-wise) and merely going off, almost happily secluded, on her own. Is it any wonder, then, that given the unpleasant energy field she found herself growing up in, she might be vulnerable enough to be compromised in her own toxic domestic tangle later on?

And this fateful upcoming turn of events would occur really before even being fully grown up at all, a teenager, meeting a man eight years her senior, a man with a band playing *live music*, but one who also had a dark side. The difference between her parents' tangle of course and her own would be that in hers, she also had a rare opportunity to use her natural gifts in a liberating way: to sing, sing, sing. When it came to her hardship-riddled childhood, however, she always took a characteristically sunny attitude about it all.

"I didn't dwell on it," she told *Rolling Stone*'s Loder in 1986. "I had my own thing going, my own world. I had to make my own way. I had to go out into the world and become strong, to discover my mission in life." Mission accomplished, I think it's fair to say.

Turner would be just as typically blunt and emphatic thirty-two years later when talking to Deborah Davis and Dominik Wichmann, the authors who helped her curate her mature memories in *My Love Story*: "My struggle began at birth, when I entered the world as Anna Mae Bullock. Ever since then I have spent my entire life fighting my way through a climate of bad karma. There was a shadow hanging over my earliest years, cast by someone more absent than present, my mother." The question of how it felt to be an unwanted child and, even more remarkably, how that child prevailed in spite of the many strikes against her forms the basic structure of her character, her later persona, and her life's convoluted narrative in general.

Indeed, this woman's earliest childhood memory was of her parents fighting, an interpersonal dynamic that simply had to have embedded itself into her psyche with a stubborn tenacity. The supreme irony is that she subsequently stumbled into exactly the same kind of loveless and threatening relationship herself. And yet this same curious combination of her private strength and personal vulnerability was also somehow captured publicly later on in her frequently revealing songs of love and loss, for all the world to share her suffering.

✿ ✿ ✿

Even if children find a way of living in their own world in order to survive adversity—especially the preternaturally talented ones prior to sharing their talents with the rest of us—the bigger world outside continues spinning its wheels unabated. Having been born into conflict and trauma, the larger world also continued to mirror Anna Mae's strife-ridden family life, with whole countries standing in for parental collisions. Just as two months before she was born Europe slid into armed conflict, two years after she arrived the entire world was consumed in a war more terrifying than any before it.

In December 1941, Japan's unexpected attack on Hawaii prompted a swift and consequential response, dragging the whole planet into a destructive binge of nationalist fervor that ironically also impacted the Bullock family personally. A sudden wartime employment boom associated with military industry and defense pants materialized, one especially helpful for formerly struggling black citizens looking for work, when a new army site opened in Oak Ridge, Tennessee, near Knoxville.

Both the prospect of fresh jobs and a cherished chance to escape from Nutbush appealed to Richard and Zelma Bullock, who oddly enough decided not to escape separately but to go together and leave their already neglected family behind. Government jobs obviously appealed to them more than farmwork ever had, and even though they hated each other, both seemed to resent, if not actually hate, their offspring almost as much, none of whom were ever really desired or especially cared for.

Alline was sent to live with the Native side of the family, while Anna Mae, much to her dismay, was sent to stay with "Mama" Roxanna and Alex Bullock, her father's stern religious parents, the dour deacon and deaconess of the Woodlawn Missionary Baptist Church. It would turn her off conventional deity worship for the rest of her life, perhaps even starting her on a search for her own spiritual alternatives. But the gospel music she encountered in the sacred church setting, now that was a different story: the fiery music provoked by faith was something she could easily relate to wholeheartedly.

I'm fond of identifying certain artists by a seemingly paradoxical epithet, *gospel funk*. Aaron Cohen, music historian and author of a history of soul music titled *Move On Up*, tends to agree with me that this certainly mysterious category in music is nonetheless real and tangible: the notion that sacred music underwent significant stylistic innovations but remained at its root a boisterous expression of fervor merely shifted from faith into funk.

"There definitely is such a thing as gospel funk—check out the two Numero Group compilations under the *Good God!* title (although these compiled records are from after Tina Turner's ascent). At this stage, I'm not sure that Tina Turner deviated too far afield from her contemporaries or influences in terms of translating the beat and repertoire from gospel into R&B, simply by changing the lyrics up, of course."

True enough, he's referring to the alteration of "Lord" into "Lover." That recursive shift from gospel to soul also involves a shift in attention, in some extreme cases even transposing Lord into Ike. But in her formative years, it was always and significantly the sacred vibe that moved her. Apart from hearing popular music on her mother's radio and attending those communal picnics, her first live musical influences were sacred ones, as emphasized in her *Woman in Rock Rolling Stone* entry identifying her influences: "Well it was a church person in the early days, Mahalia Jackson, and Rosetta Tharpe. These spiritual and very strong voices who I knew were figures in the black race, recognized and respected. But I must admit I've always covered the songs of males. I haven't really listened to that much women's music."

In Joe Smith's book *Off the Record*, stressing how little to no vocal training she's had, she referenced singing some of the McGuire Sisters songs she listened to as a young girl when she was so often brokenhearted, already apparently singing the blues. It was second nature to her, as natural as speaking: "It makes me remember just how long I have really been singing."

James Porter, Chicago-based music archivist and author of *Wild in the Streets: Tales from Rock and Roll's Negro Leagues*, a forthcoming book on black rock music from Northwestern University Press, spoke eloquently to me about Tina Turner's place in the pantheon of both great black rockers in general and exemplary black female pop artists in particular. Sharing my belief that she carried forward a considerable amount of gospel fury into her propulsive funk vibe, he also emphasized that she was always basically a practitioner of soul music, no matter how far afield her musical tastes diverged.

"Yes, Tina can still be considered a soul singer. I certainly think so. During all the style changes she went through, she never quite lost that churchy R&B feel. She may have embellished it with more rawness or sophistication, depending on the circumstances, but the soul feel was always at the core of it all with her."

The young Anna Mae was asked to join the local church choir once her community discovered how easily she vocalized, and at the age of nine or ten, she was especially fond of doing the upbeat fast-tempo hymns, quite ready, it seemed, to be a tiny star and howl about heaven even then. Her sister observed her dancing so furiously to gospel tunes that her knickers would fall to her feet without her even realizing it. Always prepared to deliver drama, she also used to come home from the movies and act out scenes for her family, stretched out on the floor to demonstrate how starlets died on celluloid. Melodrama seemed to appeal to her nature.

By the time she was thirteen, she became an accidental orphan of sorts by virtue of desertion, her parents sharing both their strong disdain for each other as well as lacking the emotional wherewithal to care for their offspring. She made a little extra money by working for a friendly neighborhood family (i.e., people who actually loved each other), Guy and Connie Henderson, as a maid, once ironically telling *McCall's* magazine, "I went to work for a nice white family as a maid. I was like their younger daughter. A lot of my training in being a woman—except for cooking—was from the Hendersons. I learned to take care of their baby, so when I had mine, I already knew everything."

The parental separation lasted through to Anna Mae's formative educational period at the Flagg Grove Elementary School up to the ninth grade, the same period during which she started singing in the church choir at Nutbush's Spring Hill Baptist Church. Family trauma continued to accelerate when her mother suddenly disappeared for a time, finally seeking liberation from her abusive father. The future echoes in reverse are hard not to note here, with Anna Mae herself eventually having later to flee precisely the same kind of emotionally terrorizing dynamic as the one that had sired her.

As kind to her as the Hendersons were, they couldn't quite teach her everything of course, such as how not to be with the completely wrong man. It strikes me that, like most cunning abusers, her future husband would quickly learn how to take advantage of and capitalize on her obvious childhood abandonment issues and use her extreme isolated vulnerability to his greatest advantage.

Shockingly, this would only be three years later, remember, when she naively wandered into what was known as "The Hole" neighborhood of East St. Louis with her older sister as an unwitting guide to the nightlife. Thus, the next seismic shift for the self-professed tomboy country girl occurred at sixteen when her grandmother died and Anna Mae was sent to the city to supposedly warmly reunite with her sister and wayward mother.

And in St. Louis, a large urban center with equally vast music and entertainment districts that must have seemed like another planet compared to Nutbush, there was yet another shock awaiting her: the young girl's fateful encounter with Ike Turner. This was the extremely unpleasant man who would loom so large in her life story and create both a nightmare of domestic déjà vu while also weirdly providing an enlivening entry into her true calling in that life.

And here's one of the strangest twists to the Tina saga. While it's true that Ike was probably a psychopath—or at the very least a misogynistic sociopath—it's equally true that without him, his music, and his initial sixteen-yearlong professional relationship, there would be no Tina. No one in the world may ever have known what would have become of Anna Mae Bullock if Turner hadn't stepped into her field of karma at just the right moment to nudge it ever so slightly a few degrees closer to the direction of her dreams.

My own theory is that Anna Mae not only still exists but has actually always been right in front of our faces and ears *impersonating* Tina Turner. And what a masterful impression she's given us of an ultimately soaring creative creature, a sheer wild pagan goddess let loose on all our senses at once. And if Tina can accurately be described as the hardest-working woman in show business (let's borrow that title for a moment from James Brown)—and I think we'll all agree she can—then it's just as clear that Ike was the meanest man in show business.

But still, Ike's admittedly bizarre legacy also includes the inexplicable fact that he gave us Tina, something for which we all need to be eternally grateful. Hell, I suspect even she is grateful, in some paradoxical way, since she knows what it meant for her to be given a rare chance to stand in the spotlight she so strongly desired. Once again, chance is the fool's name for fate.

✿   ✿   ✿

Apart from his obvious musical and arranging and band-leading skills, and they were considerable, I will maintain that it was for his special genius as a talent scout that he was sent to earth and for which he should be justly remembered. Izear Luster "Ike" Turner Jr. lived from November 5, 1931, to December 12, 2007, and the man had one of the strangest lives imaginable—almost a strange as Tina's, if a lot less inspiring. He began playing guitar and piano at the age of eight and would have been considered a creative prodigy if he hadn't been nuts. But even if he was nuts, his powers of invention were prodigious, just as prodigious as his later bad appetites would be.

Quite rightly described by *Mojo* magazine's editor Phil Alexander as "the cornerstone of modern-day rock and roll," Turner was born in Clarksdale, Mississippi, to Beatrice Cushenbury, a seamstress, and Isaiah (or Izear) Luster Turner, a Baptist minister. Turner often related a story about his father having been set on and beaten by a white mob (which he claimed to have witnessed), leaving him an invalid for three years before succumbing to his injuries, though, like most Ike stories, it might need to be taken with a pound of salt.

Blues historian Ted Drozdowski is on record as saying that Isaiah died in an industrial accident. Either way, it led to his mother remarrying to a man named Philip Reeves, a violent alcoholic with whom Ike often argued and fought physically, going so far as to knock his stepfather out with a piece of wood and fleeing to Memphis. Eventually, later in life, they reconciled, presumably when both had exhausted all of their mutual rage. The scenario does, however, allow us to speculate on the psychic impact of such a domestic environment on young Ike Jr., and we don't have to be Freud to wonder about his personal history when it comes to sexual experiences and often the merging of the two contradictory impulses: to love and to destroy.

He has recounted how he was "introduced" to sex at the age of six by a middle-aged lady called Miss Boozie. When walking past her house on his way to school, he would be invited in to feed her chickens and then be taken to bed by her, a practice that continued for several years. He claimed not to have been traumatized by these encounters, observing wryly to *Celebrity Café* that "today they would call it child molesting, to me I was just having fun," as described to Dominick Miserandino for a Hall of Famer profile piece. Apparently a favorite of questionably adjusted ladies, he also seems to have been raped twice by other women before he was twelve.

At the tender age of eight, he began to hang out at the local Clarksdale radio station, WROX, one of the few stations known to employ a black deejay, an unusual character known as Early Wright. Another deejay, John Frisella, decided to put the hang-about kid to work spinning platters, which Ike described as "the beginning of his thing with music." Before long, he was left alone to play records on his own while the adult deejay went across the street for a coffee and a smoke. Freedom of expression and low impulse control loomed large in his saga right from the beginning.

After this rather odd initiation, a few years later, while still a tender teen, he was offered the formal job of deejay for the later afternoon shift by the station manager, a job that meant he had instant and personal access to all new record releases before anyone else saw or heard them. He was known even in this early phase as someone devoted to a wide-ranging diversity in musical styles, often juxtaposing surprising combinations of songs (such as boogie mixed with rockabilly) in a form that today may be called mashups. No name existed for it at all back then, of course.

On a fateful visit to his friend Ernest Lane's house, he happened to come on the legendary Pinetop Perkins playing piano on his chum's father's instrument, something that seemed to have catalyzed an already burgeoning love of and voracious curiosity about music. He also seemed gifted with guile even as a kid, persuading his mother to pay for piano lessons, but instead of taking them, he spent the money at pool halls and went to his pal Ernest's house to watch and listen to Pinetop playing alone in an audience of two. There are, of course, worse ways to learn about music than by absorbing it at the knee of a boogie-woogie legend.

He then taught himself to play guitar by listening to old blues records, and at some point in the 1940s, he moved into the Clarksdale Riverside Hotel, run by an amiable lady who didn't rape him but did expose him to myriad touring musicians who stayed there. Among the stars who passed through the hotel he shared with them on the road were giants such as blues king Sonny Boy Williamson II and jazz titan Duke Ellington, with whom he would play music when they were touring through town. Again, there are worse ways to learn about the magic of rhythm than by hanging around and drinking with Duke.

Demonstrating the same kind of supernatural maturity (music-wise, not emotionally) as other young, gifted history makers, such as Lennon and McCartney, Jagger and Richards, and others, all of whom started playing together while only about sixteen, while still in high school (something he never paid much attention to), he joined a local rhythm ensemble, as they were then known, called the Tophatters, which included a few of his youthful friends: Raymond Hill, Eugene Fox, and Clayton Love. Turner, who could not read music, learned his parts by listening to records at home and then re-creating his parts live on the stage. The audacious kid had guts galore.

The Tophatters was a very large band, half of which wanted to play jazz while the other half wanted to play blues and boogie music, so they split in two: one group called itself the Dukes of Swing and the other, Turner's portion, called themselves the Kings of Rhythm, a band name that Turner maintained throughout the rest of his lengthy career. This precocious career at one formative stage included blues great BB King hearing them play and recommending them to the legendary Sam Phillips at Sun Studio (recording home of Elvis Presley and Jerry Lee Lewis, among others).

At this stage, he also perfected his craft by backing up Sonny Boy Williamson II, Howlin' Wolf, Elmore James, Muddy Waters, and Little Walter, some performances lasting up to twelve hours. They played straight through, no intermission, no breaks, so if one of the guys had to take a break, a fellow band member had to step in and take his instrument in hand. As reported by the *Austin Chronicle*, "That's how I learned to play drums and the guitar as well as piano; if someone had to go to the rest-room, someone else had to take his place so the music could continue."

Insane flexibility: it pains me greatly to have to say this about a guy who later turned into such a vile monster, but the young man was also a certified genius! At this point, the still only twenty-year-old musician recorded the seminal tune "Rocket 88" (named after a new model of Oldsmobile), an act that in rock music circles (which didn't really even exist yet) was the equivalent of Edison's invention of the lightbulb. It featured vocals by his band's sax player Jackie Brenston with Turner featured on a lively boogie piano and delivering an introduction that was later lifted note for note by none other than the legendary Little Richard for his upcoming "Good Golly Miss Molly" hit. Geniuses always steal from the best, so they say.

❁   ❁   ❁

While it is true that Ike and his Kings of Rhythm, during their brief recording and performing period with Brenston, have been credibly identified as a watermark in the creative invention and popular distri-bution of the musical style known as rock and roll, that uniquely hybrid mutation of several genres bent together in a raunchy romp had actu-ally already been slowly gestating for many, many years. Although it just happened to burst into the atmosphere at simultaneous times primarily in the late 1940s in America, it was already an old and almost ancient term and style by pop music standards.

From the beginning, it was commonly known, at least among music followers, that the term "rock and roll" was a euphemism for the sex act, one that had long been active in the parlance of both jazz and blues folk-lore traditions. Although it didn't surface in the public mind until the mid-1950s, the mutation of several musical motifs, including vocal jazz (itself also a slang term for sex), blues (a secular brand of gospel shout-ing with a lover replacing the deity), swing, jitterbug, boogie-woogie, and rhythm and blues, were already old when they still felt new.

There was also a huge influx of country music in rock's origins, includ-ing Ike's rockabilly, and later, when the Beatles fused the black music of artists they loved, such as Chuck Berry and Little Richard, with the semi-nal influence of Elvis Presley, then sprinkled in a dash of their own British skiffle origins, they pushed the style forward all the way into the rock age.

But its historical roots were more innocently taunting, with mariners singing sea chanteys, such as in Johnny Bowker's saucy nineteenth-century ditty about his lover demanding that he rock and roll her over.

For our purposes, 1951 was a magical year for a number of reasons. After a few decades of this fusion music that had come to be known as rhythm and blues, mostly made for black audiences, in that year Alan Freed, a corrupt radio deejay based in Cleveland, Ohio, began to play this music for mixed audiences while also first applying the term "rock and roll" to the style. But this mystery motif was already in the popular media and active among diverse ethnicities though without an official name or title. But just as more than one person invented the lightbulb (both Tesla and Edison) and more than one person invented the radio (both Tesla and Marconi), so too did more than one person invent rock and roll.

The earliest known usage of the phrase was by the Columbia Quartette in a recording of "The Camp Meeting Jubilee" around 1900, with the expressed desire to "keep on rockin' and rollin' in your arms," denoting spiritual rapture; in 1922, blues singer Trixie Smith recorded "My Man Rocks Me (with One Steady Roll)," first featuring the terms in a secular context; in 1932, the phrase "rock and roll" was heard in a Hal Roach film; in 1934, the Boswell Sisters had a pop hit with "Rock and Roll" in the film *Transatlantic Merry Go Round*; and in 1938, the western swing musician Buddy Jones released "Rockin' Rollin' Mama."

Also in 1938, Sister Rosetta Tharpe, a visionary gospel screamer who would have a huge influence on the later styles of both Chuck Berry and Tina Turner, recorded "Rock Me," originally a gospel song by Thomas Dorsey called "Hide Me in Thy Bosom," in a secular "city" electric guitar blues style. These songs and many others, including the boogie styles of both Pete Johnson and Pinetop Perkins, the early mentor of Ike Turner, were usually considered what was then called "race music"; however, in 1951, when Freed began broadcasting highly experimental tunes over his WJW AM station in Cleveland, he mixed and matched a ton of styles into his musical blender. Both he and the station's owner, Leo Mintz (who also conveniently owned a record store in classic Freed fashion), referred to the music they promoted by the now famous term "rock and roll."

According to the rock music historian Robert Palmer, whose books *Rock Begins* and *Church of the Sonic Guitar* are bibles on the subject, and echoing Aaron Cohen, "Rock and roll was an inevitable outgrowth of the social and musical interactions between black and whites in the South and Southwest. Its roots are a complex tangle. Bedrock black church music influenced blues, rural blues influenced white folk song and the black popular music of the Northern ghettos, blues and back pop influenced jazz and so on. But the single most important process was the influence of black music on white."

There is thus a straight (if jittery) line that can be drawn from a landmark artist and performer such as Ike Turner to the Beatles and the Rolling Stones and beyond, just as there is an equally straight but curvaceous line heading directly from Tina Turner to Beyoncé and Nicki Minaj. When Ike Turner created "Rocket 88" on March 5, 1951, he ignited a secret storm that would unfold for years to come. The song would be rerecorded a year later by Bill Haley in one of the first white covers of a black rhythm-and-blues song and perhaps the first recording to feature a distorted fuzzy feedback guitar, played by Ike's guitarist, Willie Kizart.

At one stage, Ike would even have a young Jimi Hendrix playing seriously fuzzy guitar with him, but he let him go because Jimi's blistering solos were "aimless and went on way too long." He had a preternatural skill at finding and using the raw talents around him, even if he was a little too conservative to fully allow his players to rock on out of bounds. But for me, apart from certain earlier Louis Jordan (known as King of the Jukebox toward the end of the swing era) and his pre-rock jive jumpers, Ike's tonal force and powerful energy were the first truly rocking rock-and-roll numbers, unleashing a primal force that would only be amplified further by his later discovery of the perfect lead singer, Anna Mae Bullock.

IKE TURNER, KING OF RHYTHM. "ROCKET 88" JULY 4, 1951, AMERICAN LEGION HALL, CHATTANOOGA, TENNESSEE

The first known performance of this seminal song was only four months after its initial release. I recently saw a vintage poster for this concert, presented like an exhibit in a museum of dreams and described in reverential tones. It offered an original relic, almost as if it were a holy grail, and in a way it is for some collectors of musical history artifacts. This unique item for sale also included a $4,000 price tag and a description that could almost be at home in a ritzy archaeology catalog, as printed in the Hake's Auction House pamphlet:

> a "22x28.25" cardboard poster advertising a "Big 4th of July Dance" at the American Legion Hall in Chattanooga Wed. July 4, 1951.
>
> Photo at left of "Jackie Brenston" w/additional text, "Singing 'Rocket 88' Featuring Ike Turner, King of The Ivories." As the auction entry continued: "This show was less than four months after 'Rocket 88' was released by *Chess Records* in 1951. The song is often cited as the first ever rock 'n roll tune and reached No. 1 on the *Billboard* R&B chart." Adding another "layer" to the immense history this piece represents is that "Rocket 88" was recorded in Memphis by Sam Phillips, who placed it w/Chess Records for release, and Phillips used the profits to start his legendary Memphis label Sun Records. Thus it remains an important artifact of the earliest days of rock 'n roll.

For many of us, though, the really crucial historical "layer" here is that with the profits gleaned from this song, Phillips went on his way to founding Sun, thus also permitting us to eventually hear Carl Perkins, Elvis Presley, Johnny Cash, Jerry Lee Lewis, Roy Orbison, Charlie Rich, and Conway Twitty (aka Harold Jenkins), among many others. Legend has it that Turner was paid only $20 for the original recording, something he would never forget. His band at the time, officially being designated by the lead singer's name, Jackie Brenston and His Delta Cats, consisted of Ike Turner on piano, Brenston on vocals and saxophone, Willie Bad Boy Sims on drums, Willie Kizart on fuzz guitar, and a young Raymond Hill, who would soon become the father of Tina Turner's first child.

James Porter is one professional listener, as well as a historian of black rock, who shares my deep respect for the humanity-challenged Ike Turner despite his obvious personal flaws. To some of us, his musical innovations were similar to the pictorial breakthroughs of a Picasso (another misogynist monster) in the art of painting. Porter says, "The evolution of Ike and/or Tina into a rock act is an interesting one. Ike, for his part, helped invent rock & roll as we know it, thanks to his involvement with Jackie Brenston's 1951 hit 'Rocket 88.' The distorted guitar on this jump-blues classic (played by Willie Kizart) was confined to rhythm, not once taking a solo, yet his riffage powered the song like the V-8 motor revved up the Oldsmobile that Brenston sang about. Even if Ike Turner had given up music after 'Rocket 88,' his rock & roll bona fides would *still* have been established right then and there."

The band known as the Kings of Rhythm has to be one of the longest continual acts in music business, let alone in rock, having played for sixty-five years all told in various versions. Turner would take along Kizart, Sims, O'Neal, Jessie Knight, and one of Ike's early wives, Anne Mae Wilson, with him to live and work in East St. Louis, where his tale as we know it today properly begins. It was there that Ike encountered the serious little weather pattern known as a Bullock storm, and they began to entrance the Missouri clubgoers at the hot little Club Manhattan.

As always, chance rules. Turner's very first song sold more than half a million copies, caused ego tensions within the band, and led to the departure of Brenston and a brief hiatus for Turner, who was about to reveal an awesome talent for scouting other talent. Ike also became a very busy session musician and production assistant for Sam Phillips and the Bihari Brothers while still contributing instrumentation to recordings by BB King, among others. Joe Bijari of Modern Records was so impressed with the spitfire Turner that he contracted him as a talent scout to find other southern musicians worth recording in the North.

Turner also continued writing original material, though without realizing it, still being somewhat green and innocent, the Bihari Brothers were copyrighting his tunes under their own name. Turner has estimated that he may have written some seventy-five hit records for the Biharis and Modern.

Then there was his uncanny skill at discovering and nurturing talent, an ability that would really come into its own over the next few years. The artists whom Turner either discovered or unearthed for Bihari included Bobby Blue Bland, Howlin' Wolf, and Roscoe Gordon, also playing piano with them on several sessions as well as on tracks by soon-to-be-big Little Milton. Around this time, approximately 1952, Turner discovered Little Junior Parker and also played piano on his first release, "You're My Angel/Bad Women, Bad Whiskey," featuring Parker's Blue Fames.

Ever the workaholic, while contracted to the Biharis at Modern Records, Turner kept on working for Phillips at Sun, for whom he cut a couple of Wolf sessions, "How Many More Years" and "Moanin' at Midnight," which Phillips sent along to the fabled Chess Records label. Turner then sneakily took Wolf across the state border and rerecorded the tracks without either Phillips's or Chess's knowledge, sending the result to Modern. Not content to simply scout talent, he even tried to poach the great Elmore James from Trumpet Records and also to record him for Modern as well.

Ike Turner ran his soon re-formed band the Kings of Rhythm kind of like a cult, exerting obsessive control of his band's every thought and gesture. Turner's discipline (a more polite word than the compulsion it really was) became legendary, with his insistence that the whole band live in one big house compound with him so he could conduct early morning rehearsals. Ironically, at this stage, Turner appeared to be a teetotaler, avoiding all drugs and alcohol and insisting that all his band members adopt this same "pure" lifestyle, fining anyone who broke his strict rules.

He also either fined or even physically assaulted band members if they played the wrong notes and controlled everything from their musical arrangements down to the very matching suits they wore together while onstage. This is the prescient talent scout, control freak, and maniacal mentor who was about to meet one Anna Mae Bullock from Nutbush, the most remarkable talent he ever had the good fortune to encounter.

But given those nostalgic memories of her sleepy childhood town that she later expressed in her wistfully rocking "Nutbush City Limits," it's extremely ironic yet also quite telling that on the very same album that featured that rural hymn to home, she also penned a totally contradictory song called "Fancy Annie." It's a raw and raunchy stomper that is slightly reminiscent of the Rolling Stones song "Brown Sugar" from their *Sticky Fingers* album, which had appeared two years before Tina's *Nutbush City Limits*.

Seemingly conflicted by nature and being pulled into two different and opposite directions, rather than only opining about her little gospel-oriented town, in this second song she also celebrated that other St. Louis–oriented Tina we're about to meet. "Fancy Annie was sweet as candy, she was never lonely cause her joint was just dandy. But Annie forgot about the hands of time, she lost her health and she nearly lost her mind. Yeah, Fancy Annie."

Thus, she had two competing myths of origin: the quiet country girl from Nutbush and the wild city chick from East St. Louis. She would really always remain in a permanently conflicted state of flux: the person she actually was versus the person Ike wanted her to be.

2

PASS ME THAT MICROPHONE

One Chance in a Million

"The only thing that remains of Ike from back in Memphis is the music. He was the best then. When I met him, I was in awe. I gave myself up."

—Tina Turner, *Nowhere to Run*, 1994

Sometimes the most important things that can happen to creative artists are those seemingly happy accidents that help them discover themselves and to find their way forward into their own careers. Maybe that's true of all of us in our lives, whether we realize it or not. For someone like Tina Turner, though, as a firm believer in the principle of karma, there are *no* accidents, happy or otherwise. Twists and turns maybe, but accidents, never.

During the course of intensive research on the trajectory of a subject, one can end up in some unexpected places. For me, it was my accidental discovery of the official record of Ike Turner's *earlier* attempts to feature a lead female performer within his Kings of Rhythm unit. Languishing in the library of the Memphis Music Recording Service and hidden in plain sight within the archives of the Sun Records label are several intriguing entries for the summer of 1953. They were a peculiar mixture of media release, public affairs announcement, and internal recording memoranda, a decade before Ike struck gold with Tina.

Among them: "Jud Phillips joins Sun Records label to help with the increasing publicity activity to promote sales for Rufus Thomas / Chess Records issues recordings by Joseph Dobbins, made in Memphis this June / Sam Phillips makes his first recordings by a white group made for the Sun label, the Ripley Cotton Choppers / Elvis Presley pays $3.98 to record "My Happiness" at Memphis Recording Services." And most intriguingly from our present perspective came the following entry: "Ike Tuner recommences bringing talent to Phillips (rather than the Bihari Brothers) for the first time since 1951, starting with Little Milton and others."

Then, for one of the archive's August entries, they list a new studio session with Ike and "Bonnie" Turner after a little context is provided: "Following the success of 'Rocket 88' in 1951, Ike Turner spent much of the next three years helping to find and record various blues musicians across the south. In 1952 Ike came back to Clarksdale and was touring with his Kings of Rhythm band, and according to Eugene Fox he came to Memphis sometime in the summer of 1953, so Ike's recordings with Bonnie are most likely dated from the same period, although as always with Ike, you're never really sure."

Thus, the record shows that during his adventures within the esoteric realm of talent scouting, he was still playing with his original band, and as early as 1952, he kind of stenciled the imprint for an early version of the Turner Revue format with the single "My Heart Belongs to You," backed with "Looking for My Baby," featuring the curious credits "Bonnie and Ike Turner" on vocals. But his voice, flat and thin, with no depth or feeling, was already indicating he was far more effective as a commanding if imperious bandleader, barking out orders to all and sundry.

The Sun archive further states that "off the back of his involvement in a raft of pre-Sun recordings, Ike Turner was frequently apportioned studio time for his own needs. As the itinerant leader of the Kings of Rhythm, he introduced into the ranks a coquettish piano player conveniently known as 'Bonnie Turner.'" Described as "one of the less chronicled female acquaintances in Ike's life, she nevertheless showed little promise on the spirited song 'Love Is a Gamble.' She was described as having traveled from Clarksdale to Memphis with her then boyfriend Ike to record demos for future single releases."

The archive entry continues to commend her staccato delivery and her pleasant enough but ultimately nondescript voice. The results, though, were not considered releasable, as she lacked both the gravitas and the power required or desired. The scouts at Sun felt it was hard to tell if she was really playing the piano. Bonnie's vocals were just not that good, and from the evidence at hand, she was deemed not that likely to ever build a career around her vocal chops.

Her only benefit, so it seemed, was that she could *appear* to play the piano well enough to allow Ike to relinquish his stool and concentrate on his new Fender Stratocaster; in fact, as the record shows, it may have been her piano playing that allowed him to browse the shiny new guitars of Houck's music store in Memphis in the first place. A nice bit of payola there.

The Sun Records archive also has an intriguing photograph of Ike and his Kings playing at the Birdcage club in 1955, in which the credits indicate members of the band and identify "singer and pianist Annie Mae Wilson," Bonnie's next vocal replacement in the Kings. He liked to keep his reserves lined up, and Ike seemed to almost collect Anna Maes as well as collecting wives. No wonder the Turner tale is a winding one.

The archive at Sun included other, similar rough pans of Annie Mae Wilson, Bonnie's replacement, who was deemed much less than stellar as well. The judgments must have been disappointing for the ladies and would have been discouraging for anyone else but Ike Turner, who appeared to have a steady stream of damsels whom he could potentially mold into gold.

In fact, if we fast-forward to 1969, with Bonnie and Anna Mae Wilson long gone and with Tina then fronting the band, Ike revisited his song "Rock Me Baby" for their *Outta Season* LP. This established that Ike's idea of how to approach the song hadn't changed much in sixteen years, but it also really proved just how much he desperately needed Tina.

Curiously, many people have identified Tina herself with two songs in particular recorded by Ike at Sun Records back in 1953 (unlikely since she was still a fourteen-year-old singing in church choirs back then), although it seems to have been "Bonnie" who did the demos and Tina who later triumphantly went on to take her place in the band, even reprising the earlier version of "Rock Me Baby" but really rocking it this time.

In Gerri Hirshey's book on soul music, *Nowhere to Run*, the two songs "Old Brother Jack" and "Way Down in the Congo," recorded at Sun Studios on August 2, 1953 (but not released until 1976), are referenced as reflections of "Tina's emotive early sessions." In that book, the author said that "Turner had a girlfriend, first known as Anna Mae Bullock, then as Bonnie Turner, and now as Tina."

Hirshey's conflation of the three singers (a Bonnie and two Annas) states that Tina's complete surrender to Ike is clearly evident on her earliest recordings. "There is nothing to connect the microphone-swallowing Acid Queen with the timorous child singing 'Old Brother Jack' and 'Way Down in the Congo,' recorded in 1953. The voice has all the confidence of a starving child singing for its supper." The author is partially correct, as there is nothing to connect the young voice of Bonnie Turner with the mature voice of Tina Turner but only because they are the distinctly varied voices of two totally different ladies.

Bonnie was Ike's first attempt at forming a Revue structure, almost a full decade before Tina's arrival on his scene but with a vocalist not nearly as strong as the one who brought him to the top of the pops later on. In between, he would attempt that ill-fated second female partnership, spookily with yet another Annie Mae (Miss Wilson). No wonder historians have been confused with Ike's dalliances. But it would be his third attempt, Tina, that proved to be the golden egg. He also had no lack of confidence that eventually he was going to stumble on just the right kind of rocking chick who was hot enough to keep up with him and his band.

He sure couldn't do the singing himself, as the Sun Records founder himself remarked. For a *Miami Herald* profile by Rod Harmon ("Ike Turner's Star Is Rising, Despite Scars of Infamy"), the great black and white record visionary Sam Phillips recalled both Ike's skills and his liabilities: "I listened to Ike sing and told him in no uncertain terms I just didn't see him as a singer. The inflections weren't there, the phrasing, none of it. But he was whale of a damn musician, one of the best piano players I'd heard up to that time, he just needed someone else to do the singing." From the inception of his career, he would be dependent on someone else to deliver the vocals, searching from person to person to find just the right one to do it.

At the time of writing her otherwise highly readable chronicle of the soul sound, *Nowhere to Run* (1984), Hirshey also shared an encounter she had with Tina at a Long Island dinner theater (prior to her comeback) in which she said the singer wasn't keen about talking about the Memphis days. But that's because it wasn't her at all in Memphis—it was Bonnie and Annie. One thing that did strike me as useful in their exchange, however, was referencing the singer's entry into a Buddhist sect known for its subtle chanting, so removed from the dry screech she's famous for. "She says her current success must be a payoff for a mother lode of bad karma: there's no other reason the first half of this life should have been so bad. No, she doesn't believe in accidents. Ike was no accident, although their marriage may have seemed like a slow-motion wreck on the highway."

But it was "Bonnie Turner" (officially listed as Marion Louise "Bonnie"), traveling much earlier on that same perilous road, with whom Ike recorded and released a few jumpy rhythm-and-blues hits, such as "Lookin' for My Baby in 1952," and this Bonnie who was in attendance at Sun Studios in 1953. I've even seen press photographs of Bonnie Turner with a credit line that actually says it was "AKA Tina." The confusion is understandable, considering Ike's wayward wanton ways. Turner was married at least ten (or twelve) times, and he often claimed to have been married fifteen times, once to someone as young as fifteen.

His first marriage, while he was still in his teens, was to Edna Dean Stewart, who passed away from a drug overdose. He then married a woman ironically named Rosa Lee Sane, with apparent mental issues, who was put in an asylum by her family. In 1953, he married pianist and singer Bonnie Mae Wilson, who was part of the Kings of Rhythm, but she left him for another man after two years. After that, he briefly married someone known only as "Alice from Arkansas," and he then became involved with the previously mentioned Annie Mae Wilson, his other failed vocal protégée, who left him for a policeman. He then quickly married Lorraine Taylor, with whom he had two sons.

By 1956, after a string of singles with multiple labels (he never stuck with only one) on Sun, RPM, Modern, and Federal, Ike had also acquired another singer, a guy this time, Billy Gayle, who sang on a minor hit with Federal called "I'm Tore Up," but Gayle would also soon leave, cementing another aggravating behavior pattern. For reasons that become obvious as history proceeds, not many people really enjoyed being around Ike Turner. His skills as a multifaceted talent were overshadowed by his already legendary temper and violence. As Tina later once told *Vanity Fair* magazine, "He had a very, very bad reputation. He was already known as 'pistol-whipping Turner.'"

Apparently not yet maritally content, long after his relationship with Tina ended, he also married a former Ikette, Margaret Ann Thomas, in 1981. After his eventual release from prison, he was met at the iron gates by blues singer Jeanette Bazzell, another Ikette, who also married him in 1995. Finally, in 2006, he married his "music collaborator" at the time, Audrey Madison, yet another Ikette, who also divorced him before his death in 2007.

It was Thomas, with whom he had rekindled a friendship, who found him unconscious at his home the day he died. He seems to have liked getting married; he didn't like *being* married obviously, but he enjoyed *getting* married. Sometimes I almost think the cause of death could have been accurately listed by a coroner as twofold: being Ike Turner and marriage.

In a sense, he was also kind of a Bill Cosby predator figure of his time but without administering quaaludes or other noxious substances to have his way with women. Inexplicably, given his character flaws, in Ike's case, his only seduction substance was the overwhelming force of his own charismatic personality: Ike *was* the drug he administered, and he was also the noxious substance.

And in that combined spirit of both consequential karma and accidental happenstance, the initial moment of collision between sixteen-year-old Anna Mae Bullock and twenty-five-year-old Ike Turner would prove to be both providential and bewildering. He was already considered something of a legend in the music business by 1956, but their shared legend together—and then her own legend alone—was only just about to materialize. All that it took for the sparks to begin to fly was Anna Mae's heartfelt declaration that the singer and his band "put her in a trance." Little did she know that she was only the latest in a long line of starry-eyed young ladies who had been similarly mesmerized by Ike.

※   ※   ※

Anna Mae generally followed the lead of her elder sister Alline when it came to playing kids' games together in the country, and when she was growing up into mature girlhood, she also followed her lead right into the dens of inequity that peppered a hopping city like St. Louis. That's where all the exciting new adult games were taking place.

Remember, the two country-girl sisters learned all about music from only two limited and drastically divergent sources: the gospel sounds of sanctified church gatherings (which could get plenty raucous and kick up quite a ruckus, including much frenzied dancing) as well as the tiny tinny radio they listened to while cooking up sliced potatoes on the top of their family's old kitchen stove. The sounds they heard sweeping across the nation during the mid-1950s were enough to get the blood of any kids stirring faster, and the Bullock sisters were no different, just more distant from the urban din back then. They were, however, definitely ready to rock and roll.

Anna Mae also used to enjoy incorporating some of the twangy energy she heard on their father's wooden radio into her own personal fantasy plays, which she conducted at her mother's bedroom dressing table when she thought no one was watching (though her mother later commented on her boisterous little performances with some disdainful amusement). This girl just seemed to have been a born performer from the beginning.

She would pull the two side mirrors together so that they enclosed her little frame and pretend to play piano by pounding on the counter surface with wild abandon and acknowledging the invisible crowds' applause with dainty bows. It goes without saying that this motif would later explode into the actual screams of gigantic adoring crowds in stadium-scale performances once she underwent her radical transformation into the mature Tina.

As a matter of fact, if it's accurate to claim Ike as the inventor of a new hybrid of boogie, blues, and rockabilly that came to be known as rock and roll (which I tend to believe since it took Little Richard six years to lift the opening bars of "Rocket 88" and launch a revolution along with Chuck Berry's similarly lifted guitar solos, himself a mix of Ike Turner and the incredible Sister Rosetta Tharpe), then I'm quite comfortable claiming that Tina Turner was almost the inventor of *rock* music per se and stadium rock for sure in tandem with rock's other official inventors, in my opinion, the Rolling Stones.

I've always been mystified when listeners link together or discuss Tina in the same soul music context of James Brown, Aretha Franklin, or Sharon Jones, for instance. To me, she was never, ever, really, a soul singer at all, although her bluesy brand of sensual rocking and rolling was soulful for sure, and, yes, she did deliver the occasional soul-based song exquisitely.

Aaron Cohen feels that despite many distinctions in her evolving styles over the years, Tina Turner was still basically a soul music artist, albeit one who stretched the parameters of what that might mean. As he remarked to me, "I believe so, but also my definition of 'soul music' is perhaps more broad than most others' definition. But I would certainly consider her a soul singer by any description: coming out of gospel, bringing that style of singing to black secular music, the call-and-response between her and her band, that's all what anyone would consider soul, or certainly R&B. Anyway, if Tina Turner singing 'Knock on Wood' in the late 1960s isn't soul, then what is?" I sense a rhetorical question there, and fair enough.

Ike was of course the exact opposite of soul music. He didn't have a soul bone in his skinny body: strictly boogie blues and almost a jitterbug vibe until Tina took him in a whole new direction of her own. It was that old wooden radio on the stove that really started Anne Mae on the road to both self-expression and liberation as well as a little perdition thrown in for spice. For her, things "started getting crazy" in the midst of 1956, a year when all of America seemed to be in the grip of the new kind of music: rhythm and blues mingled with rockabilly and country, the exotic amalgam of black and white emotive sound structures being introduced predominantly or most publicly by Bill Haley and the Comets and, soon enough, the earth-shattering arrival of Elvis.

Rock and roll was decidedly and defiantly one of the first totally urban music styles after jazz. Any city seemed like a big city if you're from Nutbush, an unincorporated little town without any city limits. For Anna Mae, though gigantic by comparison to Nutbush, St. Louis proper was a somewhat sedate place in the mid-1950s. But East St. Louis, now that was a whole other thing. That was where the action was, especially Alline's kind of naughty action, and it never seemed to stop—cathouses, gambling dens, uncountable music clubs and bars, roadhouses, juke joints, and constant nightlife that continued on all through the day and started all over again every night.

There were tantalizing temptations for a young, rather small, and wide-eyed country girl with an older sister she idolized who could guide her through the stunning bright lights of the Blue Note, the Birdcage, the Sportsman, the Lakeside, Perry's Lounge, Kingsbury's Lounge, Garrett's Lounge, and others, sometimes on the same night. There was lots of *lounging* going on; it was a new way of life. Many of these joints (that's the only word for them) didn't even feel the need to have keys to lock up since they stayed open twenty-four hours a day and all yearlong. Who needs holidays when life already is a holiday?

For musicians (a special breed to begin with), East St. Louis provided the ways and means to be what could only be described as *ridiculously happy*. And at the epicenter of it all, holding court at the Club Manhattan like a reigning monarch, was lanky and languid Ike Turner, the leader of an exciting rhythm group that Alline couldn't stop raving about. Still only sixteen, Anna Mae was in awe of her sister, who was already frequenting the clubs and dating dangerous dudes who picked her up in huge Cadillacs and Lincolns. One of them, Leroy Tyus, owned a club suggestively called the Tail of the Cock, where Alline was a barmaid, but she was just as well known all across town.

On the weekends, after her various dude dates ended, she and her girlfriends would go to see Ike Turner performing at Club D'Lisa (you didn't bring boyfriends to see Ike because they wouldn't like him, and he definitely didn't like them), and then after hours, from 2:00 a.m. until forever, he would sit on the throne-like stage at Manhattan directing the action in the room as if he were making a Fellini movie, which, in some strange way, maybe he was. Anna Mae, dressed up in her sister's clothes and dolled up with makeup trying to look older and more serious than she really was, found it to be the ultimate jumping joint, almost as if every little hole-in-the-wall club down south had been smashed together into one circus-like arena up north.

Two hundred and fifty seats for squirming patrons (yes, mostly women) waiting for Ike to strut his stuff from the stage set up in the center of the room with the tables encircling it and a gigantic painting of the Kings of Rhythm hanging up on the wall—it must have felt like

Las Vegas when Elvis was there, otherworldly, heady beyond description, especially to this young rural girl pretending to be a more urban adult. The band would already be playing when Alline and Anna Mae arrived, following their custom of warming up the crowd before King Ike emerged.

And when he finally did, Anna Mae later recalled for Kurt Loder, you could feel it. "He had the body then that David Bowie had—great. His suit looked like it was hanging on a hanger. I thought, what an immaculate-looking black man." But for her, even so young, she knew he wasn't really *her type*. For one thing, his teeth and hairstyle were all wrong, looking like a wig had been glued on, and on closer inspection, she was able to notice that, for her tastes, he was simply *ugly*. But there was still just *something* about him. "Then he got up onstage and picked up his guitar. He hit one note. And the joint started rocking."

The dance floor was crammed with sweaty people gyrating, with Anna Mae sitting there gob smacked, wondering why so many women liked him given what she thought he looked like. But she continued closely studying him while listening to his amazingly tight band, glued together sonically as only a band that has played a song 10,000 times can be. She was, as has been reported many times, entranced. She and all the other couple of hundred swaying dames and girls were stunned by his magnetism and waiting for a chance to catch his eye—which was just the way King Ike liked his kingdom to roll.

In an odd way, she was hooked right from the start. It wasn't love at first sight, not by any means, more something like wonderment. Sooner or later, it seemed inevitable that she would have the opportunity to be up on that stage singing out in the midst of those swirling lights and all those twisting bodies. It took a little while, as the inevitable often does, but it was, she decided, going to happen, and her sister was clearly the way to help it along.

In yet another sequence of apparent karmic influences (as Tina Turner would later undoubtedly feel given her evolving philosophical and spiritual inclinations), sister Alline had been dating, among her many beaus, the drummer of the Kings of Rhythm, Eugene Washington. Gene began to notice over the coming weeks that his girlfriend was always showing up with her younger sister, then still a gangly junior at Summer High School. Washington, who felt the vibes coming off the girl like electricity but also knew very well Ike's tastes in ladies (generally big and round, all around), felt that she was way too skinny and underfed by country standards to ever really garner much attention from his majesty.

But the erstwhile rhythm man and longtime member of the Ike cult was smart enough to know that he needed to cultivate the friendship of Alline's mother and to gain her trust and affection (today I believe we refer to this cultivation process as *grooming*)—or perhaps I should say, as a proficient enabler, that he was devious enough to do so. He actually audaciously asked her mother, whom he had gotten to know somewhat, if Anna Mae could go to the Manhattan as long as he looked after her (kind of like enlisting the protection of a crocodile when you think about it). And Anna's mother, never known especially for her maternal instincts, gave her consent.

As the drummer, Washington had a platform raised above the rest of the band, and from this perch, he was able to observe the young fan and her restless yearning to sing along. He even went so far as to dangle a microphone off the edge of the stage to pick up the chirps and warblings of perhaps the most enthusiastic audience member. Anna Mae became a regular at most of the clubs where King Ike was appearing and somehow struck up a friendship with the bassist in the band, Jessie Knight, among others, in what seemed like a pronounced attempt to penetrate the inner sanctum of Turner's kingdom.

She even pressed her sister Alline to ask Eugene Washington to ask Ike if she could try a song sometime, which he mumbled some disinterested assent to but never really followed up on because (even Anna Mae was certain) she was not his type of dame. Finally, her patience wore thin, and during an intermission one night—in a quiet spell when most of the band was hanging out, smoking or drinking, but Ike was up alone onstage playing the organ by himself—Anna Mae recognized the song he was tinkering with, a BB King tune called "You Know I Love You."

Washington returned from outside, by now half plastered, and began playfully offering the microphone to his girlfriend Alline, who, though a fairly reckless party girl, wouldn't have been caught dead singing in public. Observers can recall what happened next, and certainly Anna Mae will never forget it since it was that moment when destiny stands up and screams, "You!" She took the mic and started singing along, "I love you for myself but you're gone and left me for someone else, when night began to fall I cry alone . . . ," causing Ike to pull up short, jump offstage with a wailing "Girl!," pick her up off her feet, and demand to know what else she knew how to sing. Anna Mae's response was as guileless as it was accurate when she quietly remarked, "Well, everything they play on the radio I guess."

✻   ✻   ✻

Knowing the Anna Mae we've all heard of today, it's hard to imagine a teenager, someone who had never sung professionally, wanting so badly to climb onstage with this strange but alluring guy who had been around for years already. But knowing the later Tina, we might at least imagine her gumption at thinking, as quoted by Maureen Orth in a *Vanity Fair* profile, "I was of course very excited. Very competent too, because I've been a singer all my life." Right, all sixteen years of it so far.

Turner was utterly blown away by the raspy voice coming out of this skinny kid, someone he was already nicknaming Little Ann in a deceptively friendly manner. Orth also referenced the technique Ike employed, what I would call using self-pity to gain sympathy from the obvious raw talent in front of him. "My problem is, people always took my songs away from me, and my singers always leave me." He was so knocked out by her voice and energy that he couldn't believe she was only a teenager who sounded like an old Bessie Smith howler. "When I got there," Tina explained to Orth, "Ike was so shocked, and he never let me go."

So Ike played some songs she knew, the band began to mull back in and join in as she sang "Since I Fell for You" and did a duet with Jimmy Thomas on "Love Is Strange." It sure is. Her mother Zelma of course wanted none of it once she discovered that her daughter had already been singing semiregularly instead of doing what she expected her to do: be a nurse or a maid. Oddly enough, in a few short years, Anna Mae would indeed be a nurse and a maid but with only one patient: Ike.

He sent his second failed attempt at a singer, Anna Mae Wilson, over looking for his new young discovery, much to the horror of Zelma. Then, afterward, he again sent his loyal drummer to come across as a chaperone since, like all characters of his ilk, he needed to befriend the girl's mother in order to have full and easy access to the girl (at this stage, only to her voice). He then also went over in person himself to visit and charmed her mother, as he was somehow able to do with most people, promising that he'd personally take care of her and make sure nothing bad ever happened.

As reported in *Off the Record*, her voice was indeed remarkable and maybe even one worth conniving over. "When I started singing with Ike, I was basically patterning myself after most of the male singers I was around, like Ray Charles and Sam Cooke. I think my voice is heavy because my mother's and my sister's also is. I think the raspiness is the natural sound. But the style really came from mimicking my surroundings. The pretty way of singing is not my style, I like them rough."

She was so young when she started, despite the strange maturity of her voice, that she didn't really see what was going on in the dynamics of their blossoming relationship at all. She even stipulated to all and sundry that Ike was very good to her when she first started her career, going so far as to claim that since she was still in high school and singing only on weekends, they became close friends and had what she thought was a fun life.

She also actually felt sorry for his sob saga, something he was counting on no doubt, and she could even empathize with him (her inherent skill), which was something I'm sure he carefully calculated and amplified. "He was broken hearted because every time he got a hit record on somebody, of course *they* got to be the star," was how she put it to Gerri Hirshey in a *GQ* magazine piece. "The man was very nice to me, way before our relationship really started, I promised him that I wouldn't leave him." That was almost a prophetic statement on her part.

At first, their relationship was kind of sibling-like, in a foreboding sort of way, but Ike wasted no time, partly because he was a brilliant talent scout, partly because he was a cad, and totally because he suddenly saw and heard what was missing in his earlier protégées Bonnie and Annie Mae Wilson. Turner went out on a shopping spree and bought her new clothes as stage attire. To me, what he decked her out in was almost a kind of female impersonator costume: hugely high stiletto heels, nylons, and skintight, clingy, sequined miniskirts. That's when I think he truly felt the future arriving, and he jumped on board.

No doubt all of the other patrons of the Club Manhattan, especially the women who always had an impossible-to-understand attraction to

Ike, looked on this scrawny kid with disdain as she suddenly assumed a regular role onstage. Disdain is putting it mildly perhaps; it was undiluted hatred for someone they assumed was only stealthily cashing in her meal ticket. But nothing could be further from the truth.

Anna Mae was simply soaking up the exciting glamour and enjoying the attention bestowed on her for what she always knew was an innate vocal gift, and it was really King Ike who was the one who saw his one-way ticket away from the dives of St. Louis. He dreamed of going onward and upward to the legitimate theaters and concert halls he so coveted, such as the Regal Theater in Chicago, the Howard Theater in Washington, or the holy grail of all music performance cathedrals, the Apollo Theater in New York.

He may have been nuts, but he was also right (almost always), and the other members of his Rhythm Kings knew it too when they heard it in Anna Mae: something out of this world, a magical sonic ingredient you can't just concoct no matter how good a musician you were. Loder characterized it very well: "Her voice combined the emotional force of the great blues singers with a sheer, wallpaper-peeling power that seemed made to order for the age of amplification." From my perspective, she was also about to accidentally invent rock music.

Drummer Eugene Washington couldn't believe his ears either, noting that women don't usually get away with this degree of raw power, unless they were Bessie Smith maybe, and he was fully aware that up until that point, he and Ike and the other Kings were basically delivering solid but simple and down-home boogie-swing numbers. This was a whole new ball game, and it was the real deal, an original style, not just them doing covers of other people's music anymore. Ike could now write it, and Anna Mae could dish it out. It was a match made in you know where.

Moving swiftly after he inadvertently "discovered" his future singing sensation, their very first appearance as Ike and Tina Turner was as the opening act for a BB King concert on January 9, 1956, at the Café Royale in Lake Charles, Louisiana. A vintage poster identifies King performing his hit "Every Day I Have the Blues" and featuring special "guest" (singular) Ike and Tina Turner, with the freshly minted Tina being still only seventeen years old.

At this stage, another musician of Ike's unit, Raymond Hill from his "Rocket 88" days, was doing the duties of being her first official "boyfriend." They moved in together, and he stayed for a while, but then he moved on, amiable but maybe not fiery enough to match "Little Ann," as Anna Mae was still known personally during this period. Ike stepped in, and even though he'd gotten his other girlfriend pregnant, he became seriously unplatonic with Anna Mae to the point that when she too became pregnant, Ike's girlfriend Lorraine naturally assumed that it was Ike's. She knew how much Ike liked to get people pregnant.

But pregnant with Raymond Hill's baby, not Ike's, Anna Mae's conflict with Ike's jealous girlfriend was still amplified. On August 20, 1958, recent high school graduate and eighteen-year-old Anna Mae gave birth to Hill's son Craig (who sadly would kill himself in 2018), while on October 3, Ike's girlfriend Lorraine gave birth to hers: Ike Jr. This was obviously a freight train moving at faster and faster speeds, heading who the hell knew where. But I honestly suspect that both Ike and Anna Mae knew exactly what each wanted from the other and what they were going to get out of the deal—up to a point. By this time, Raymond Hill was already history, so Anna Mae briefly took a job as a nurse's aide in the maternity ward of Barnes Hospital to try to make maternal ends meet.

Ike, as usual, was fighting tooth and nail with his band members, the singers (especially Lorraine), and anybody else who was foolish enough to get in his overheated way. The next thing she knew, "Little Ann" was officially named lead singer of the group, so she dutifully moved back out of her mother's place (not liking it much with her anyway) and into Ike's house and cultish musicians commune in East St. Louis. There was already an ominous note hanging heavily in the air. That was when Anna Mae felt it: the first time she definitely knew that Ike Turner was assuming a huge role in her life.

It must have felt like she was the still child star of her own movie, except it was her real life. Rather ominously, she characterized it later on as, without fully knowing it at the time, Ike *moving in on her life*—a curious turn of phrase and one that couldn't possibly bode very well for all concerned. To mark the occasion, he raised her salary to a whole $25 a week. To make it all truly official, though, he'd have to turn her into Tina Turner. And that's just what he did.

CHITLIN' ROYALTY

Touring Mania

"Her vocals sounded like screaming dirt . . . it was a funky sound."

—Juggy Murray, Sue Records, 1959

Basically, blues, jazz, rock and roll, soul, and funk all evolved out of turning adversity into art. The Chitlin' Circuit was the fond name of a collection of performance venues throughout the southern, eastern, and upper Midwest areas of America that provided commercial and cultural acceptance for African American musicians and other performers during the era of racial segregation. The name derives from the soul food item *chitterlings* (stewed pig intestines) and is also a play on the Borsht Belt, a resort area that was popular with Jewish entertainers from the 1940s and 1960s. The live concert touring club circuit provided employment for hundreds of black musicians and eventually brought about the birth of rock and roll as a central if unintentional side effect.

Music is also very often integrally connected to major social issues, as Aaron Cohen stressed in *Move On Up*. "A generation born at the tail end of the African American Great Migration created its art while contending with segregation, integration and deindustrialization. Music ran alongside civil rights activism, and some performers contributed to that crusade." Tina Turner would definitely be among the most influential of them all.

The circuit term ironically memorializes the cultural history of black people, who were often given only the intestines of the pig to eat as opposed to the bacon or ham, thus coming to symbolize acquiring a taste out of necessity but coming to like and identify with it. Ike and Tina Turner came to represent a certain kind of majesty within this supposedly humble entertainment environment that helped elevate it into a cultural phenomenon. Their Revue would create among the first major crossover opportunities for mass white audiences to absorb black musical motifs. They were also probably the busiest performers on earth during this time.

Aaron Cohen's comments to me on the intertwined nature of geographical and cultural influences are revealing in this respect. "The vast African American migration from north to south and the music that resulted is, indeed, too vast to adequately describe. But it was often multi-directional from the 1940s through the 1960s, with urban northern performers and musicians influencing Southern artists as much as Southerners brought their sounds up north (musicians going back and forth, producers and arrangers from Detroit working in Memphis and vice versa).

"What's interesting in Tina Turner's case is that she seemed to be more global than exclusively American. Maybe that eclecticism came through in her embrace of Buddhism, but I can't say for sure. Maybe this international personal vision served her particularly well enough so she could have numerous inner resources to draw from as she staged her huge comeback later on in the 1980s."

The touring circuit was a powerful but also a dangerous context for performers, as Cohen also clarified to me: "While this may be a broad statement, I always understood the 'chitlin' circuit' to be the loosely (very loosely) organized network of performance venues for African American audiences that sprung up during segregation and, to a limited extent, still exist today. The circuit itself was filled with crooks and thugs (of all colors) and I have heard that, actually, Ike Turner was accomplished at not just forcefully dealing with these characters, but making sure that his entire band got paid. Not sure if that's true, but I could see how Tina Turner would have seen him as a protector in this environment, at least, initially."

For Toronto-based music journalist and author John Corcelli, the astonishing growth and evolution of musical styles connected to geographical shifts is a powerful one. Corcelli concurs on the essential ingredient of these North–South artistic "trade routes" in constructing a uniquely Yankee musical sensibility. "When it comes to race-relations in the United States, Turner had to find her own artistic path. Sadly, many of the great American black singers had to play gigs that were 'politically correct.' That said, a gig is a gig, and if you choose to make your living in concert performances, you're no worse for wear by doing so by any means necessary.

"To me, Turner paid her musical dues by rigorously playing the 'chitlin circuit' and she emerged out of it as a kind of rite of passage, just as so many black performers that came before her had done. My main observation regarding that vast cultural migration is that our entire understanding of contemporary American music would not ever have been created without it. *All American music is rooted in dreams*, as the great Duke Ellington once said."

James Porter, always an astute chronicler of black rock music, certainly feels that African American artistry is beyond geography and far outside the scope of merely northern or southern sensibilities. The dream of freedom, whether political or musical, disregards arbitrary borders. "To me, that means one thing: limitless cultural aspiration. You don't have to be bound to one specific idea of blackness. You can redefine the medium as you please without having someone from on high tell you it's not black enough. Or white enough. I think this was a by-product of the African-American cultural migration—mentally, musically and physically. The downside of this is that some of the grittier southern sounds, like the blues, were left behind, with the incorrect perception that it was synonymous with hard times. Even so, there still were vague traces of the blues in all mainstream black music, at least until the disco era."

Despite their close working and living relationship, however, I remain convinced today of something I've always suspected: I seriously doubt that Ike Turner ever had any romantic interest in Anna Mae Bullock whatsoever. Conquest perhaps but only in the very broadest sense of the word. I don't think he found her attractive at all in the customary sense, but he did have a profound and sudden awareness that she was a prodigy, probably because he was one too (or used to be). He needed her to fulfill his long-held dream of music world domination, even though he was a small thinker and likely just wanted more club dates, a few more record sales, and more expensive drugs.

Meanwhile, back when the 1950s was drawing to a close, Ike was going through other fresh singers as if they were loaves of bread, looking for the right equation, always utilizing the Kings of Rhythm with interchangeable vocalists. He tried Brenston again (the voice from "Rocket 88") on "You Keep Worrying Me," Tommy Hodge on "I'm Gonna Forget about You," and Betty Everett on "Tell Me Darling," and finally he tried using his new protégée, Anna Mae Bullock, mostly in the background still, on their next throwaway single tune.

The first time her dry, breathy voice was heard on a recording, although still doing scenery chores, was in the novelty song "Box Top" in 1958, released to a silent response by a little local St. Louis label, Tune Town, and while still being listed on the single as "Little Ann." It was an inauspicious beginning perhaps by the standards of what came afterward, but everyone has to start somewhere. Besides, what came afterward came almost immediately and with a force and fury that rivaled the upcoming British invasion in sheer intensity if not numbers.

Never one to avoid complicating his life further, by 1959, he'd split with his girlfriend Lorraine and started more of what he had promised Zelma he would never do with her starstruck daughter. Anna Mae wasn't happy, she hated his blatantly philandering ways, but she felt stuck. Her main mistake was when it became more personal, and in fact, had it not become intimate and later violent, they possibly could still have stayed together. One thing she realized clearly, though, was that she *was* addicted to a drug of sorts, but it wasn't Ike she was addicted to; it was performing live music that she craved so powerfully that she'd be willing to put up with Ike, at least for a while.

Sure enough, near the end of 1960, however, Anna Mae did become pregnant, this time more obviously with Ike's child, and as if like clockwork, Lorraine moved back into the scenario, causing Anna Mae to leave Ike and his Virginia Place home yet again and take a little house back in St. Louis proper, where she hired a woman to look after her first son, Craig (Raymond Hill's), while she went to work. While pregnant, Anna Mae naturally still continued Ike's usual dizzying round of hectic club dates as well as live appearances on some college campuses.

On the morning of October 27, she gave birth to her second baby, Ike's son Ronald, but only days after the birth, Ike insisted that she leave the hospital to perform with him in Oakland, California. She had to stay in the hospital, on doctor's orders, so Ike hired an impersonator (who turned out to have been a hooker) to portray Tina, as she was by then known. Forever afterward, Tina would be haunted by the pop conspiracy rumor that she herself was in fact a prostitute.

By this time, Anna Mae wasn't just the featured occasional singer with his band; she was indeed the full-time star vocalist. This is the period during which Ike was restlessly trying to repeat his early success nine years earlier, continuing to repetitively copy the same tired formula over and over, never seeming to realize that he might try striking out in a new direction if he wanted a new hit record.

Ike merely saw his main chance to do something he'd already been trying to accomplish for the past decade or so with other female singers when Anna Mae just happened to show up at the edge of his stage. Once he began to coordinate his career-making campaign, he simply then related to her in the only way he knew how. He didn't seem to know any better, or else just couldn't help himself, being unable to maintain a strictly platonic business or creative relationship. His concept of male–female relations, after all, was rather narrow and thuggish to say the least: have sex with them, marry them, make them pregnant, and hit them, pretty much in that order.

By then, she was already in the early transformative stages of becoming someone else, living with Ike (and Lorraine) almost as if they were her adult chaperones. But soon enough, two inevitable events occurred: Ike broke up with Lorraine and with Little Ann, who still believed he was looking out for her best interests (like a brother and sister, was her innocent assumption). Little Ann still naively but seriously believed she was in love (or a kind of love) with him despite the fact that sexual relations with him repulsed her, and she relented mostly because of everything she thought he was doing to help her in her life and music career.

In addition to all the frenzied touring, she then participated in the second inevitability, a new Ike song single, ironically titled "A Fool in Love," which was being recorded on the fly. This second time, it was a surprise hit. Ike had sent the tapes to some of his St. Louis deejay friends who also shared them with one of the few record labels owned and operated by a black entrepreneur, Henry "Juggy" Murray, of Sue Records. Murray was instantly taken with Little Ann's voice. "Smitten with the kitten" was how he put it.

The label owner traveled to ostensibly meet Ike in East St. Louis, where he encountered him in his usual domain of Cadillacs and young (usually white) girls. But actually, it was really Anna Mae he wanted to meet, and he did, then also stunning Ike by slapping down a contract with a $25,000 advance on the table and declaring that Ike should abandon his intended plan of rerecording the track with a male vocal. "It was," he announced, "really only Anna Mae that made the song work the way it did."

The record promoter apparently knew in the first moments of hearing the tape that this was going to be a hit, even though Ike had been rejected many times by other labels he had tried before Sue Records. Ike was puzzled by Juggy's certainty but was probably impressed and a little awed by his aggressive confidence. He wondered why this new guy on the scene believed so strongly in a song no one else cared about, to which Juggy responded that they didn't know what he knew. He is also known to have historically observed, in Loder's Turner testimonial, that "Ike was a musical genius, but he wouldn't know a hit record if it fell off the Empire State Building and hit him on the head."

Murray was also the one who suggested (always one to follow his own intuition faithfully) that Ike should seriously consider making Anna Mae the permanent up-front lead singer of his show, not just a backup singer, that she was way too good for that secondary role. That was all Ike had been waiting to hear, for about ten years in fact, and just as intuitively as Juggy, he pronounced that the new single would be released with Anna Mae as the lead vocalist. But even more propitiously, he heralded the newborn existence (in his head, at that very moment) of a whole new group name to replace the Kings of Rhythm identity that he'd worked with for so long.

The new single would be credited to Ike and Tina Turner. This was obviously a huge surprise to Anna Mae Bullock, who wasn't at all sure about adopting a stage name he'd concocted in reverence to a white blond television heroine named Sheena (of the Jungle) he grew up fantasizing about. She was even less sure about how deeply she was getting involved with a guy she didn't even really like (even though she had convinced herself that she loved him in order to get by) and despite the fact that she recently had the spawn of Ike living inside of her body.

Yet she was also still enthralled by what she, a nobody little country girl, had achieved as a result of his looming presence in her life as a show business mentor and manager. Especially impressive was his stated intention of moving to California, where he said the action was, if the new record was a hit, something that both appealed to and yet daunted her at the same time.

✿   ✿   ✿

Not very long at all into the rapidly accelerating arc of their performing career, including his plan to pay her rent expenses but keep all the money they made for himself (a decision that even a still youngish neophyte knew couldn't possibly be correct or fair), came her earliest encounters with what one might call the real Ike, the one concealed beneath his disguise of slick suits and magical rhythms. First, she didn't like her name being changed. She had tried to explain that she didn't really like the arrangement, that it was unfair, and also that she didn't actually want anything more to do with him anyway. "Click" went a secret button in his head.

A danger switch went off, one likely connected to his dream of making his third female lead singer in a row the one who made him rich, and he suddenly beat her up for the first time, using a shoe stretcher (later on, shoes themselves would be a preferred method for pounding on her), leaving her with a swollen eye and a fearful realization that her life had taken a sinister turn.

Now of course, this unsavory and even sordid side of their story has been more than amply chronicled in the 1993 film *What's Love Got to Do with It?*, featuring a grippingly dramatic Laurence Fishburne and Angela Bassett portrayal, following the well-documented and much-publicized personal testimonial of the singer in 1986. These aspects were naturally expected to be contentious, and they were, with Ike loudly lamenting for two decades his false treatment amid a pack of lies and Tina stoically standing by her side of the story. Like most abusers, he went to his grave in a state of denial about his own toxic behavior, preferring to blame everyone else around him.

From our vantage point now (and even back then as I recall), the salient question was this: which person in such a dynamic would one expect to have a firmer grasp on their memory and therefore the accuracy of the narrative, the one who was blotted out on cocaine and ego rage or the victim, who was repeatedly brutalized in a lifestyle of coercion? End of debate, I'd say. As Tina put it so wistfully in *My Love Story*, "Living with Ike was a high wire act, he'd jump on anything, just to fight. I had to tread carefully. In a perverse way, the bruises he gave me were markings, a sign of ownership, another way of saying—she's mine and I can do whatever I want with her. I knew it was time to leave but I didn't know how to take the first step."

It's but another opportunity for us to focus on two things that don't matter more but that matter at least as much: first, how his warped genius as impresario-producer brought her into our collective experience and, second, the singer's contribution to pop music history during her duet persona and especially what she accomplished as a solo artist in her post-hostage phase. When dealing with a person as a subject who was willing to undergo even emotional privations to artistically express herself publicly, it's always the music that matters most to us because that's clearly what mattered most to her.

But like many women, she first convinced herself that she had done something wrong, that she didn't fully appreciate him, that she didn't want to walk out on him just when his career was taking off, and that she could work harder to make things better between them—a common litany of excuses. The main thing she was forgetting of course in her strategy of personal rationalizations was the fact that it was *she herself* who was the secret of his success, not him, just as the eccentric Juggy Murray had predicted. Thank goodness for Juggy and his gentle persuasion regarding Anna Mae being the real star.

Immediately following their first hit, "A Fool in Love," and with truly sizzling ambition, Ike figured the time was right to do two things: get even busier on the road while also getting back into the studio. The important thing to remember about Ike and Tina at this stage is that her future husband and manager was proceeding on the assumption that his dream was coming true but that it all might easily end soon, so he had to perform, write, and record as if there was no tomorrow just in case there wasn't.

A steady stream of songs was feverishly cooked up somewhere in the back of his busy mind, especially singles, which tumbled out of his brain like leaves from a tree. All told, they eventually released sixty-eight singles in their time together, with twenty-seven LP albums, twenty compilation records, and twelve live LP albums. Obviously, some were better than others, but all were compelling and captivating to some degree, especially if they primarily featured the torchy gifts of his young new girlfriend from down south.

In December 1960, the group's next single, ominously titled "I Idolize You," rose to number 5 on the R&B charts and number 82 on the pop charts listed by *Billboard*. The year 1961 saw Sue Records release their debut album, *The Soul of Ike and Tina Turner* (although I'm one who questions whether it was actually soul music), with a horde of quickly popular songs, such as the equally ironically titled "It's Gonna Work Out Fine."

James Porter told me that it was the inherent nature of rhythm and blues that it would eventually erupt into rock, simply by unleashing its core values at a higher volume. "When Ike & Tina first started to make noise as a duo, it was during a time when the distinction between rock & roll and rhythm & blues was marginal. Prior to 1965 or so, even the smoothest of vocal groups were referred to as 'rock & roll,' even though modern ears might hear them as rhythm & blues today. While Ike & Tina's earliest releases were right in the R&B mode of the time, occasionally glimmers of 'rock & roll' would come blasting through. Witness the blazing guitar intro to 'It's Gonna Work Out Fine' for instance." There is indeed a blurry yet strong lineage linking these genres that precludes any easy classification, and with Ike and Tina, we can certainly witness powerful purveyors of the subliminal threshold between these two styles.

Tina remembered this early period with undiluted dread when discussing the details for *Vanity Fair* and flatly stated that she would have loved to leave him at this stage, but "I was caught in his web." This was also the period during which he began regularly clobbering her out of nowhere, and if she dared to ask him what she had done wrong to provoke this bad treatment, he would pound on her even more.

Recalling this time for a *GQ* piece later on, she explained that there was a constant pressure to produce more hit singles and records and that even though it was *she* who had made *him* a star, she was the innocent one being terrorized. "I just went home, put on an ice pack, and I found a way to sing over the next few days. I just kept going."

Marriage for Ike had always been a means to an end. In his attempts to control whatever profits he had accrued through her talents, he also enlisted Tina's assistance in protecting them from former wives seeking shared income by simply marrying his young new singer. Ike's constant appetite for more hit records seemed exceeded only by the public's appetite for more Tina tunes. On Cenco Records in 1964, he released *Get It* as well as *Her Man His Woman* on Capitol Records.

He also went on a big binge of one-offs: *Ike and Tina Turner Revue Live* on Kent Records, *Ike and Tina Live Volume 2* on Loma Records, and a different version with the same title on Warner Bros., the last of which climbed to an impressive number 126 in *Billboard*. That year would be their true recording borderline: a kind of holding pattern before and after their upcoming wall-of-sound experience with the equally loopy producer Phil Spector. Ike would embrace that pinnacle too, and even though it didn't really involve his input, he could always find some way to take credit for it.

Ike was shifting into overdrive. One of the tricks that Art Lassiter, Ike's frontman for the Kings of Rhythm, was already up to in his own career was stealing Ray Charles's idea of a backup group of cute chicks to add some spice to his performances, a trio he called the Artettes after Ray's fem format called the Raylettes. Guess what Ike decided to call his own trio of cute chicks to back up his new singing sensation Tina once "A Fool in Love" started to burn up the charts. Never one to reinvent the wheel unnecessarily but instead to simply make improvements on its existing design, he naturally stole the already stolen idea and named them the Ikettes.

"A Fool in Love" was an extraordinary debut, raw and gritty pulsations with hugely thumping bass lines and a sharply articulate tapping drumming tempo, all with the newborn Tina Turner yelping away to her heart's discontent on top of the mix, just where she belonged. It still packs a punch all this time later: there was just some simple but lasting magic in it that seemed to come out of nowhere. A seeming case of sui generis, ex nihilo, born from nothing, in a class by itself, unique as a species that does not appear to fit into any other species.

It's kind of like a blind date between Mahalia Jackson and James Brown or perhaps a double date between Ray Charles and Rosetta Tharpe. It is one of Tina's most important songs because as her first outing, it set the template for absolutely everything that would came afterward. Two minutes and thirty seconds of blissful sorrow, with a B-side of "The Way You Love Me" for dessert, and on her very first featured vocalist stint, she had made it into Ike's first national hit, one of the first rhythm-and-blues tracks to cross over to pop charts and go on to become a million seller.

Ike's first hit a decade earlier had of course not been credited to him, inappropriately, and it had left him struggling solely as a regional act. This time, with Tina fronting his band, there would be no mistake, and years later, *Rolling Stone* would correctly characterize it as one of the blackest records to ever creep into the *Billboard* Hot 100 since Ray Charles arrived.

Featuring a scorching lead vocal by Tina, instrumentation by the Kings of Rhythm, and background vocals by Robbie Montgomery, Sandra Harding, and Frances Hodges, while being led on the piano by its writer and producer, Ike Turner, the tune just cooked. This is also the song that would begin their physically punishing tour of one-night circuit stands, including their first primal descent into the Apollo Theater, resulting in the group's stunning presentation on *American Bandstand* to the utter amazement of very young, conservatively suited Dick Clark. It also had a lasting impact on Tina, who would continue to perform the song far later on in her solo career, including even during her final concert tour in 2000.

While it rose up through the rhythm-and-blues charts that summer and fall, Tina was in the hospital with a bout of hepatitis contracted after making the record, further complicated with a case of jaundice while convalescing, and she found herself staring at the ceiling in bewilderment while their new hit single played out on the hospital's radio. "He's got me smilin' when I should be ashamed, got me laughin' when my heart is in pain."

Needing his prime supernatural resource to be back in action pronto, Ike had her sneak out of the hospital at night, sending one of his henchmen to pick her up, and he forced her to create an improvised stage costume from a baby-bump–concealing sack shape with loads of chiffon on top, hop into a station wagon, and be driven all the way to Cincinnati.

This was the first live show feature by Ike and Tina Turner as a duet, now formally called a Revue, with "A Fool in Love" climbing to number 2 on the R&B charts. The tour picked up as much steam as the song had, bringing them to the Apollo Theater in New York on a huge star-packed bill with Hank Ballard and Lee Dorsey and with the blossoming eight-months'-pregnant Tina teetering in tow.

Appearing at the fabled Apollo was basically like going back to church in black musical culture. As Lucinda Moore observed in the *Smithsonian* magazine, "For more than 75 years, entertainers, most of them African-American, have launched their careers, competed, honed their skills and nurtured one another's talent at the Apollo Theater. Along the way, they have created innovations in music and dance and that transcended race, and ultimately, transformed popular entertainment."

The Apollo had previously been a burlesque house for whites only but opened to racially integrated audiences in 1934, with a wild reputation as a stage on which performers sweat to win the affection of a notoriously critical crowd and an "executioner" shoos unpopular acts away. During the first sixteen years of its existence, almost every notable African American band of the era appeared, including many in the mid-1950s who helped shape the history of rock-and-roll music. Godfather of soul James Brown appeared there in 1959, and observers said they could feel the whole building pulsating.

But Tina's later appearance would lift the building right off its foundations. As Moore described it, "Wearing microscopic skirts and stiletto heels, she exuded a raw sex appeal on stage that far surpassed, and preceded Madonna or Beyoncé, or anything they did to draw attention to risqué display." Later on in the 1970s, hard times would hit the famed venue as a result of heavy competition from larger arenas, such as Madison Square Garden (where Tina would also eventually play), and the theater closed its doors in 1976 (the same year Tina closed her doors to Ike). Luckily, however, in the 1980s, the Inner City Broadcasting Corporation bought and renovated it, secured its landmark status, and revived its beloved amateur night competitions, which continue to thrive to this day.

Portia Maultsby, editor of the book *African American Music*, remarked that "it was a testing ground for artists, a second home, an institution within their community almost at the level of the black churches." Indeed, Tina took the Apollo back to testifying in a big way, and the Revue by then had passed into a kind of pop scripture. Tina would do two classic things at the Apollo in addition to singing the big songs of the moment for her and Ike: she would both testify and signify, in an almost gospel-funk manner, on behalf of James Brown, a hero of hers who had made that stage hallowed ground, and yet also stake out her own claim to a special place on that ground. She delivered a blistering rendition of his "Please, Please Please" that almost topped the original in terms of passion and pleading.

Their crossover timing could not have been better—or perhaps "luckier" is the better word. The big time was either beckoning or had already arrived, almost too rapidly to really notice it. So that meant it must be time for a little road trip to Las Vegas, where else? Curiously, another accident of fate happened during this period, one that would impact the style of Tina's persona from then on through her more hard rock and even later solo phases. This was her decision to bleach her hair while Ike was out of town, having flown back to St. Louis to stand trial for a bank robbery he was allegedly involved in. Bleaching was a popular trend at the time, but the hairdressing salon left the heat on too long, and when the cap came off, so did almost all of Tina's reddish, kinky hair.

The hair incident led to her having to resort to a variety of blondish wigs to cover it up, which she quickly began to actually enjoy as a style statement, even encouraging the Ikettes to do likewise so that all their long locks would be twirling and swirling in unison during performances, another signature look she inadvertently created. Her sense of style was always just as innately theatrical as her singing.

The music itself, *her* music with her distinctive howl, had also begun to be identified with the Turner enterprise. She now had "the look" to go along with "the sound," and the show business roller coaster was really starting to gain momentum in a way she had never dared to imagine. One of the great things about the digital age that we now occupy is that all these original recordings, often with sparkling visuals to accompany them, are available easily on YouTube, and it's a stunning guided tour of her and their musical evolution to swiftly view and listen to these early songs in rapid succession.

The most eye- and ear-opening historical exercise is to start with Ike's "Rocket 88" from 1951 and then jump to "A Fool in Love," "Poor Fool," "I Idolize You," and "It's Gonna Work Out Fine" (with its witty spoken-word banter intoned not by Ike but by Mickey Baker), all from 1961, then hop over to "I'm Blue" from 1962. The head-spinning acceleration of hits was something of a delirium, as was the couple's relationship, which featured an ever-escalating cascade of those other kind of hits for which Ike is now quite rightly notorious.

There was obviously a cognitive dissonance or disconnect in Tina at this stage that made it seemingly impossible to differentiate one kind of hit from another. Forget about divorce per se (that was still more than a decade away), and with Tina suddenly the center of attention by this time, Ike continued to employ his most effective strategy for controlling the women in his life who proved most useful to his aims and intentions. Following the birth of their son in 1960, in 1962, he officially married her in order to cement the name change he'd already foisted on her.

Unaware of what was really going on behind the scenes, besides all the trappings of apparent success for her daughter, her mother back in St. Louis was naively delighted with the news. Meanwhile, Ike always claimed that he married Tina only in order to prevent *her* ex-boyfriend, fellow King of Rhythm Raymond Hill, from returning to her. But then, Ike claimed a lot of things. The marriage to Tina may not even have been legal at all since they did it so quickly in Tijuana while he was still seemingly married to another wife or two (or three).

Tina was apparently in a permanent state of shock, the kind most people experience during actual warfare, the kind that leaves some victims afterward with what we today have come to call posttraumatic stress syndrome for years to come. But it was deeply submerged and sublimated, privately pushed far below that very intense wave of success shimmering brightly on the surface of her public life. All she could do—or so she thought—was to surf that wave.

✿   ✿   ✿

As always, chance favored the well prepared. Ike had been stealthily maneuvering for this moment not only since he hit his early stride ten years before with Jackie Brenston and his "Rocket 88" but really since being a teenage deejay at WROX in Clarksdale and even since being tutored at the piano stool by the great Pinetop Perkins. Ike always borrowed from the best; in the case of his early hit, he borrowed from Pete Johnson and Big Bill Turner, and now he was borrowing from Tina Turner. With Tina providing the vocal chops he'd been missing with both Bonnie and Annie earlier on and his Ikettes providing the sexy visual appeal and nonstop gymnastic gyrating, he was practically tasting the big time. He wasn't about to let it slip away this time.

Timing was everything, and it's not even something we can control, no matter how gifted we might be. The early years of 1962 and 1963 also offered up the frenzied national dance crazes to Ike on a sterling platter, with a youth-fueled appetite for wild abstract dances without much physical contact between the two partners. Moves like the Twist, the Pony, the Stomp, the Mashed Potato, the Hully Gully, and the Monkey were ideally suited to the quivering legs of Tina now, being shadowed by her bewigged and miniskirted Ikettes.

The composer's limits, however, soon began to be evident when he started recycling older Ike rhythm-and-blues material more and more often for the new pop era by merely dressing it up in shiny new clothes. It seldom worked out well for him. "Tra La La La La" was a retread of Ike's old theme song "Prancing"; "You Shoulda Treated Me Right" jumped around nicely; "Sleepless" was a slow, heavy-duty blues grind; and "I'm Blue" was presented as the debut single by the Ikettes, shooting up to number 19 in the pop charts during February 1962.

All of them benefited greatly though from the public desire to dance dance dance. And when the crowds watched Tina and her girls spinning in hot shimmy heaven, they even got to imagine that they too were really dancing up a storm. She was a vicarious life force for every anxious libido. But her life now was all about "The Tour," a never-ending merry-go-round that makes today's young "stars" feel like a slow-motion cakewalk.

The only tours even remotely more frenzied of course were those conducted by a certain new pop group in 1963–1964 called the Beatles, a transcendentally talented pack of archetypal gods who brilliantly re-processed the jittery black rhythm-and-blues music of Chuck Berry and Little Richard for unsuspecting but hungry white audiences. The one black group, however, that was able to reach the pale audience with un-diluted power and grit was the Ike and Tina Turner Revue. In 1964, in the midst of Beatlemania, their tight little rocker called "I Can't Believe What You Say" reached the top of the charts. "Top-ermost of the pop-ermost," as John Lennon himself once sarcastically said.

The song is only one minute and forty-four seconds long, but the way Tina shakes, it makes it feel like it takes a whole week. An old video of one performance shows her in front of the band shimmying up a storm, with Ike twitching spasmodically behind her in his white gangster suit. It also showed us all without a doubt that she would soon be breaking out of his stylistic kitchen and baking up a whole new cake of her own recipe. These kinds of numbers were still peppy rhythm-and-blues pop tunes of course, and it was still four years away from her transition to serious rock music, a shift that would come about with songwriting help from Phil Spector in 1965 and from John Fogerty in 1969.

The chance to shift more gears, professionally at least, came when Ike's contract with Juggy Murray expired, but rather than acknowledge that it was Sue Records generally and Murray specifically that got him where he was, Ike started playing around again with the Bihari Brothers. He was always fond of double dealing, both his women and his business associates, so he signed a $40,000 advance with Juggy, bought a new house, but didn't especially provide any product that Murray could re-ally release. It was his classic rope-a-dope technique.

Ike's new ranch house in Valley Park Hills, on the southern edge of Los Angeles, was a place where black artists who made it big went to live, people such as Ray Charles and Nancy Wilson. So when Ike got some fresh cash, he naturally wanted to assume a position in that privi-leged enclave, and along with his cars and other possessions, he brought his new and popular wife to show her off as well. She brought out her children from St. Louis, Craig and Ronald, along with a woman to take care of them while she was back at the circuit grind working again, back out on the endless road.

The Revue at this stage had an almost ritual routine in its approach to touring: roughly ninety days and nights of clubs around Los Angeles, locations such as the Cinnamon Cinder and the 5-4 Ballroom, and with mixtures of black and white audiences in San Diego and San Francisco. This schedule was followed by another ninety days and nights of sheer mind-bending one-night-stand appearances across America, and hot on the heels of that out-of-town binge would come another ninety-day frenzy of local dates all over again.

After a year of constant motion, the Revue would get a special treat: one week off, but it was a week during which Ike made them all come in early for rehearsals and recordings. No roadies did grunt service to help out, and the band members had to lurch their own equipment with them everywhere. No one asked any questions, and no one knew any different or any better. It was a movable feast with a movable beast.

It's always tricky dealing with the dark side of certain artists whose work is still so important, as Aaron Cohen so honestly acknowledged to me. "While I would not make any excuses for his atrocious personal behavior, and I'm sure that the stories about him are true, he was an incredible musician, a sharp songwriter and he had a terrific tremolo-laden guitar sound.

"He also kept coming up with fresh musical ideas from the mid-1950s into early 1970s, a longevity shared by relatively few. Ike also was a great bandleader, and keeping these groups organized while dealing with all of the obstacles on the road was no easy feat (until his drug abuse got way out of hand). Thinking about how he still played 'Steel Guitar Rag' at the Chicago Blues Festival some eighteen years ago still blows my mind. Meanwhile, he was also an important scout for musical talent, whether he was working at Sun Records or his noticing the potential in Annie Mae Bullock. But I don't know how to properly balance, recognize, and address all the good he did for music with the harm he did to those around him." Who does? It's a permanent puzzle.

Once again, James Porter also wanted me to realize the full extent of Ike's brilliance as a player, one that is often overlooked in the chaos of his personal life. "Ike & Tina became fully realized as a 'rock act' around 1969. Paying full tribute to the blues was probably the hippest thing you could do back then. The guitars were emphasized, Tina carried herself like she wanted you to know where the rock stars got it from, and the lyrics were spiced with social commentary, sexual frankness, and references to getting high. This gave them an identity for the remainder of the 70s (until their 1976 breakup).

"They'd found a permanent home with Liberty/United Artists and established a sound that owed as much to earthy blues and rock experimentalism as to their own earlier soul backbone. By his own admission, Ike considered himself more of a behind-the-scenes man, but during 'I Smell Trouble,' for once Ike is in the spotlight doing an extended guitar run, proving that he wasn't just the equal of a Jimmy Page or a Jeff Beck, he was the source!"

The Ikettes in particular were always worked harder than anyone else and paid much less, a paradox considering that they helped Tina consolidate the flashy and sultry fem vibe for Ike. Usually a trio but occasionally a quartet, they morphed over the years into interchangeable goddess statues whose job was to attract attention and be as ornamental as possible in addition to also being superathletic dancers of course. After being ripped off from Lassiter's Artettes, the original Ikettes consisted of Robbie Montgomery, Venetta Fields, and Jessie Smith, later evolving into the Mirettes on their own.

Chafing at the constant workload and also under the sway of Ike as his concubines, they struck out independently for a while in 1964–1966 with a string of respectable hits on Modern Records: "The Camel Walk" in 1964 and "Peaches and Cream" and "I'm So Thankful" in 1965. They could be heavy, and some listeners have likened their swagger to the funk style embodied by the gritty visionary Betty Mabry-Davis a little later on.

Naturally enough, when "Peaches and Cream" became popular, Ike himself chafed and sent out a different group of Ikettes onto the road— Janice Singleton, Diane Rutherford, and Marquentta Tinsley—for a Dick Clark caravan of stars while keeping back Montgomery, Fields, and Smith for himself in the Revue. It would be Singleton and Rutherford who sang backup vocals for Tina on Phil Spector's upcoming breakout hit for her, "River Deep, Mountain High."

Meanwhile, Ike hired separate women over the years to be Ikettes as his fancy dictated: Pat Arnold, Juanita Hixon, Gloria Scott, Maxine Smith, and, later on, Pat Powdrill, Ann Thomas, Shelly Clark, Rose Smith, Edna Richardson, Stonye Figueroa, Ester Jones, Claudia Lennear, Linda Sims, and Paulette Parker. All of them deserve recognition for ever working with Ike at all and special acknowledgment for helping Tina be Tina, even though there was frequent friction due to his blatant infidelities.

Once free of Ike and on her own of course, she obviously ceased using the concept of Ikettes, preferring instead to refer to her dancers as her "flowers." How any of them survived the grueling work schedule and internal tensions of that body-and-mind–punishing Revue is anybody's guess, but of course one other recreational side of the music business has always been open and obvious for everyone to see.

The musical band itself was often high as a kite (no surprise there), but the Ikettes were also fond of smoking joints to help their energy levels, and Ike often gave Benzedrine to Tina (who didn't approve of any "poisons" at all) to help (or force) her get through the constant vocal demands of his perpetual recording sessions.

Ironically, Ike himself was still strictly a coffee-and-cigarettes kind of guy, maybe some alco-fuel to pretend to relax, but, as has been indicated, early on he disdained drugs and fined or beat up his staff if he caught them using. I suspect that a control freak of his stature didn't enjoy the loss of control that drugs implied, at least until he soon enough entered his mature phase and discovered cocaine, which he snow-shoveled by the pound.

But for some reason, he let his Ikettes smoke weed all they wanted, perhaps deeming them "special," and he even started to supply them with heaps of pot on the road to keep them happy—or as happy as they could be while working for Mephistopheles. But after practically everyone in the industry wanted to offer the original Ikettes some club appearances and recording gigs, with the popularity of their "Peaches and Cream" outing hitting its stride, Ike created his veritable revolving door of alternate Ikettes to keep them all in line through job insecurity.

In September 1965, when their spritely but basically Supremes-cloned tune "I'm So Thankful" was rising in the pop charts, the main Ikettes smartly navigated their way out of his possessive clutches. By then, however, bigger and bigger and yet bigger things were looming on the mutual horizon of Ike and Tina Turner, with something deep and high—and totally crazy—rapidly brewing in the wings. Enter, stage left, Phil Spector.

4

PUBLIC ROMANCER

Deeper and Higher

"I must have sung that song 500,000 times, I was drenched in sweat,
I had to take my shirt off and stand there in my bra to sing."

—Tina Turner, *Rolling Stone*, 2003

It's all about the music; it always was. His, theirs, and hers: it was a collective contribution to musical culture that is mind-boggling and heartwarming at the same time. The number of albums produced and concerts presented by Ike and Tina Turner, while together and then on her own as a solo act, is vertiginously lengthy. Ike and Tina Turner's sixteen-year recording career together resulted in several masterpieces in multiple genres as they evolved their artistic style and creative sensibilities from basic rhythm and blues with a soul inflection to more complex rock and roll with a bluesy feel and finally to a heavy-duty funk-rock mode with a crossover pop appeal.

One element in common among these varied threads was the sensually charged torch song format of Tina that encouraged listeners to lose their sorrows by getting up and dancing them away. Their music unleashed a kind of involuntary joy, one still closely akin to the religious rapture that originally birthed gospel, soul, and funk in the first place.

The other shared focal point between records is the puzzling fact that even though Ike was clearly a psychopath, he was nevertheless a very talented psychopath, one who had a knack, at first, for clever and snappy large-band arrangements, hyperstylized instrumentation, and frequently compelling production values, all of which were under his creative sway from the very beginning. All of this single-minded ambition and wholehearted devotion to nonstop action is almost inconceivable by today's lumbering standards.

The key to their best recordings (or one of them anyway) is how connected they are to their live performances, often overlapping dramatically, and indeed, as famous as they are for studio records, they are in a way even more widely appreciated as one of the most sizzling live acts in the entertainment field. This comes from playing live more than 300 days of each year ever since they had first launched. And though many of their early and middle-period albums will be enjoyed by lovers of hard-core rhythm-and-blues music, the finest ones they released were definitely their live records, and that's the best place for a new generation of listeners to find out what the big deal was all about.

Among them, the peaks are probably *Ike and Tina Revue* Live at the Club Imperial and Harlem Club in St. Louis, 1964; *The Ike and Tina Turner Show*, 1965; *In Person with the Ikettes*, 1969; *Ike and Tina Turner Festival of Performances*, 1970; *Live at Carnegie Hall*, 1970; and *The World of Ike and Tina Turner*, 1973. Several examples of their best live records as barometers of their overwhelming stage shows are well worth examining in passing.

In 1963, they started upping the ante while still recording with Sue Records and releasing, in quick succession (speed was always of the essence with Ike), *Dynamite!*, *It's Gonna Work Out Fine*, and *Don't Play Me Cheap*, all produced by Ike. By 1964, they were already a smashing success and were among the few American entertainers (along with the Beach Boys) who had any chance in hell of competing with the British invasion of the Beatles and the Rolling Stones then well under way or, at the very least, of holding their own amid their powerful cultural onslaught.

IKE AND TINA TURNER REVUE LIVE AT THE CLUB IMPERIAL, ST. LOUIS

Released November 1964, Kent Records. Personnel: Kings of Rhythm, Ike Turner, Tina Turner, Stacey Johnson, Vernon Guy, Venetta Fields, Jimmy Thomas, Bobby John, Robbie Robinson. Produced by Ike Turner. Duration: 35:49.

Please Please Please (James Brown and Johnny Terry) 6:54 / Feel So Good (Junior Parker) 3:12 / The Love of My Man (Ed Townsend) 3:55 / Think (Lowman Pauling) 2:24 / Drown in My Own Tears (Henry Glover) 7:31 / I Love the Way You Love (Berry Gordy) 3:12 / Your Precious Love (Jerry Butler) 2:30 / All in My Mind (Maxine Brown) 3:30 / I Can't Believe What You Say (Ike Turner) 1:59

On October 27, 1959, at the Club Imperial in St. Louis, the then newly minted Ike and Tina Turner show would launch an endless series of club circuit appearances coupled with a rapid-succession release of singles and albums designed by Ike to fully capitalize on the obvious gold mine he had prospected for and found in his latest girlfriend and soon-to-be wife. This iconic venue is presently in danger of being demolished despite being worshipped in a manner similar to the little cardboard poster from his "Rocket 88" age. This live record captures some of the alluring frenzy of their early club dates in their home base of St. Louis.

The Turners recorded some early songs for later hit albums there, among them *Ike and Tina Turner Revue Live*, and they regularly played there on Tuesday nights to wild acclaim. It's a stunning demonstration of their raw power, originally released only in America and subsequently released worldwide on different labels, then later rereleased as "Please Please Please" in 1968, with the CD issue featuring additional tracks from the album *Festival of Live Performances*. This record was proudly identified by the declaration "some of the early pop rock n' soul recordings that made this band a household name."

Soul Magazine's promotion editor Warren Lanier in his liner notes observed about Tina, "Several years ago the recording industry was hit like an atomic bomb blast by the exciting songs of Ike and Tina Turner, if you missed this spectacular unit in action you can still be a witness, so if you think your heart can take it, drop this on the turntable and enjoy the greatest moments in their musical entertainment magic . . . as Tina, the bronze bombshell, exploded all over the stage at the Club Imperial. She actually tears you apart and leaves you breathless when closing out the Revue's appearance." This is a great listening entrée into their sizzling world of early momentum for a band obviously headed skyward.

The years 1964 and 1965 were also notable for their crucial contributions to the tricky format of live concert albums, not always the most dependable mode for even the best musicians but by far the best way to get as close as possible to their sizzling live performance energy without actually being in the theaters they rattled so emphatically. The best examples were *Live: Ike and Tina Turner Revue Live* on Kent Records and *Ike and Tina Turner Show Vol. 2* on Loma Records as well as the studio release *Get It* on Cenco and an early *Greatest Hits* package released back on Sue Records, their original youthful home.

❖   ❖   ❖

Once again, destiny would step into the fray, this time disguised as a legendary producer who utilized the whole recording studio itself as a single musical instrument. Phil Spector, a great musical innovator from the early and mid-1960s, invented a special sonic quality that made his records as unique as they were memorable: booming, reverberating echo and massively lush orchestration, with gigantic chiming avalanches of sorrow and joy in equal measure in the melancholy girl groups of his era. The Ronettes, the Shirelles, the Crystals, the Shangri-Las, and others all had Spector's distinctive and signature huge analog sound and frenzied doubling up of instrumentation that would give those mournful little two-minute pop symphonies both their charm and their long-lasting technical prowess.

Among Spector's other historic achievements in the same domain were the hugely popular Righteous Brothers hits, all of which utilized what had by then become his own personal brand, often imitated but never duplicated: big, shimmering architectural monuments to the raw emotional impact of overwhelming, reverberating sound waves.

He was one of the first and finest examples of the producer as artist in popular music and was well known in the music industry for inventing a unique aural aura all his own. And it would be Spector, already a historic creative titan at the time, who would contribute to utterly renovating and re-launching the Ike and Tina Turner Revue, helping them to inaugurate their unexpected rock phase.

As usual, two unrelated elements came together like alchemy to do so: first, the fact that the Turners had reached an impasse with their usual brand of boogie-blues rock and roll, especially within the limited scope of Ike as a songwriter, and, second, the fact that Spector had been around and at the top of his game for so long that song styles and tastes were shifting slightly away from his earlier boy-meets-girl/bad-boy-woos-girl sonic soap operas.

Spector's contribution to the future of music was his gifted use of clearly white arrangements sung by voices who were in some cases blacker in tone that even Motown could muster while regularly using well-tempered jazz musicians as his pop posse, most notably the famous Wrecking Crew session geniuses, such as Hal Blaine and Carol Kane. He then processed it all through a cataclysm of disorienting audio effects that came to be known as the "Spector wall of sound," which could paralyze the mind while freeing the heart.

In an excellent study of Spector and his historic influence called *He's a Rebel: Rock and Roll's Legendary Producer*, Mark Ribowsky opened his own examination of the producer as artist with this single salient fact: "Phil Spector, a little man with a Napoleon complex, faced his own private Waterloo in early 1966," referring to the fact that by that year, Spector had all but played out his welcome on the world music stage and needed to craft a new and even more elaborate masterwork to stem the rising tide of changes in musical taste swirling around him. His history was already something for which he was rightly considered a musical deity, but soon enough and completely without warning, Ike and Tina would religiously move into the sonic church that Phil had built—and all for just one amazing song.

Ribowsky has more than adequately characterized the magic of the sound that Spector invented, a sound so powerful and seductive that it would still haunt producers for the next half a century, especially the one that Amy Winehouse was later then woozily leaning on: "Phil Spector did do overdub background vocals on his records to create a swirl of voices that aped his instrumental tracks, but his true love was *live* music, a rhythm section blaring and wailing its brains out the way great jazz combos did.

"At Gold Star Sound Studios in Hollywood, a titanic rhythm section of the kind Spector had become famous for—four guitars, three basses, three pianos, two drums and a small army of percussion—became one, as only it could in a live, massed monolith. The room, Gold Star's Studio A, was saturated in sine waves; they bounced off the walls and the low ceiling and came tumbling out of two echo chambers before being sucked into a tape machine.

"When mixed down, the sound was not of this earth, and it wasn't a melody as we know it. It was a mood, a feel, aural poetry, and sheer rock-and-roll heaven. Even the ludicrous teenage themes of Spector's early records sound like the Ride of the Valkyries elevated to Valhalla by a tide of inspired commotion that was the Wall of Sound, or as Spector himself would have preferred, 'a Wagnerian approach to rock and roll, little symphonies for kids.'" This was a nearly ideal description of what would later become the Turners' breakaway shifting of gears in 1966, "River Deep, Mountain High."

Spector had been born in the big-band era of 1940, and he was only twenty-five when he had already changed the face of popular music forever with a constant stream of hits that topped the charts twenty-seven times from 1961 to 1965. Perhaps most personally telling for Ike and Tina Turner would be one of his later hits, the Righteous Brothers' huge, booming anthem of sorrow "You've Lost That Lovin' Feeling." "Spector was a visionary, not a revolutionary." Ribowsky clarified, "He didn't change the system, he used it." What Spector did was not invent a new kind of rock and roll, but he brilliantly enhanced the old one, using the same simple song arrangements but with more and more instruments, until it almost reached the breaking point.

In Tom Wolfe's article on Spector, "The First Tycoon of Teen" for the *New York Herald Tribune* in 1965, during a period just then undergoing the seismic musical shifts of the Beatles' *Rubber Soul,* Spector was already having to defend his deceptively simple songwriting approach to operating as the American Mozart. "This music has a kind of spontaneity that doesn't exist in any other kind of music, and it's what is here now. It's unfair to classify it as rock and roll and condemn it. You know? It's very today. Actually it's more like the blues. It's pop blues."

Pop blues would also become perhaps the best term to describe what Ike and Tina Turner were already then putting down. It was usually incredibly speeded up into a frantic dance mode, but it was still inherently a female blues take on the classic torch lyrical tradition. The bluesy torch song is indeed a unique genre, one that would be lovingly handled again and again by great female singers on into the 1960s and 1970s, right up to those churning and burning anthems of angst that Tina was good at delivering.

The Spector sound was also tailor made for Tina's uncanny vocal skills, a sound that can best be summarized as a big vibrating wall: atmospheric, echoing, reverberating, shimmering, sweet, dark, brooding, dangerous, and ultimately hypermelodramatic. Melodrama in its pure musical form, Spector's reimagining of the classic torch song for Tina's voice and soul was almost a tidal wave of desires denied, deferred, or derailed—a perfectly crafted heartbreaker aria, the spiritually anguished sound of mini-operas about desperately trying to win back someone you've lost but can't let go.

But by the time Tina Turner got hold of that torch when it was her turn to carry it forward, passed to her by the eccentric recording pioneer Phil Spector, it sounded like something no one in this world had ever heard before.

❋   ❋   ❋

In 1965, Ike and Tina Turner had been signed to something like their tenth record label, with often more than one at a time given Ike's graspy predilections. Loma Records was a small subsidiary of Warner Bros. being run by Bob Krasnow, a deeply appreciative white lover of black music who had been working briefly with the great James Brown. In light of the politics of the times, however, Brown felt it was incorrect for him to be working with a white producer, so Krasnow was on the lookout for a similarly energetic black performer to get behind.

The only performer I can imagine him encountering who might fit the bill might be Tina Turner, as kind of a female James Brown, who Krasnow observed had the power of Mr. Dynamite but with much better looking legs. After touring every day of the year and doing maybe five high-octane shows a night, the band was so tight that he was quite ready to record a handful of singles for them, none of which went anywhere in the charts. That was when the equally restless Phil Spector, searching around for a new way to revolutionize the music world for the third or fourth time, happened to call him.

Asked if he and his team had Ike and Tina on board and replying in the affirmative, Krasnow was stunned to hear the high-pitched lisp of Phil's voice announce that he wanted to make a record—with Tina. Emphasis on the word "Tina." Like everyone else in the know, Krasnow held Spector in a kind of reverence for all the reasons he rightly deserved. He had already had ten big hits with the Righteous Brothers as 1965 began to draw to a close when the mellow duo decided to leave him and go to Verve Records. For equally well known reasons, artists could work with Spector for only so long before they burned out or imploded. He was the only music professional I can think of who might be as nuts as Ike was.

Yet he was then and still is now (even though he's serving a life sentence for murder) revered for his almost mystical sound production skills, and at this stage of his career, he needed a boost. A friend had recommended that he take in a show of Ike and Tina at the Galaxy Club on Sunset Boulevard, and he was taken aback, which took some doing for a pro of his stature. He immediately added them to the lineup for a revue of his own being staged at the Moulin Rouge with a slightly schizoid roster of other artists appearing: the Byrds, the Lovin' Spoonful, Ray Charles, Petula Clark, and Donovan.

Mesmerized by Tina, bowled over by the band's performance in keeping up with her in her miniskirt and flashy go-go boots, and hearing that little bell in his head going off to the tune of *hit song*, he went off to the fabled Brill Building in New York to collaborate with the supersonic pop maestro duo of Jeff Barry and Ellie Greenwich (writers of such monsters as "Be My Baby," "Baby I Love You," "Chapel of Love," "Leader of the Pack," and "Do Wah Diddy") and returned with his shared song with them, "River Deep, Mountain High," in hand. The great Darlene Love, for whom he had concocted "A Fine, Fine Boy," loved what little she heard of his new secret tune, but he explained that this one was not quite her thing. This was to be Tina's thing.

Notice that he didn't say "Ike and Tina's thing." In fact, he worked out some business stipulations with Krasnow, reportedly offering Ike $25,000 (shades of Juggy Murray's old offer of a stately sum to work with Tina as well) to let him *have* Tina and her voice and for Ike never even to set foot into the studio during the process of his making "River" into what he thought—or hoped—would be his pièce de résistance, his masterwork. Tina loved the song, especially since it wasn't the usual simple-structured Ike rhythm-and-blues–oriented format but rather a complex tower of rock power and especially since it wasn't written by Ike and he'd have no role in its fabrication process.

That process was, as always with Spector, a mysterious one, with Phil building up acres and acres of instruments crashing headlong into a blistering finale of unimaginable intensity. At first, she literally couldn't imagine how her voice would end up audible amid this intricate roar, but she had yet to experience the otherworldly skill with which he could manipulate vocals as deftly as he could musicians and their instruments. She guessed there might be seventy-five players in the studio at any given time until finally she created, after so many takes and retakes that she lost count (almost losing consciousness as well), a rough vocal track for him to use.

The main man at Loma Records, Krasnow, who would eventually end up as a head honcho at Electra Records much later on, recalls being stunned by the way Ike treated his obvious gold mine of a talented singer when he encountered them at this time, as recalled in *Vanity Fair*. "He treated her like she was his maid, she was in the kitchen with a wet rag, down on her hands and knees wiping the floor wearing another rag on her head." In a strange way, Tina actually *was* Ike's maid in more ways than one.

The down-to-earth person Krasnow encountered was one whom most people saw, someone with a sensual public persona but with private mores that are quite old fashioned and traditional. When one met her, Tina could be your girlfriend, your sister, your best friend—she could fulfill all these emotional markers at once. Yet when she gets up onstage in performance, she has the ability to powerfully stimulate you by bringing lyrics to life in a way that is uniquely hers alone.

Phil Spector had more than a few things in common with Ike Turner, not the least of which was a prodigy background and an intense relationship with his own lead singer, Ronnie Spector (née Bennett). Krasnow has mentioned to *Rolling Stone* that "at one point Phil had every single big studio musician in Hollywood in there, and of course most of the famed Wrecking Crew, with Hal Blaine and the brilliant bassist Carol Kane."

All this for just one track, for only one side of a single, not even for an entire album. "River Deep, Mountain High" was indeed a Spector masterpiece with sound so deep and heavy that you almost lost yourself in it. When Ike finally heard the track, Ike was gob smacked, there's no other word for it. He was so impressed that he couldn't describe it; this was in another league altogether, hell, in another dimension. In the vernacular of musicians, he was bummed out by it big time. He thought this was impossible to do, maybe because it usually is impossible.

It is generally agreed that Tina gave the performance of her life for this quirky producer. As per his usual obsessive technical laboring, Spector took months to complete the pressing he was satisfied with, with Krasnow reporting that he was brought sixteen different pressings to consider, each more compelling than the last, which, as he characterized it at the time, only dogs could hear the differences on.

At long last, in the late spring of 1966, the magical musical period in which *Revolver* by the Beatles came out, "River Deep, Mountain High" was finally ready to be unleashed. George Harrison himself, in fact, considered it one of the most perfect recordings ever made, a pop song so well crafted that nothing whatsoever could be done to improve on it.

Indeed, Spector, never one known to be that modest, was fairly certain that this song was going to be the first number 1 chart-topping hit for Ike and Tina and effusively told them so. Amazingly, though, to many at the time (but almost to everyone else since then), it wasn't—it was a complete flop, at least by established Spector standards. Larry Levine, the gifted audio engineer who had worked with him on the overall construction of his wall of sound, was equally stunned by the mediocre response of most music trade publications.

He felt that basically Spector, the boy wonder who had amassed maybe twenty-five chart-topping records in a row, was due for his turn at some cutting down to size by critics and industry types. Other producers, musicians, and the music-loving public at large of course saw it and heard it quite differently. It was embraced as the glittering production and performance peak it really is. Yet it still didn't really sell. It climbed to number 88 on the pop charts during the summer and then began to slide.

Spector was crushed and deeply disappointed. Levine thought that Phil just felt so vulnerable and depressed that he withdrew into himself, didn't want to make any more music, and just kind of permanently retreated behind his already ubiquitous dark glasses and hid away in self-imposed silent exile.

When Spector had first played the intended Tina song for her, singing along on a guitar, she was mesmerized, as reported in *New Musical Express*: "Wow! Jack Nitzsche's arrangement was really something else! I was knocked out by the Jeff Barry/Ellie Greenwich and Phil song." After all the hard work she put in on the song "River Deep," Tina was still stunned, especially by the awesome complexity of its recording style.

In the *Best of Tina* DVD film, she expressed her amazement at its sonic architecture: "He was so much behind that project—it was something he strongly, strongly believed in. I've got to tell you—it was an army of backing vocals—it was a choir. The room was chock-full of singers." But alas, despite how complex it was (or maybe even because of it), the industry couldn't relate to it, and listeners were puzzled by its waves of instruments and voices. On the official Tina Turner website, her historical comments clarified why: "It was too black for the pop stations and too pop for the black stations. But at least it showed people what I had in me."

Her version of its B-side, "A Love Like Yours," swept up the U.K. charts to become a number 16 hit, largely as a result of touring abroad: "We were breaking the chains that were holding us back from a mass audience," by which she meant a white audience. Now all she had to do was find a way to break the chains holding her to her thuggish pimp. It was a tough ride of course, especially because of her own sense of loyalty no matter how misplaced it might have been.

For the first seven years of her troubled life with Ike, she felt obliged to be loyal to him because of how he had helped her in the early days. Naturally, she found it difficult to separate his attitude and behavior from what he had done for her professionally, but her confusion was also compounded by fear, just as everyone else around him in his clique also shared that strangely seductive hold he seemed to exert over people.

This odd cult-like environment was observed publicly by myriad people in their circle: the fact that he ruled his roost by a vicious intimidation so severely that if any of his own band broke some of his compulsive rules, they could be fined or fired, assaulted, or pistol-whipped.

Tina was also naturally disappointed by the song's public and critical responses, feeling that it was her entry into a whole new side of her musical persona (which it actually was, as time would show) but that the audience just wasn't quite ready for so radical an evolutionary leap.

As often happens, though, with musical releases in one country or another, "River Deep" was quite a smash in Europe, where there had always been a healthier appetite for black music in general, for innovative pop in particular, and especially for a dish named Tina. But regardless of its reception in some quarters, 1966 was still their biggest creative and commercial turning point, especially for Tina, after personally diving so deep and reaching so high.

RIVER DEEP, MOUNTAIN HIGH

Released in 1966. London Records. Recorded at Gold Star Studios. Produced by Phil Spector and Ike Turner. Personnel: Tina Turner, vocals; Barney Kessel, guitar; Carol Kaye, bass; Jim Gordon, drums; Claudia Lennear and Bonnie Bramlett, backing vocals; Harold Battiste, piano. Engineer: Larry Levine. Arranged by Jack Nitzsche, Barry Page, Perry Botkin. Cover: Dennis Hopper. Duration: 37:06.

River Deep, Mountain High (Jeff Barry, Phil Spector, Ellie Greenwich) 3:38 / I Idolize You (Ike Turner) 3:46 / A Love Like Yours (Eddie Holland, Lamont Dozier) 3:05 / A Fool in Love (Ike Turner) 3:13 / Make Em Wait (Ike Turner) 2:22 / Hold On Baby (Jeff Barry, Ellie Greenwich, Phil Spector) 2:59 / Save the Last Dance for Me (Doc Pomus, Mort Shuman) 3:02 / Oh Baby (Ike Turner) 2:46 / Every Day I Have to Cry (Arthur Alexander) 2:40 / Such a Fool for You (Ike Turner) 2:48 / It's Gonna Work Out Fine (J. Michael Lee, Joe Seneca) 3:14 / You're So Fine (Lance Finney, Bob West, Willie Schofield) 3:14

A gorgeous studio recording peak, *River Deep, Mountain High* is thirty-seven minutes and six seconds of sheer sonic spectacle, with the title song lovingly handcrafted at Gold Star Studios by Spector. Sharing production duties with Ike for the first time in both their careers, it was released again in 1969 on A&M Records with a different track listing and song selection. *Pitchfork* named it number 40 on the best 200 records released in the 1960s. It's a good place for the uninitiated to begin any exploration of their joint collaboration.

I've always been partial to Ben Fong-Torres's insights into Tina in general and this record in particular as he explored it in *Rolling Stone* way back in 1971, when the impact of this record was still intensely fresh. "'River Deep, Mountain High,' to hear that song for the first time, in 1967, in the first year of acid-rock and Memphis soul, to hear that wall of sound falling toward you, with Tina teasing it along, was to understand all the power of rock and roll. It had been released in England in 1966 and made Number Two, but in America, nothing. 'It was just like my farewell,' Phil Spector says. 'I was just sayin' goodbye, and I just wanted to go crazy for a few minutes—four minutes on wax.'" Alas, that's always felt like Phil's attempt at explaining away why his homeland didn't quite *get* what he was up to at all.

Ben's appreciation for Tina's true superstar stature is also very adept, placing her in the pop and rock pantheon where she belongs, close to the Rolling Stones, largely because when she's onstage, many people compare Tina Turner to Mick Jagger. But Tina, in fact, when observed more closely, is much more aggressive and more animalistic than even Mick. She owns whatever stage she stands on.

Equally revealing, given what the couple was going through at the time, was Tina's comment in Phil Agee's book *Tina Pie* that no matter what was happening to her personally, "I always go on. Whatever's bothering me—I don't care how bad it is—I drop it when I go on stage. You know that kind of hypnosis—I don't know what it's called—where you induce yourself into a trance? Self-hypnosis? Yeah, that's it. I hypnotize myself, and I forget."

But the unique sonic sensibilities of "River Deep" had to compete that same year even with themselves via the familiar-sounding *Soul of Ike and Tina Turner*, released on Kent again, which by now was far from anything easily recognizable as soul music. The year 1967 showed them once again to be masters of live concert albums with *Festival of Live Performances* on Kent, and 1968 offered up *Ike and Tina Turner* on

London and the quiet little rocker called *So Fine* on Pompeii. But 1969 would be their magical year.

No less stellar a band than the Rolling Stones, British musicians who were deeply enamored of black blues and rhythm-and-blues sounds by artists such as BB King and Tina Turner already were about to embark on a fall tour of the United Kingdom. Mick, Keith, and the lads thought it would be a fine idea to invite the whole Ike and Tina Turner Revue along to open for them in their large-scale concerts. And it was with them that Tina Turner began to fully solidify her newfound persona as a Rock Goddess.

That, coupled with a live U.S. clip of a "River Deep" performance on the English *Top of the Pops* television program, started Tina on her road to rock royalty, with Ike now more or less along for the ride, a disgruntled figure in the shadows, while the spotlight spent more and more time focused brightly on her. But despite Ike's long slide into the oblivion he had largely brought on himself, the up-and-coming Rolling Stones were all ready, willing, and able to give Tina the recognition they believed she truly deserved.

Porter also emphasized to me the passionate inspiration that later so-called rock artists, especially the white ones, such as the Stones, would glean from their supposedly more mild antecedents. "Historically, whenever the white rockers looked to R&B for inspiration, it was usually with an emphasis on the raw and the raunchy. An Otis Redding, say, would be more adaptable to a garage-rock format than a Jerry Butler. Ike & Tina, with their high-energy live shows and guitar-based sound, were a natural for rock bands to pick up on. Even though their live shows had the formal precision of a Las Vegas revue, Ike's guitar and Tina's screaming voice detonated with rock & roll dynamite. They were almost a total natural to open shows for the Rolling Stones and to later headline the rock festivals and ballrooms."

Apart from Mick Jagger admitting that she taught him to dance properly onstage, Keith Richards also harbored a not-so-secret fondness for Tina when he got to know her on tour. He can often be witnessed practically ogling her gutsy presence onstage. For the British rock band so in love with black blues music, it was almost as if she took them back to drama school and demonstrated what show business was really all about.

Richards also had no illusions about what made the Turner Revue so special. He knew it was all Tina and not the ersatz Svengali that Ike imagined himself to be. It was equally obvious that Ike saw himself as another Phil Spector, the driving force behind the star. But he was also a force of another kind, a nasty pimp capable of pistol-whipping musicians in his own band—someone you don't want to be around, let alone mess with.

Richards's fellow Stone, bassist Bill Wyman, was especially fond of dating young Ikettes, and he concurred on the *Best of* DVD from *Image Entertainment*, "I heard horrendous stories from The Ikettes about what was going on in the background. It was almost unbelievable actually. They changed so quickly, The Ikettes, every time you saw them, it was a completely different set, because they just couldn't deal with what was going on."

And yet for all its stylistic bigness, there is still a basic irony to this Spector signature song having been composed for her if not about her since its odd sentiment is rather telling indeed: "When you were a young boy did you have a puppy that always followed you around, well I'm gonna be as faithful as that puppy no I'll never let you down."

❖   ❖   ❖

After her instantly legendary working relationship with Spector and the remarkable song that was birthed by him, all the other subsequent producers they worked with had to up their game technically. This was not a conscious choice or effort on their part; it was simply an alteration of the soundscape that became a natural new part of their sonic scenery. Each song after this one also tended to be bigger in scope and scale just as a matter of course, with a good example being their upcoming version of the wonderful John Fogerty song "Proud Mary," a song that is pretty much associated with her now much more than his own Creedence Clearwater Revival version. And needless to say, all of Tina's solo records *after* she liberated herself from Ike were to be crafted in the most grandiose proportions production-wise.

Although Spector was fairly obliterated by the less-than-stellar reception of his volcanic masterpiece, Tina took it in stride, happy just to have the opportunity to break out on her own (as coproducer) and away from her increasingly paranoid husband. Meanwhile, Ike was likely pleased just to have the Phil episode, during which he had zero control over anything to do with the project or his wife. In his claustrophobic mind, there was room for only one rooster in the yard no matter how brilliant everyone claimed this interloper was.

The near-mystical associations with Spector continued on unabated, however, in the music world, with his mythology blossoming only once, he withdrew to his castle overlooking Sunset Boulevard. *Rolling Stone* editor Jan Wenner once asked him how he managed to so skillfully create the sonic environments in which only his records thrived, and his answer was typically both laconic and bombastic at the same time: "When I went into the studio, I created the sounds that I wanted to hear." His unique Tina sound was still a big hit in England, where the Rolling Stones took them on tour in September–October for twelve straight dates in addition to another twelve or so on their own at select clubs scattered around the country.

The Stones tour launched at Albert Hall for a live concert was also being recorded for *Got Live If You Want It*. After six songs, however, the hall erupted into a near riot with adoring fans storming the stage, a shocking glimpse of a whole new world for Ike and Tina, who were basically down-home chitlin'-circuit veterans at heart suddenly thrust into pop at the top. Tina hit it off quite nicely with the bad boys of rock and roll of course, especially Mick Jagger, who firmly believed in having an opening act that forced his own band to raise their game in order to top them, something Tina did easily.

Ike as usual didn't get along with Jagger or Richards apart from accepting their worship as an early black rock and roller who had inspired them in the first place. Adoration he could get into; equivalent respect, well, that was something else again. He also didn't much appreciate the fact that Jagger, Richards, and Wyman were all dating his Ikettes, as that kind of rooster competition *really* irked him, maybe even more than the musical kind.

What England really offered to Tina was a chance to finally see a potential life beyond Ike, what she perceived as a new life, a new way of living, of being. And the more exposure she got on independent non–Ike-controlled venues and shows, such as the popular program *Ready Steady Go!*, the more she liked what she saw, especially since the vast new white audiences were focused largely on her and her fellow singers and dancers and less on the sinister glowering presence of her dour puppet master.

One of the psychics she frequently consulted for guidance in her life and career even told her that she predicted that she would become one of the biggest of stars and that her partner would fall away like a leaf from a tree.

The psychic also saw the number 6, which apparently told Tina that even though Ike was beating her up more and more often, she should hold on for another six days, another six weeks, or another six months, which of course morphed into another six years.

So hold on she did, through the follow-up to the Stones tour and on into France and Germany and a raft of newspaper and television appearances. Fans and critics alike went bonkers over her zesty stage show yet also adored her still kind of quiet, humble approach to the whole carnival she was living in.

The frenzied touring continued—that was naturally where the big money was in the business anyway, something that at least kept Ike off her back, busy counting his cash. The road was still the same old show business grind, with one new change: the press was constantly following *her* now, extolling her style and her personality as well as their music. Subsequent to "River Deep," she was now seen by the public and the media not just as a vital part of the Turner Revue but also the central sun around which they all orbited.

Ike's hyperactive label hopping also continued on through the following year of 1969, with *Cussin', Cryin' and Carryin' On* on Pompeii, *Get It Together* and *Get It–Get It* on Cenco, and *His Woman, Her Man* on Capitol, rounded out by *In Person* on Minit, the only album to achieve good sales, reaching number 142 on *Billboard*—a cyclone of compositions. The bigger she got of course, the angrier Ike got, now resorting to twisted wire coat hangers as his tool of choice in his raging attacks on her.

However, privately, Tina's growing depression had already deepened into a disturbing darkness as early as 1968, the ominous year before her Stones triumph. That year, on what she described as "an ordinary day," she finally reached her breaking point and made a secret suicide attempt. She had become pregnant yet again by Ike, but so had one of his nonsinging Ikettes, a kind of managerial type named Ann Thomas, originally one of her friends, allies, and protectors before joining the Ike cult. Tina decided then and there that she would not submit to giving birth to another of his children and instead chose to terminate the pregnancy altogether.

Around this time, he began to exhibit truly psychotic and scary behaviors, exacerbated by his increasingly heavy drug use, resorting one time to using his guitar to clobber her, breaking it, and then complaining that she had ruined his guitar and using his fists again. She confided to those who would listen that Ike by this time had lost whatever marbles he had left, beating her with phones, with shoes, and with his preferred coat hangers.

One time, just before a show, he punched her in the face and broke her jaw, but she had to go onstage and sing anyway, trying to annunciate the words gurgled in the blood gushing around in her mouth. She was, she firmly believed, ready to die. She went to her family doctor complaining of a nonexistent sleep disorder and requested some extremely strong pills, fifty of them. On the way to some club with her whole entourage, she got a glass of water in the bathroom and swallowed all fifty of them at once.

The pills started kicking in when she was in the backseat of the limo, and the whole crew dashed her off to Daniel Freeman Hospital in Inglewood, California, desperately needing to get her stomach pumped. When she finally woke up afterward, *his* face was glaring at her. She wasn't at first sure if she was dead or alive until he barked out that she was trying to ruin his life. Fifty full years later, in *My Love Story*, she still vividly recalled the weird experience of coming back to life against her will.

She described how the emergency doctors moved into action. While pumping her stomach but unable to get her to respond to them, Ike apparently asked if he could talk to her. Her subconscious mind heard him (so she said), the voice got through the fog, and her heart immediately began racing again. The doctors remarked that he should keep talking, that they had a pulse, and the next thing she knew, she woke up wondering why she was in a hospital bed. She fell asleep again and then woke up the next day, looking right into the face of Ike Turner, telling her, "You should die, you motherfucker."

"As soon as I was released from the hospital, he forced me to go back to work. I was weak, had terrible stomach cramps, and yet had to go through the whole show with a smile on my face. When we finished, the Ikettes held me up and helped me to the dressing room. There was Ike, fuming, 'You should die motherfucker,' he said again. 'But if you die, you know what you would do to me.'"

That's the moment when she shifted finally from disliking the man, fearing the man, to hating the man, who had actually plucked her practically out of high school and propelled her into an admittedly exciting (at first) merry-go-round of music and show business. "I was unhappy when I woke up. But I never tried to do it again because I made the realization, one that changed the course of my life. I came out of the darkness believing that I was meant to survive. I was here for a reason. I knew there was only one way out of this nightmare, and it was through the door."

❄   ❄   ❄

It was like Tina Turner was a thoroughbred racehorse who couldn't stop running or wasn't allowed to. It probably wasn't lost on her that one of the most daring and successful films released in the year 1969 was Sydney Pollack's *They Shoot Horses Don't They?* But for her, 1969 was the usual mixture of good and bad, great and terrible, since they were starting to get the big gigs now in Las Vegas in the same International Hotel lounge where Elvis Presley was launching his own huge comeback.

Also as usual, it was producer Bob Krasnow who suddenly appeared like some musical angel and offered up a song he thought she could work wonders with: Otis Redding's "I've Been Loving You Too Long" (which Ike hated and didn't want her to do, perhaps for obvious reasons). Krasnow and his instincts were just as right as he always was. That Redding song, delivered with almost unbearable longing and pathos by Tina, became one of their biggest hits in years when it climbed to number 68 on the pop charts in May 1969.

It was also featured on an accompanying album, *Outta Season*, with other blistering blues numbers. Once again, she delivered a cover version of a song, one that she totally took away from the originator and made all her own. Krasnow then engineered more momentum for the pair, especially for her, by following that hit in quick succession by *The Hunter*, yielding more chart hits, among them the title song as well as one that became a kind of symbolic signature song for her: "Bold Soul Sister."

In the summer of 1969, while the Woodstock festival was capturing the attention of the nation and world, the Turners were on a veritable binge of often overlapping releases, shot out into the airwaves as if the world were about to end. They were not part of the Woodstock lineup per se that summer, but they did headline a similar hippie festival in October, the Lake Amador Gold Rush Festival, with a somewhat more blues and folk flavor and to a healthy and respectable but not as out-of-control audience of about 50,000 fans.

As always, they were going places, but for Tina, they were places she had already been with Ike, tried-and-true but tired rhythm-and-blues tunes of catchy but limited appeal to her newly evolving tastes. Enter her old Brit friends the Rolling Stones again, as if on cue. They had become the biggest rock act in the world, rivaling if not eclipsing their mates the Beatles, who by then were trying to make what would be their final masterpiece before splintering apart into solo careers.

In August 1969, the Stones released "Honky Tonk Woman," and at roughly the same time, the Beatles released "Come Together," their great *Abbey Road* opener. Tina desperately wanted to sing both tunes onstage, something that completely mystified Ike, who by now was being left far, far behind her stylistically. The year 1969 was also a banner musical year in general not just for the drastically new incarnation of Ike and Tina Turner's Revue taking shape but also for rock and pop music in general across the charts.

This was definitely also the beginning of the period in which Tina's tastes were seriously evolving and maturing and moving way beyond her rather conservative husband's grasp of what music was, what it could be, and where it was going. She was tuning in to rock music, with the help of the Stones and others, groups that were reinterpreting and repackaging musical motifs that were originally black in the first place. "Honky Tonk Women," a song that must have felt like it was literally written for and about her, a raucous southern babe playing in little juke joints of ill repute, was just such a flick of the switch for her career style-wise.

So it was the perfect chance to try out what she considered her new black rock vibe in front of the ideal music lovers for her new spirit when the Stones asked her (and the Revue of course) to join them for their U.S. tour to promote *Let It Bleed* and expose their new guitarist, Mick Taylor, late of many a great British blues bands, such as John Mayall's, to replace their recently deceased founder, Brian Jones.

The tour would play thirteen cities and eighteen shows, starting in November at the Los Angeles Forum, again being filmed for a theatrical documentary. Also on the bill with the reigning British kings of contemporary pop music would be one of their old black idols, BB King, and one of their new black heartthrobs, Tina Turner, and her girls and her band. One of our most important pop critics of that era, Ralph Gleason, described the whole extravaganza best I think in the new little music magazine he had just cofounded: *Rolling Stone*.

The second night's outing, at the Oakland Coliseum, he referred to as an intense experience that "may very well have been the best rock show ever presented." Gleason raved about the erstwhile senior statesman of the blues BB King, who was followed by Ike and Tina Turner's Revue, who preceded Mick and the boys. For Gleason, she was definitely the most sensational female performer on any contemporary stage of the time.

One can only imagine her husband's reaction to such accolades and especially Gleason's response to another showstopper that Tina did: the Otis Redding song that Ike hated more than any other. "The climax to her act was the most blatantly sexual number I have ever seen at a concert." She famously caressed the microphone erotically while twisting and squirming and letting out animalistic vocal noises that closely simulated an orgasm.

It would be a performance later included in the Stones' film *Gimme Shelter* and one that she would find hard to live down for many years afterward, thinking not only that she might have gone too far but also that Ike was behind her in the shadows trying to capture some of her attention with grunting and groaning sounds of his own. She found the whole thing embarrassing and almost pornographic, but of course the audience lapped it up.

Luckily for Tina and her band (yes, it was truly now hers), they missed the notorious later Stones concert at Altamont Speedway near San

Francisco at which four people had been killed, but the Stones tour still injected another boost of rocket fuel into their forward motion. When 1970 arrived, Ike and Tina were still buzzing from being exposed to an immense white rock audience, with "Bold Soul Sister" reaching number 59 on the pop charts in January of the new year, a year filled with an ever-accelerating public profile for both the Revue itself and Tina in particular.

Ike signed a new contract with Minit Records, an affiliate of the giant United Artists outfit, which would represent them for the rest of their time together. Meanwhile, the two songs that Tina loved and had to beg Ike to let her do, "Honky Tonk Women" and "Come Together," were paired as a single that peaked at number 57 on the pop charts. Tina had been right again. The album that both of those songs were on stayed on the charts for nineteen weeks, a great run. Ike was kept very busy counting *his* money, which he frequently liked to have near him in stuffed suitcases.

While Ike was busy counting, he barely noticed that his wife's health was falling apart totally. Her doctor told her to stop working so much, but "Doctor" Ike said to keep going despite her contracting bronchitis (never fun for a singer), which actually turned out to be tuberculosis, leading to rounds of biopsies and spinal taps that revealed glandular infections and a collapsed lung. When she woke up in the hospital, there were flowers waiting there for her from "Mick Jagger and the Rolling Stones" but none from her husband.

Her illness lingered for quite a while, and in a sense, it appears that it never really left her at all. How could it since she immediately returned to the road, crammed with antibiotics, appearing at several planned concerts with a couple of other gigs suddenly squeezed in between those ones by Ike. They made their regular appearance in Las Vegas to open for Elvis, obviously a huge deal for any musician, anywhere, anytime, especially for Ike, who liked to fancy himself as an artist operating at the same level of influence as the King.

The only trouble was, it was his Queen Tina who was getting all the kudos. And Ike was also getting more and more edgy the more money he made and the more drugs he could spend it on. It was clearly time, in his addled brain, for him to create his very own recording studio so he could publicly demonstrate that he too could be a Spector (more like a specter, though, in his case).

Yet on top of everything, they still had time to record and release a machine-gun–like series of albums: *Cussin', Cryin' and Carryin' On* on Pompeii, *Get It–Get It* on Cenco, *Her Man, His Woman* on their new home (or one of them at least) of Capitol, *Outta Season* on Blue Thumb, *Ike and Tina Turner and the Ikettes—In Person* on Minit, *The Fantastic Ike and Tina* on Sunset, *Get It Together* on Pompeii, and, rounding out the year, *The Hunter* on Blue Thumb again.

The years 1970 and 1971 saw their competing "together" releases, *Come* and *Workin'* on Liberty, and three amazing live concert records: *Live: On Stage in Paris* on Liberty, *Live at Carnegie Hall: What You Hear Is What You Get* on United Artists, and *Live: Something's Gotta Hold on Me* on Harmony. But it would be the live recording master-piece of their Carnegie Hall appearance that would be most beneficial for listeners today to behold. That one, all by itself, captures the essence of her lightning in a bottle.

IKE AND TINA LIVE AT CARNEGIE HALL, WHAT YOU HEAR IS WHAT YOU GET

Released July 1971, United Artists. Personnel: Ike and Tina Turner, Kings of Rhythm. Produced by Ike Turner and Bonnie Barrett. Duration: 59:26.

Piece of My Heart (Bert Berns, Jerry Ragovoy) 3:38 / Everyday People (Sly Stone) 2:10 / Doin the Tina Turner 1:20 / Sweet Soul Music (Arthur Conley) 1:00 / Ooh Poo Pah Doo (Wilson Pickett) 4:05 / Honky Tonk Women (Mick Jagger and Keith Richards) 3:05 / A Love Like Yours (Ed Holland) 3:43 / Proud Mary (John Fogerty) 9:50 / I Smell Trouble (Jessie Hill) 7:57 / I Want to Take You Higher (Jeff Beck) 3:35 / I've Been Loving You Too Long (Otis Redding, Jerry Butler) 8:35 / Respect (Otis Redding) 5:03

Making it in your hometown is one thing, but New York, New York, is really where's it's at—always was, always would be. Just as the popular song famously implied, if you can make it there, you can make it any-where. But in terms of documenting that New York emergence live on vinyl, their triumphant return on August 15, 1971, was a true gem. The record they made of their appearance there in the hallowed Carnegie Hall is a live masterpiece, and it's also a crash course in what made them great as a performing unit.

After having commanded the revered African American venue of the Apollo, the only conceivable place to top it would be the equally revered Carnegie Hall, where she once again somehow managed to even out-sweat the Godfather at the incongruously formal classical concert site, with the historical detonation captured on this stellar live album.

As Laurie Stras pointed out in her book *She's So Fine: Reflections on Femininity in 60's Music*, "Instead of vamping on the theme of lost love as Brown does, Tina actually stops the music altogether and tells the audience a story of lost love as a spoken monologue, with the inflections and tone of a black preacher in church. Tina makes her story incredibly personal when she stops the music.

"'I'm going to stop the music for just a few minutes now because I want to talk to you about love and hurt. I want you to sing along with me now if there's anybody in this house that's ever been hurt.'" The music starts to roll again, but then she declares theatrically that she has to stop it again because she wasn't quite through talking about love and hurt. The crowd went nuts.

Discogs offered a fair assessment of the remarkable occasion when this raucous unit stormed into Carnegie Hall. "At the top of their worldwide fame, having crafted their incendiary version of Creedence Clearwater Revival's 'Proud Mary' and opened for the Stones on their tour, their visual appeal was equally impressive. Not intimidated by the formal ambience of New York's legendary concert hall, the nine-piece ensemble ripped through a display of their soul-drenched funk-inflected down and dirty brand of r & b, taking the rock originals to new heights in their cover versions."

This live record famously captured her comment that she never does anything "nice and easy," she always does it "nice and rough," and also included her almost unbearable sexual innuendos with the microphone during "Been Loving You Too Long." Equally telling, however, and totally spooky was Ike's repeated refrain that he inserted into the tender Otis Redding song he so despised. When she intones those intense lyrics about being tired and wanting to be free but her lover's feelings have grown stronger with time, "I've been loving you a little too long to stop now," the song turned into a classic call-and-response soul motif. But when Tina purred, "I can't stop now," Ike's improvised response was not of course part of the song at all: "Cause you ain't ready to die." How romantic.

Her partner should obviously have been listening more closely to the lyrics of the other Redding song that Tina had transformed here so tellingly. Doing a job on "Respect" that I actually prefer to the already amazing Otis and Aretha versions and at about three times their speeds, she once again took that song away from both Redding and Franklin and made it her own. She just needed to spell that word, "Respect," out more loudly for her husband. And soon.

5

PLEASE RELEASE ME, LET ME GO

Proud Tina

"One good thing about music, when it hits you, you feel no pain. So hit me with music."

—Bob Marley, "Trenchtown Rock," 1975

During their creative and commercial peak from the mid-1960s until the mid-1970s, one of Tina Turner's biggest achievements was certainly the sheer tenacity to continue making important musical statements while in the midst of times of emotional and physical trial as well as great personal danger. She simply seems to have refused to give up being the person she had become, much to the chagrin of those who knew her backstory, either because she saw herself as a survivor who could weather any storm or because she was a perfect example of Stockholm syndrome. Was she deluding herself into accepting the person holding her hostage?

We'll never know her motivations, and it's not my place to speculate. The music, however, continued its forward momentum in a remarkable example of her classic against-all-odds optimism, and while we are entitled to wonder at the psychological underpinnings or contradictions in the character of a hostage, we're not entitled to judge them. The music she made with her partner speaks for itself in a confident voice, and the music she made after her liberation from him during her stellar solo career has since entered the lofty annals of artistic mythology. What goes around comes around, from one funky generation to the next.

I recently encountered a key observation regarding resilience that feels like it applies directly to us when trying to assess the valuable life lessons learned by Tina Turner and that she left for us all to ponder. The first observation has to do with suffering and its values and was made by the conceptual artist Barbara Bloom, whose work frequently uses broken objects or obstructed images in order to convey the fragility and ephemeral quality of memory. Bloom, in her book *Broken*, was referencing the Eastern aesthetic known as *wabi sabi*, which highlights imperfections or damage, irregularities or rough patches, of objects and even experiences.

Included in this notion is the practice of *kitsukuori*, which means "to repair with gold," the art of repairing shattered or cracked pottery with gold or silver lacquer and the understanding that the object is more beautiful for having been broken. This concept involves the acceptance of imperfections in our experiences and embraces the fact that all of us are in some way broken. Instead of hiding the broken element, *wabi sabi* tries to strengthen the damaged areas by highlighting and even accentuating the healing process.

I believe it's immediately apparent that Tina Turner's whole approach to learning from and growing beyond her traumatic early life has much to do with this practice of accepting damage and emphasizing its potential blessings. Turner is obviously a case of rough patches in life experience, which she used to her advantage both during the traumas and subsequent to her deliverance from them. I believe her later songs were the gold lacquer she used to fill the cracks in her earlier life.

One question we often grapple with: how do we differentiate between the art someone produced and the person who produced it? Without dispensing with the vital importance of an individual's biographical experience in the making of their craft, there might be some truth to D. H. Lawrence's admonition to "never trust the artist, trust the tale. The proper function of the critic is to save the tale from the artist who created it." Yet even though we can to some degree separate her personal narrative from the art she made, we risk overdoing so at our peril as appreciators. We're still left to wonder about the lyrical content of the songs she served as a vehicle for—the message she was transmitting in those songs—by which I mean, *who* exactly is she singing about?

Many listeners have noticed and remarked on the peculiar fact of how often Ike's songs repeated the same central subjects, themes, and motifs over and over again. Apart from having a limited range of ideas, I suspect it was also a kind of deep unconscious urge for recognizing something in which he himself was complicit. I wouldn't call it guilt exactly since I think he was probably incapable of that particular human emotion, but, nonetheless, how often can the motif of *the fool* recur without at least some meager meaning trickling into his addled psyche?

Generally, it was the singer who appeared to be assuming the title role; however, I believe it was secretly the insecure writer who felt that diminishment, almost in this order: "A Fool in Love," "Poor Fool," "A Fool for a Fool," "Poor Little Fool," "Foolish," and of course the ultra-obvious "A Fool for You." I mean, really? One has to wonder why this message, coupled with the abuse, took so long to finally sink in for Tina, but better late than never I guess.

She was obviously too busy performing and recording to stop for any much-needed introspection at the time. And again, that's the way Ike liked it. As much of a control freak as any composer or bandleader who ever lived, though, Ike Turner must have found his grip on the creative situation loosening literally day by day as Tina became more and more the star attraction in his little carnival act. He ended up being the side-show geek. Such a weird mixed blessing: his dreams of success coming true were also precisely the very circumstances that were threatening to crack open his dream completely.

Two memorable things in this regard occurred toward the end of 1970. First, after performing an incendiary version of John Fogerty's song "Proud Mary" in their live concerts and television for more than a year, Ike decided to bring Tina into the studio to finally let her record her own version, which she totally transformed from the songwriter's earlier delivery and once again made it all her own. She not only created a sterling rendition that has become synonymous with her name but also felt that hers was even more true rock and roll than the original, much as she enjoyed Creedence Clearwater Revival. Fogerty's *Bayou Country* album would yield another surprising pop rock hit for Tina Turner, by then almost being identified as a de facto solo artist, still long before she would actually be one. When it was released early in 1971, it rapidly rose in the charts to become their biggest hit to date, selling more than a million copies by May.

It also won Tina her first Grammy Award for best rhythm-and-blues vocal performance. Whether or not you're one who believes in the principle called karma (actions and their consequences, both positive and negative), as the devoutly meditative chanter Tina was and still is, it certainly seemed that whenever Tina needed someone or something to lift her up and move her forward to the next spot on her chess board, they always materialized magically right there in front of her.

In Jan Wenner's *Rolling Stone* piece on Tina, the grateful original writer of the song, John Fogerty, was effusive in his praise for helping to make his tune the second-biggest single song ever for either one of them: "Tina Turner doing my 'Proud Mary' is one of the most electrifying images in rock and roll. Thank you beautiful Tina, for shooting my song into the stratosphere."

As Aaron Cohen expressed it to me, pretty accurately I think, "Not to disparage John Fogerty, but Tina Turner certainly put dimensions to 'Proud Mary' that I'm sure he couldn't ever have possibly envisioned."

Cohen tends to share my estimation of what her chief characteristic was as a singing talent. "Empathy and, of course, sexuality, have been essential to her talents as an interpreter." She certainly was an invitation to embrace our most visceral feelings by being an open channel for them herself. Indeed, she had certainly transformed both the song and herself in the process, explaining in her opening lines about her version, which by then had practically become part of the song's formal lyrics: we're going to start this out doing it nice and easy but then change it up a bit because we never do anything "nice and easy, we always do it nice and rough." Who can ever forget watching footage of the Revue doing this blistering song on the innocent and unsuspecting *Ed Sullivan Show*?

Certainly not John Corcelli or I. Not being a singer-songwriter herself but instead rather a gifted interpreter, in considering what she did to transform "Proud Mary" from a Creedence Clearwater Revival song into whatever we can call it in her hands, Corcelli was succinct and to the point. "She took the song and made it her own. In fact, I heard Ike and Tina Turner's version *before* I heard CCR's. Their classic performance on the *Ed Sullivan Show* still stands as the definitive version of it for me." Hear hear.

Aaron Cohen also hits the target right on when he identifies what made Tina stand apart from her many talented female peers. "What strikes me as unique about Tina Turner was something I hadn't thought about until I saw her on an episode of *The Dick Cavett Show* from the early 1970s (1971 or 1972). She mentioned that her main vocal influences were male singers, like Ray Charles. And that got me thinking about her androgyny. Physically, nobody watching her would think she's trying to look male (like, say, Grace Jones), but the more I thought about it, that androgyny does come through in her voice. And I also wonder if that's why she formed such strong affinities with male rock singers who also played around with gender roles, such as Mick Jagger and David Bowie."

Again, something unique in her basic vocal approach is what tended to make Turner's impact on the distinctive spectrum of black rock so significant stylistically for Cohen. "Certainly her androgyny was a big contribution to black rock, and white rock, too. And since Ike Turner was as great a guitarist as any of the more recognized names in rock were, Tina Turner's voice alongside his guitar lines were a big contribution to expanding the parameters of what made black rock what it became." Naturally, to me, the stellar name of the alluringly androgynous Prince comes immediately to mind as a big inheritor of both Ike's guitar and Tina's vibe, merged impossibly into one singular black genius.

The second notable development that year: a combination of recording "Proud Mary" in a prohibitively expensive commercial studio and also raking in those massive profits from the hit inspired Ike to finally indulge in his long-held dream of opening his very own recording studio. He had more or less had it with rehearsing at home in his living room and hurrying the sessions along at sites that were booked by the hour. His dream or, more accurately, his delusion was that in his own studio, he could create a personal hit factory along the lines of the great Phil Spector, whom he both envied and despised in equal measure.

He planned to call it Bolic Sound Studio, playing on his wife's maiden name in a rather ironic tribute to the source of his creative and financial freedom. He could just as easily have named it Bullock Studio: that would have been the most appropriate way of spending the large sums of money that she was bringing in and that he was about to invest in a little building on Le Brea, only a few minutes from his View Park Hills location. It was completely remodeled, renovated, soundproofed, and equipped with what he thought he deserved to have: state-of-the-art equipment, including an almost $100,000 control board. This was, he believed, a sound investment (pun intended) since he firmly, if delusionally, believed that fresh hits would soon be pouring out of the place.

He even allowed himself the luxury of two complete and separate sound studios in the building, including a large space that he would rent out to big-name stars he deemed worthy. Eventually, it was used on multiple occasions by no less a stellar rock star than Frank Zappa, so it must have been technically proficient. Given how drastically different their music tastes and temperaments were, that must have been quite the intriguing business arrangement to be sure. Zappa recorded some great albums right there in Bolic Sound, including his big hit *Apostrophe*, with Tina even doing some backup vocals for him on his *Overnite Sensation* album.

Ike also built a smaller studio for his own private use, meaning for the recording of his now famous protégée Tina. Ever hyperconscious of both privacy and security and being more and more paranoid daily, he also even created a private sanctuary (or party room) behind a totally sealed-off security vault door. His control fetishes also demanded that he install an intricate system of closed-circuit television cameras everywhere for both security and paranoia purposes. Naturally enough, for Ike, he also kept a small arsenal of guns, both pistols and even machine guns, strategically placed hither and yon.

This combination did not bode well given the mountains of cocaine he was now also able to indulge in privately in addition to his now well-documented poor husband skills and frequent volcanic rages. Luckily for the nominal name behind the studio at least, push never came to shove and shoot, although after Tina did manage to eventually extricate herself from his control and file for divorce (still five years away at this stage), her car was frequently found torched, and bullets were often fired into her independent home away from home.

The year 1971 was dawning as one of his and their biggest yet, with summer seeing their latest Revue album, *What You Hear Is What You*

Get, peaking at number 25 on the charts. Both were also both featured in a film documentary filmed in Ghana, Africa, called *Soul to Soul*, celebrating the fortieth anniversary of that nation's independence, and each delivered a song performance in the Milos Forman film *Taking Off*.

However, one big drawback to this year was the first high-profile public exposure of the couple's marital troubles and Ike's own obvious mental problems in the still-stunning Ben Fong-Torres *Rolling Stone* cover story of October 14, 1971. Even if he was embarrassed by all the public attention this brought, for the first time lifting the lid on what Tina's life with Ike was like, and though angry of course, he didn't seem to possess any customary human gene for shame at all. He just went farther up coke mountain as if it was his personal Everest and contented himself with counting his bigger and bigger acres of cash.

That article both may have contributed in some small way to making him rein in his proclivities slightly (the Tina violence, not the coke romance) and may have resulted in giving Tina the strength of public awareness and the support system she'd need when she eventually made her escape from the Ike cult. But as the money poured in and the adulation for his now megastar spouse reached a peak, his own popularity as the leader of a formerly successful Revue began to slide. Their next album, the first created in his "hit factory," *Nuff Said*, did not crack the Top 100, and the next single they managed to get out, "Up in Heah," struggled to reach number 83, while a second factory-produced album, *Feel Good*, ranked even lower.

Things were not exactly going as the black Spector had planned. Tina had obviously realized by then that the times were changing and that musical styles and tastes were evolving (as were her own), but she also noticed that her husband never changed either his music style or his stage show. It was basically the same one he'd been doing when she first approached his stage back at the end of the 1950s. Tina was also impressed by the feminist movement and the notion of women's liberation, although she found it ironic: most women were trying to get liberated from housework, while she was trying to simply stay alive.

One rare hot late hit would arrive, a little belatedly, and such an ironic and paradoxical hit it was: a hot-blooded dance song and album celebrating her family's southern roots in Tennessee. The aforementioned "Nutbush City Limits" arrived at number 22 in the pop charts in the fall of 1973. It was the final Top 30 number the couple would ever have together, and her husband couldn't fail to notice the fact that it was all about *her* childhood origins and *her* personal evolution.

Another song similar to the title tune was also penned by Tina for the same album, "Club Manhattan," chronicling the place where she was introduced to Ike, a supercharged tune that chronicled her origins with him: "Over in E. St. Louis there's a swingin' little club called Manhattan, and the band on that stage are kings of rhythm," in addition to several other first-time-ever self-written songs: "Daily Bread," "Help Him" (a strange Tammy Wynette–cloned song), and one that has a distinctly gospel feeling, although it's gospel funk to be sure: "That's My Purpose." "Some of us are livin' in an earthly heaven and some of us are livin' in hell. But I was put here to love you and that's my purpose," she chirped, almost as if she really meant it.

Personally, I interpret that song's message as meaning she's here to love all of *us*, not "him." Meanwhile, Ike's own strange tune for the album also contained a not-too-subtle and somewhat ominous message to his partner: "Get It Out of Your Mind." But for me, one of the most salient aspects of a jaunty little rocker like "Nutbush City Limits" is that the little town in question was not incorporated by the county, so actually it had *no official city limits* anyway, only the designation that everything beyond it was merely not Nutbush.

In a weird sort of way, Nutbush was everywhere she went, and thus she was still living in Nutbush, even in Europe, since she couldn't really leave it, and as a then thirty-four-year-old worldly woman instead of the naive country girl, she also certainly knew the time was past ripe for a big change. She had, however, finally reached the real city limits and actual borderline between Anna Mae Bullock and Tina Turner.

For Aaron Cohen, her major achievement as a musical artist was fully using the instrument she was born with. "Her voice on those late-'60s/early '70s recordings as part of Ike & Tina Turner, as well as her dynamic stage presence, would be my favorite among her accomplishments. But I also can see how people who have been victimized in personal struggles look upon her as an important role model." True, in her appetite for liberation, she's kind of an all-purpose goddess in that respect and also utterly limitless.

❖   ❖   ❖

Somebody up there likes me: that must have been her constant refrain around this time. No matter how bad things got, they also still got better somehow. The office of record producer Robert Stigwood contacted them to inquire about her availability for a film he was helping to finance for the eccentric British director Ken Russell, the notorious maker of *The Devils* and *Women in Love*, among many others. The film was a cinematic interpretation of the Who's bombastic rock opera *Tommy* from 1969, a record she had heard of but had never really heard.

It had an all-star cast: Elton John, Eric Clapton, the Who, Oliver Reed, Jack Nicholson, Ann-Margaret as Tommy's mother, and, in the role of the Acid Queen, Tina Turner if she wanted it. No mention of Ike. Filming in London was quite a hoot and allowed her to reunite with her old Las Vegas pal Ann-Margaret, who then asked her to stay on after shooting wrapped to partner with her in her latest television musical special. Their duets together on "Nutbush City Limits," "Honky Tonk Women," and "Proud Mary" were also smash TV hits.

Meanwhile, back in his toxic Bolic studios (which by then maybe should have been called hyperbolic), Ike had recently boosted his capacity from twenty-four to thirty-two tracks, possibly in the hope that by mimicking Spector's skillful overdubs, he could catch some of the same magic in his own. But all it allowed him to have was way too many different versions of songs without knowing how to sort through all the coke-addled experiments he had indulged in.

Once someone throws hot coffee in your face, it becomes abundantly clear (if it hadn't already been) that he didn't love Tina for herself at all but rather was merely obsessed with not losing control of her and, by extension, of the comfy creative lifestyle she made possible. Any young person seeking a crash course in their dynamic allure would be well served by getting these mid-career discs. As popular as they were, however, it was never lost on Ike that their *most* successful and beloved songs and albums were usually the ones that had *not* been entirely written or produced by him. That made the big boss man all the more impossible to get along with, if that were even possible given his pathology.

Nuff Said and *Feel Good*, both released on United Artists, quickly consolidated their superlative groove in 1972, but the vibe had started to wear a bit thin by this stage, along with their relationship, which had never been on anything but shaky ground from day one anyway. By then, they were largely together in name only. *Tina Turns the Country On*, her unique (if slightly surreal) solo effort from 1974, was a clear indication that she was way more than ready to get along without *workin' together* with Ike.

At last, she had struck out on her own, musically at least, with her unlikely but catchy country-flavored album of cover songs, which had to be satisfying at some level. It did not of course exactly turn the country on, being mostly a lame cash-grab attempt on Ike's part, though most listeners were impressed by her stylistic flexibility and utter lack of professional guile. Even when she flopped, people still admired her authenticity and perseverance.

For John Corcelli, it was her very mutability as an artist that also made her so special. "Clearly Turner certainly made the perhaps surprising transition from R&B to Rock and then smoothly to Pop, but my guess is that she also brought everything from those earlier musical worlds *forward* with her into Pop itself as an art form. And she somehow managed to accomplish this remarkable feat while not compromising anything at all along the way: she was true to herself regardless of which style she embraced. By doing so she also contributed greatly to the stylistic evolution of each successive genre she touched."

Aaron Cohen feels it was her dedication and energetic devotion to sheer hard work that made her triumph in the end over any slight vocal limitations she may have had. "Tina Turner didn't have the range of Aretha Franklin, or the family lineage of Mavis Staples, but she worked incredibly hard to make the most of the voice she had. And she added a physicality and theatricality to her performances that few of her contemporaries, of either gender or any race, had. She also made singers with rougher vocal qualities fit into the soul era (as did Etta James), but it's something I couldn't imagine Mary Wells or Tammi Terrell ever accomplishing. Tina doing so likely helped set the stage for Bettye LaVette's reemergence later on."

I agree and also believe that she laid the groundwork for a niche to accommodate a funky performer as raw as Betty Mabry-Davis as well, not to mention certain female rappers. Her rather amazing creative flexibility was also one of the ingredients that most impressed John Corcelli. "I think Tina's most significant artistic accomplishment has been her ability to transcend categories altogether. In fact, Turner has firmly established her place in popular music precisely by never making compromises artistically. *She* has also shaped her own career and was never molded by her handlers or record executives. We must remember that Ike had always tried to 'control' her artistic career right from the start. When she broke free from his grasp, she finally took full control of her own repertoire and made much better and higher quality creative musical choices. That very willingness to take risks musically has given Turner's fans a solid and satisfying discography. After all, only Tina Turner could have sung 'What's Love Got to Do with It.'"

But it would take a while for Tina to fully come into herself, perhaps not surprisingly, and to find her own footing once she made the attempt to present herself as a truly solo artist (on two albums while still with the Revue band) and another two follow-up solo albums while caught in a weird kind of transitional period of stylistic searching.

As I've suggested, her first two efforts were quite odd and almost kitschy really. Any way you look at it, and even being as charitable as possible, *Tina Turns the Country On!* is a slightly bizarre pastiche of wonky western tunes on which she appears dramatically out of place, mostly because she is. And *Acid Queen* (1975) is a novelty send-up supporting her then recent acting turn in the Who's campy Ken Russell film, an album for which she deserves kudos just for keeping a straight face throughout. It's a respectable choice of hard rockers for her to cover, however, mixed incongruously with a second side dish of more mediocre late Ike tunes.

TINA TURNS THE COUNTRY ON! (UNITED ARTISTS RECORDS)

Released in 1974. Produced by Tom Thacker. Personnel: Joe Lamno, bass; Michael Bolts, drums; Mark Creamer, guitars; Glen Hardin, piano; J. D. Minnis, steel guitar; Tom Scott, saxophone; Terrance Lane, percussion. Engineers: John Horton, Fred Borkgren, Steve Waldman, D. B. Johnson. Duration: 33:49 (but feels like a small eternity).

Bayou Song (P. J. Morse) 3:22 / Help Me Make It through the Night (Kris Kristofferson) 2:48 / Tonight I'll Be Staying Here With You (Bob Dylan) 2:58 / If You Love Me (John Rostill) 3:00 / He Belongs to Me (Bob Dylan) 3:59 / Don't Talk Now (James Taylor) 2:58 / Long Long Time (Gary White) 4:42 / I'm Movin On (Hank Snow) 2:37 / There'll Always Be Music (Dolly Parton) 4:10 / The Love That Lights Our Way (Fred and Marsha Karlin) 3:15

Don't get me wrong, now. If you made it this far in the book. you know how much I respect this artist. However, everyone sometimes make a big mistake, and this was hers—or, rather, theirs since it was her husband's idea: a somewhat crass attempt to expand their audience base using his primary commodity: her. But country? I'm not a big fan, it's true, but I definitely know great country when I hear it (Kitty Wells, Patsy Cline, Tammy Wynette, June Carter, and Dolly Parton before she went pop), and this isn't it. They even tried describing it as country rhythm and blues, a contradiction in terms if ever there was one.

It was a tricky venture as your first debut album on your own, even if you are dissatisfied with your usually popular rhythm and blues going through a slump in sales. Weirdly, it still managed to garner a Grammy nomination for Tina for best rhythm-and-blues female vocal performance in 1974, a fact that still mystifies me to this day. This record of course did not fare well and has never been released on CD. Count your blessings perhaps, although I totally understand why completist Tina fans would want it in their collection since I have a healthy compulsive streak myself.

It should also not be confused with myriad other strange Ike attempts to cash in, even after she'd left him, with other blurred-line releases of dubious distinction, such as *Tina Turner Sings Country*, *Soul Deep*, *Country My Way*, *Good Hearted Woman*, *Country in My Soul*, *Stand by Your Man* (really!), *Country Classics*, *You Ain't Woman Enough to Take My Man* (poor Tammy!), and *The Country Side of Tina Turner*, all of which represented Ike's persistence, if nothing else, in scraping every scintilla of sound she'd ever left behind her in his home-based Bolic Studio.

ACID QUEEN (UNITED ARTISTS RECORDS)

Produced by Denny Diante, Spencer Proffer. Released in 1975. Personnel: Tina Turner, vocals; Ike Turner, arranger; Ed Greene, drums; Henry Davis, bass; Ray Parker, guitar; Spence Proffer, guitar; Jerry Peters, keyboards; Joe Clayton, congas; Alan Lindgren, synthesizer; Sid Sharp, strings; Julia Waters, Kim Carnes, Maxine Waters, vocals; Denny Diante, percussion; Ray Milano, recording and mixing. Duration: 35:29.

Under My Thumb (Mick Jagger, Keith Richards) 3:22 / Let's Spend the Night Together (Mick Jagger, Keith Richards) 2:54 / Acid Queen (Pete Townshend) 3:01 / I Can See for Miles (Pete Townshend) 2:54 / Whole Lotta Love (Willie Dixon) 5:24 / Baby Get It On (Ike Turner) 5:34 / Bootsy Whitelaw (Ike Turner) 5:06 / Pick Me Tonight (Ike Turner) 3:13 / Rockin and Rollin (Ike Turner) 4:02

Well, at least it's not country and western (sorry Dolly). Although another kind of blatant attempt to cash in on her frenetic cinematic *Tommy* turn (but why should we hold that against her really?), it did have all the makings of something heavy duty. I wish they had confined the songs to all Townshend material rather than mixing and matching famous hard rock hits and then diluting it all with a side plate of tired Ike raunch odes past their prime. "Bootsy Whitelaw," his ode to a jazz trombone legend who influenced him early on, is a strange choice of subject to include in an acid queen operetta. I would have loved her to do not necessarily all *Tommy* material (that would have been too trite perhaps) but maybe some other Who masterpieces, such as "Happy Jack" (a favorite of mine) or "A Quick One while He's Away."

As Robert Christgau remarked in his *Rock Albums of the Seventies*, "Her rock myth reconfirmed cinematically, Tina quickly turns out two from the Who (only fair), two from the Stones (who else?) and one from Led Zep ("Whole Lotta Love" is brilliant). With bass lines lifted whole from the originals, the singing almost doesn't matter. And what rocks out most mythically? Ike's cleverly entitled 'Baby Get It On.'" The latter tune, which is already almost (but not quite) as disco influenced as Tina's next two truly solo albums would be, was the last moderately successful rhythm-and-blues single ever for the pair together.

✿   ✿   ✿

The period 1974–1975 was still another banner one of sorts for the troubled partnership, as they were descending into their inevitable downward spiral—and for mixed reasons. Those years would see one last excellent live record, a double album: *The World of Ike and Tina Turner!* from United Artists, which won a Grammy Award for best album package, in addition to a truly oddball effort, *Let Me Touch Your Mind*, also from United Artists, as well as *Ike Turner Presents the Family Vibes—Strange Fruit*, with vaguely eclectic but overused synthesizers by Ike in one of his sinister pseudopsychedelic side projects with his original Rhythm Kings band in tireless tow.

Also in 1974 came two still respectable and notable entries to their catalog, both equally historic. *The Gospel according to Ike and Tina Turner*, their nineteenth studio record, featuring new arrangements of traditional gospel tunes (something every secular blues/soul artist tends to do sooner or later) but again overly reliant on Ike's new fetish for synthesizers. Still, it was nominated for a 1975 Grammy in the gospel category! And finally, literally *finally* (almost), came an album called *Sweet Rhode Island Red*, their last studio recording before they separated, which includes several new songs by Tina as well as covers of reliable Stevie Wonder tunes.

One reason I tend to use the world "finally" in italics (or certainly tongue in cheek when it comes to Ike) is the fact that he then released almost more albums of her music *after* she left him than he did when they were together, mostly using alternate takes, unissued songs, B-side rejects, or literally anything else containing her voice that was gathering dust in his Bolic Studio vaults.

His obsession with making her constantly record would pay off for him for decades to come, even if the releases were by then less than up to their usual high standards. Without her around, he couldn't seem to tell the difference anyway, and, besides, she was his prized thoroughbred champion, or so he thought, and he wasn't about to let anything she voiced ever go to waste. By my count, some thirty vault recordings on different labels, many of them European, found their way into the world after her grandiose comeback without him.

He would have released her reading from the telephone book if he could have done so. *Delilah's Power*, an album produced after she left (except for the title song, which was already a single from two years before, when they were touring in Europe), was released one year after she escaped him, in 1976, in order for him to capitalize on his soon-to-be ex-wife's Midas touch. During this time, Ike was spending more time at Bolic Sound than he was with Tina and their children at their home in Inglewood. Tina, meanwhile, had looked inward to alleviate her own problems and soon found solace after her introduction to the contemplative teachings of Buddhism and chanting.

In July 1976, Ike intended on signing a five-year contract with a new record company, Cream Records, for a reported yearly amount of $150,000. The contract had a key "personal" clause, meaning Ike would have to sign the contract in four days, thus keeping Tina tied to Ike for at least five more years. She couldn't take five more minutes. On July 2, 1976, the Ike and Tina Turner Revue traveled by plane to Dallas, where they were to perform at the Dallas Statler Hilton. While on the airplane, the two became embroiled in an altercation that led to a physical fight in their limousine.

The duo presented different accounts as to what went on that day. Ike accused Tina of being negligent to help him with a nosebleed due to constant cocaine, with his incongruous solution being to do even more cocaine. Tina claimed Ike was annoyed that she was eating chocolates while wearing an all-white outfit, causing Ike to slap and punch her. The couple did agree on one thing, however: that Ike had been up for five days straight on a cocaine binge.

Following Ike's punch, Tina recalled fighting back for the first time, scratching and kicking him. Ike seemed stunned, alleging to a musician associate friend that the two "went around like prizefighters for a while." Both Ike and Tina were bleeding by the time they arrived at the hotel. After going up to their suite, Ike retired to a sofa. Once Ike had fallen asleep, Tina grabbed a few toiletries, covered herself, and escaped from the back of the hotel, running across an active freeway before stopping at a local Ramada Inn hotel.

She claimed that she later hid out at several friends' homes for a time, insisting on helping them with household chores and duties regardless of their attempts to prevent her from doing so. Christian Wright characterized her combination of haughty and humble very well in *Trouble Girls*. "Tina Turner had been a star but she had never been a diva.

When the friends putting her up would tell her to stop cleaning, that the maid would do it, she persisted, she needed to pay her way. She didn't think less of herself for it, she said, because it helped her survive. She was proud of it."

On July 27, 1976, Tina Turner filed for divorce on the grounds of irreconcilable differences. About time. Ike and Tina fought for a year in divorce court arguing over money and property. By late 1977, Tina decided to stop her pursuit of any financial earnings, including an apartment complex in Anaheim, California, and another apartment elsewhere, stating to her lawyer that her freedom "was much more important." Tina also agreed to retain only the use of her stage name, which came in handy for her upcoming reincarnation.

The divorce proceedings ended in November 1977, and the divorce was officially finalized in March 1978. Having the self-awareness of a clam, it simply never occurred to Ike that it wasn't the fault or flaw of the people around him for "abandoning" him all the time but was actually simply the result of his being such a horrible human being. That would have required too much self-reflection.

"Tumultuous: it's an interesting word to choose in considering Turner's artistic endeavors in music and movies," John Corcelli told me. "While I'm not comfortable with that word as an overall appropriate descriptor of her life, that said, she is definitely an artist who has taken a lot of personal struggle and, as blues artists often did, expressed her pain through her music. So, from that perspective it works. Nevertheless, I think Turner has enhanced herself to her audience as a significant means of recovery. Her time with Ike was undoubtedly regrettable, but her relentless pursuit of her own identity, as best heard in *all* of her music, has been a total validation of who she is, both as an artist, as a woman, and also as a person."

Indeed, assessing the crucial but distressing role of Ike Turner has always been a challenging one. For Corcelli, it is mitigated by a few key and indisputable facts. "On strictly musical terms, Ike has earned his place in music history as one of the founders of a 'sound': that Gospel/funk/Pop mix that made the Ike & Tina Turner Revue such a spirited success. The fact that he mistreated Tina has done more to tarnish his own reputation, and deservedly so, but I think it unfair to see his overall contribution to music through the prism of domestic abuse."

True enough, his is a problematic legacy, and like many artists, his work is best left to be considered separately from his character or personality. Ironically, though, it often amazes me that it was that very corrosive character and challenged personality that somehow prompted or provoked his ex-partner to seek a solo career at all in the first place. So somehow (and paradoxically), his own psychological problems also made for just as huge, if accidental, a contribution to our collective cultural history as his original musical mix of motifs had previously done.

In terms of what was about to befall each of the ex-partners, I found myself remembering an obscure quote from Robert Louis Stevenson in an elegy he penned shortly before composing the aptly titled *Strange Case of Jekyll and Hyde*, an observation that applies perfectly to the Ike and Tina situation: "Sooner or later, everyone sits down to a banquet of consequences."

It was high time for Tina to be resurrected in her own image.

※   ※   ※

Karma is a funny thing, except when it isn't of course. Some kind of exotic deliverance had seemed to manifest itself out of nowhere—and from a surprising and ironic source given her circumstances. It was a gift of reflective and restorative energy late in 1974 that would hold her in good stead later on. It would still be two full years until crunch time came in her volatile relationship with the obviously atrociously violent husband whom fate had placed by her side. In fact, it was that same psycho-husband who one day brought an attractive Jewish woman home and introduced her to Tina.

She naturally assumed it was just another of his ongoing parade of secretaries, assistants, managers, and fleeting Ikettes, but this one was different, and she also didn't last long in the fold. However, Valerie Bishop stayed just long enough to introduce the depressed singer to a unique brand of meditational practice involving the contemplative breath techniques of chanting, known as Nichiren Shoshu Buddhism. As has been suggested, it would lead to long-term implications for her that continue to this day.

This practice was also apparently validated for her by a close friend of hers who was a dancer, Jackie Stanton, and involved *shakubuku* as the first stage of its subtle and calming teachings. Bishop left her with a book, some beads to use as an aid to meditation, and also the main mantra used by this particular sect, founded by a thirteenth-century radical Buddhist master, Nichiren, part of the Mahayana school during the Kamakura period.

This teaching revolves around the notion that all people contain within them the innate enlightened state known as Buddha-nature, or awakened awareness, but it is dormant and generally concealed by limited frameworks, such as identity and ego, and is definitely clouded by personal sufferings, leading to fear, confusion, and inhibition. Its most common and visible tenet, apart from undertaking faith in the Lotus Sutra, a key philosophical text in the Buddhist canon, is the mind-tranquilizing practice of chanting: in this case, the chanting of *nam-myo-ho-renge-kyo*, which basically means an expression of homage to the truth in the sutra teachings as exemplified by Nichiren himself, something of a radical and prophetic figure historically.

Tina began chanting (while still living with Ike) at first as a means of calming her distressed mind, then she developed a serious interest in the meditative means of subduing illusory projections that might allow a person to transcend one's current limited condition, in her case the posttrauma of victimhood. She did this practice of course when her abusive keeper wasn't around, acquiring also a *butsudan*, a small cabinet or reliquary containing symbolic necessities, such as candles, water, incense, and scripture rolls, similar to the Western notion of an altar. This was all minus the notion of worship since there is no inherent deity in Buddhism apart from a kind of divine consciousness associated with purified human awareness.

Her husband of course was not known for his depth of philosophical or spiritual understanding, and he reacted with a combination of fear and loathing, demanding that she get rid of her shrine cabinet and knock off all her muttering. He was most likely misinterpreting the meaning of things, as he usually did, and in his self-saturated drug haze perceived a nonexistent voodoo quality to the whole affair, something that obviously could not be explained away. But the beauty of her new practice was that it did not require any outward signs of activity and could be carried on silently and internally as a means of mastering her own assumed limits.

Sixteen-year-old Anna Mae Bullock in her Sumner High School, St. Louis, class photo from 1958, at the time she first met Ike Turner and began performing. *Photofest*

Promotional image for their dynamic 1961 debut album, *The Soul of Ike and Tina Turner*, on the Sue Records label. *RGR Collection/Alamy Stock Photo*

Ike and Tina Turner with The Ikettes in 1966, at the time of their momentous collaboration with producer Phil Spector. *Pictorial Press Ltd/Alamy Stock Photo*

Appearing at the Summer Schaefer Music Festival in Central Park, New York, 1967. *Photofest*

Live at the Musikhalle Theater in Hamburg, Germany, 1972. *Heinrich Klaffs/Wikimedia Commons*

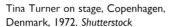

Tina Turner on stage, Copenhagen, Denmark, 1972. *Shutterstock*

Tina watching suspiciously
as Ike hams it up,
Stockholm, Sweden, 1976.
*Roger Tillberg/Alamy Stock
Photo*

Performing in 1976. *Shutterstock*

During her separation from Ike in 1977, performing at a dinner theater prior to their divorce in 1978. *Kent/Mediapunch/ Shutterstock*

Tina, footloose and fancy free in 1980, on the way to her mega comeback. *A. F. ARCHIVE/Alamy Stock Photo*

Performing with close friend David Bowie at the NEC Arena in Birmingham, England, on the Private Dancer Tour, 1985. *Photofest*

Filming a video in 1986 featuring Robert Cray and his band, prior to her Break Every Rule Tour. *Brendan Beirne/Shutterstock*

Tina Turner and Eric Clapton, Wembley Arena, London, UK, 1987. *fattkatt from england/Wikimedia Commons*

Tina with her new paramour Erwin Bach, 1989. *Trinity Mirror/Mirrorpix Alamy Stock Photo*

Tina performs with Mick Jagger, with the Temptations in the background, The Rock and Roll Hall of Fame, Waldorf Astoria, New York, 1989. *Alan Davidson/Shutterstock*

Studio Portrait, 1990.
Johnny Boylan/Shutterstock

Tina Turner, Bryan Adams, George Michael, and Sting, Fourth Annual Rainforest Foundation benefit concert at New York's Carnegie Hall, 1993. *Ron Frehm/AP/Shutterstock*

Tina Turner and Elton John perform a duet during the VH1 Fashion & Music Awards show in New York, 1995. *Adam Nadel/AP/Shutterstock*

Tina with good friend Oprah Winfrey at the opening night of *The Color Purple*, Broadway Theater, NYC, 2002. © *Andrea Renault/Globe Photos/ ZUMAPRESS.com*

President George W. Bush congratulates Tina Turner during a reception for the Kennedy Center Honors in the East Room of the White House, Sunday, December 4, 2005. From left, the honorees are singer Tony Bennett, dancer Suzanne Farrell, actress Julie Harris, actor Robert Redford, and singer Tina Turner. *White House photo by Eric Draper*

With husband Erwin Bach, German Media Awards, Baden Baden, 2005. *Frank Rollitz/Shutterstock*

Tina Turner 50th Annniversary Tour, Birmingham, 2009. *Philip Spittle/Wikimedia Commons*

Tina: The Tina Turner Musical press night, Aldwych Theatre, London, UK, 2018. *David Fisher/Shutterstock*

Tina with Adrienne Warren, opening night on Broadway, Fontanne Theatre, NY, 2019. *Andrew H. Walker/Variety/Shutterstock*

A lifetime later, when she spoke to Minerva Lee in 2018 for *Lotus Happiness* magazine, she emphasized the power of what she called the miracle of *daimoku* to enhance life, something she had experienced firsthand. She recalled how a friend had confided that Buddhism would not only transform her life but also, in her case, save her life, literally. So she continued her practice of meditation, even in the midst of her ongoing violent abuse by Ike, especially her chanting, up to three hours a day in a clear attempt to remedy trauma in the present moment, while it was still going on.

In the midst of these personal transitions, just prior to her separation, the film *Tommy* was released in early 1975, pretty much to the bewilderment of critics but to the amusement of pop music fans. It still garnered an Academy Award nomination for Ann-Margaret, who was indeed stellar in the role of Tommy's mother, especially in the infamous baked beans scene. *Melody Maker*, a music magazine rather than a film magazine of course, lost its marbles and called it a work of art but also sang the praises of the surreal performances of both Ann-Margaret and Turner. It must have depended on what drugs the audience had taken prior to viewing.

The hit records of the Revue and its dazzling duet had pretty much dried up by this stage anyway, with "Baby Get It On" reaching number 88 to a deafening commercial silence. Basically, no one wanted to get it on with the pair anymore. What followed was a soap opera of mammoth proportions: Tina tried to leave him, once for a few days, a second time for a few weeks, and then finally, on July 4, 1976, during a Bicentennial celebration week in Dallas, where they were supposed to perform, she lulled him to sleep and took off into the night. She stayed at the house of their joint attorney, someone she trusted, until she realized no one who worked for Ike could actually be trusted.

She moved into a house of a girlfriend of hers, the sister of jazz musician Wayne Shorter, who lived on Lookout Mountain. Then she moved from place to place like a fugitive on the run from mafia hit men, carrying a .38-caliber revolver in her purse. After one last meeting in a car with his thuggish attorneys, she clarified that there would be no going back, it was over. Subsequently, Ike sent all four of the children, her two and his own two, to live with her. She had to look after them as well as pay back promoters she owed for walking off the final Revue tour, so she took any little gig she could find, especially the tried-and-true cabaret circuit, where oodles of people were ready to see her with or without her maniacal mentor.

Having agreed to give up all claim on creative or commercial rights and only wanting to start again from scratch, she smartly decided that her living her life itself was more important than any of the *things* in that life. She collected some royalties from BMI for some of her own songs, then arranged to front her own band, a real rock band this time, and recorded her first post-Ike solo record, *Rough*, which didn't exactly set the world on fire. But it was only her opening salvo.

Tina was obviously openly sharing her pleasure in doing what most people take for granted, making all her own decisions, whether about big or little things. Once the divorce finally came—she had cut her hair and had gone shopping, even though she had no money. She got through it, though, and she was really and finally having fun. It was a freedom that—unless you've been in some form of bondage—is hard to explain or understand.

As Lee too reported it in *Lotus Happiness*, "It was a full sixteen years of abuse—and two years of chanting—before Tina left Ike forever in 1976. What does the four-word Buddhist chant that helped her mean? 'Nam' is devotion, 'Myo' is mystic, 'Ho' is law, 'Renge' means lotus blossom, 'Kyo' means sutra (teaching)." It also helps to read the original Lotus Sutra on which Nichiren based his primary teaching and practice. It is not overly academic, intellectually complicated, or philosophical, though it is deep and largely focuses on compassion for all suffering fellow sentient beings. This teaching emphasizes that both suffering and joy are facts of life and that both can be either amplified or reduced by our own responses to whatever we might encounter.

As Tina put it to Lee, "When I first started chanting is also when I started using my head, I started thinking—I'm not going to kill myself, there's nothing here for me. This person doesn't even realize that I am helping him, that I have tried to be good and kind to him. I didn't have anybody, really, no foundation in life, so I had to make my own way. Always have from the start. I had to go out in the world and become strong."

Looking back on that transformative period in her life was a touching experience. "I slowly started to feel like myself again. And now, forty-five years of chanting has opened a door inside of me, it changed my life for the better. I've left a good body of work as a rock singer, and I've made it very clear that it was all because of my spiritual practice."

She has also proven to be very bravely adept at confiding her personal troubles with the whole world, enabling the rest of us to do the same. Her new calm, peaceful, much looser attitude toward her life even permitted her to do downright silly projects just for the sheer fun of it. The impact of her shift of attention away from her abuser and toward herself and toward her inner nature was immediately evident to everyone around her, everyone except the main source of her suffering of course.

In 1978, she had a hoot being involved in Robert Stigwood's happy but shapeless cinematic take on the Beatles' Sergeant Pepper motifs, in which he tried to repeat his *Tommy* success but didn't quite match it. Critics were not impressed with the film but were always touched by Tina's presence on-screen, seemingly regardless of what she was doing there. Her own much more relaxed psyche appeared to be coming across to the camera as well.

She was ready for new challenges, even if some of them required a certain amount of humility and patience until she had paid her solo dues. That was all right with her, though, since prior to her solo career, she had already *overpaid* her dues and knew she deserved some payback sooner or later. But her eventual payback was already on its way, big time.

6

NICHIREN NIGHTS

The Baptist Buddhist

"Trouble is a part of your life—if you don't share it, you don't give the people who love you a chance to love you enough."

—Dinah Washington, in *Queen: The Life and Music of Dinah Washington*

All of us have passed through transitional phases in our lives, periods of uncertainty when we're in between those recognizable landmarks that provide meaning and stability. Naturally, few of us have experienced the degree of radical instability encountered by a person like Tina Turner or have had to weather the storm seemingly caused by decisions we made in the beginning and those we felt forced to make later on. This is a stage in her narrative when she embarked on a nebulous journey into no-man's-land, with quite literally *no man* to navigate her course as there had been since she was sixteen. She may have been without a map but she certainly wasn't without a compass.

Such a time, when one is caught in a kind of interval zone of interrupted choices, is also a time when we can best examine how we got where we are while trying to figure out where to go next. That same compass, the internal and intuitive one that had gotten her *here*, would also take her *there*, wherever that was. She was already counting her blessings over having escaped from an exotic kind of creative and personal captivity, but soon she'd also be able to assess the rich possibilities inherent in her freedom.

Several of the music critics, musicians, historians, and journalists I interviewed about her musical and cultural contributions had quite different and yet parallel interpretations to share about her ongoing trajectory. It's a path I myself identify as a sequence of *cadence and cascade*. Cadence is a pattern or rhythm that we all follow in our lives, whether we know its shape or not, while cascade is a series of processes that unfolds over time and usually becomes clear only in retrospect. Crystal clear in fact.

Without a major label other than small affiliates of Capitol/EMI (at least her British fan base was still active), she was also tight with Festival Records in Australia, where she had a kind of cult following (but the good kind of cult this time). With the decade fast coming to a close, 1979 found her utterly at loose ends when fate once again intervened in the most unlikely of shapes. Olivia Newton-John, hot off her *Grease* hit, wanted Tina to appear in one of her popular television specials, and John's manager, Lee Kramer, was someone whom one of Tina's dancers and close friends had recommended to her. He was, she said, on the lookout for fresh new talent to promote.

While Tina may not have been exactly new, she was definitely fresh. Through Olivia Newton-John, Lee Kramer would also meet a young Australian management wizard named Roger Davies, and the two of them agreed to fly to San Francisco late that fall to take in her stage act at the Fairmont Hotel, where they caught her on her final night. By this time, she was mightily struggling to mount an earnest comeback, and her name had slipped slightly off the public's radar.

The adventurous agent Lee Kramer had to explain to his new partner Roger Davies that, yes, Tina Turner was still around, still performing, but this current incarnation wasn't really a *comeback* per se at all since it didn't involve the Revue or her mentor. It was actually way more exciting for precisely those reasons, and it was more like a coming out of a dark closet, an evolving emergence. It was *all* her now.

She was clearly fishing around for a new creative direction, which sometimes takes a little time, and she wasn't necessarily overly disappointed that the spotlight had yet to come back to her. As she expressed it in *Off the Record* by Joe Smith, "Once you've experienced a type of bondage and then gotten free, you really learn what being free is all about, and it's about just being comfortable with yourself. So I didn't put any value on not having an immediate hit record or not being in the limelight as much. I was fine where I was, I watched myself, it was a studying time after Ike."

This was an astute observation from someone who had become so famous so young that she hadn't completed any further educational pursuits after high school. So instead of any higher formal education, she had become a *student of herself*. She was also about to become a graduate, not just from the school of hard knocks but one with a master's degree in triumph.

Her first two valiant attempts at a post-Ike persona, 1978's *Rough* and 1979's *Love Explosion*, suffered from disadvantages similar to her country music record and her acidic monarch outing. In the second case, it was to be her brave but ill-advised flirtation with pseudo–disco dance music, not a great fit for either her dancing talent or her vintage voice. She wasn't alone in experimenting with other such styles of course (that's what lots of great artists do), and sometimes it'll click, other times it won't. But the great ones don't ever stop experimenting. So she just kept on chanting.

ROUGH (UNITED ARTISTS RECORDS)

Produced by Bob Monaco, Jill Harris, Conway Recording Studios. Released in 1978. Personnel: Rick Kellis, horns; Ken Moore, piano; Airto Moreria, percussion; Dennis Belfield, bass; Michael Boddicker, synthesizer; Peter Bunetta, drums; Al Ciner, acoustic guitar; Denise Echols and Venetta Fields, vocals; Bill Oz, harmonica; Ron Stockert, clavinet; Willie Smith, organ; Gerald Lee, strings. Duration: 41:15.

Fruits of the Night (Pete Belotte, Edo Zanki, Vilko Zanki) 4:05 / The Bitch Is Back (Elton John and Bernie Taupin) 3:30 / Viva La Money (Allen Toussaint) 3:14 / Funny How Time Slips Away (Willie Nelson) 4:08 / Root Toot Undisputable (Gary Jackson) 4:29 / Fire Down Below (Bob Seger) 3:13 / Sometimes When We Touch (Dan Hill, Barry Mann)

3:54 / A Woman in a Man's World (Hal David, Archie Jordan) 2:41 / Night Time Is the Right Time (Leroy Carr) 6:21

On the plus side, at least it wasn't called *Nice and Rough*. By now at least, she was also free to make her own mistakes rather than being led to them by an impresario who fed parasitically on her talents. The downside? Disco is the place where rhythm and blues, soul, and funk went to die. So instead, she is led down the thorny path by new producers who fed parasitically on her talents and by the curious social party wavelength of the times themselves. So it goes. But the forced marriage of blues and disco makes for a weird outcome here, as does the peculiar mix of song selections, as if curated by a schizoid club manager or crazed deejay.

Her third solo effort had a trio of distributors, perhaps in keeping with its multiphrenic tracks. You also know trouble is on the way when the songwriters chosen are as varied as the drastically eclectic selection of Elton John, Willie Nelson, Willie Dixon, Bob Seger, Hal David, and the ever-saccharine Dan Hill. Now there's a brain salad for you. And of course, the clever punning of Bernie Taupin's gentle mockery of his longtime creative partner Elton John's personality (The Bitch is Back) works perfectly when Elton delivers it but not quite so much when Tina's persona is asked to do so.

This is also her actual first solo record where there was absolutely no involvement from Ike, so that alone also forgives it somewhat. But alas, as with *Acid Queen* before it, this one too failed to reach the charts or receive any certifications, selling rather disappointingly, and though converted to CD in the 1990s, it currently remains out of print—perhaps a blessing in disguise. Oddly, it arrived just when major upheavals in music had happened simultaneously: the death of Elvis Presley and the ascent of punk. You'd never know it from *Rough* and *Love Explosion*, however, comfortably nestled in the cold embrace of disco.

LOVE EXPLOSION (LIBERTY RECORDS), RECORDED IN EUROPE

Produced by Alec Constandinos. Released in 1979. Personnel: Tina Turner, vocals; Jean-Claude Chavanat, guitar; Tony Bonfils, bass; Bernard

Arcadio, keyboards; Andre Ceccarelli, drums; Manu Roche, percussion; George Young, Lawrence Feldman, Michael Brecker, tenor saxophones; Lew Del Gatto, baritone; Pat Haling, strings; George Rodi, synthesizer. Engineers: Mike Ross-Trevor, Scott Litt, Geoff Calver, Peter Kelsey. Arranged by Raymond Knehnestky. Remixed at Trident Studios London by Peter Kelsey. Duration: 36:05.

Love Explosion (Lenny Macaluso, Pat Summerson) 5:55 / Fool for Your Love (Leo Sayer, Michael Omartian) 3:24 / Sunset on Sunset (Billy Livsey, David Courtney, Richard Niles) 3:35 / Music Keeps Me Dancin' (Lenny Macaluso, Pat Summerson) 3:49 / I See Home (Allee Willis, David Lasley) 5:19 / Backstabbers (Leon Huff, Gene Macfadden, John Whitehead) 3:34 / Just a Little Lovin' (Barry Mann, Cynthia Weil) 3:12 / On the Radio (Victor Carstarphen) 3:49

Okay then, we won't hold it against her that she allowed the anesthetic use of synthesizers; after all, almost everybody by the late 1970s was doing so. And it's also totally permissible to use artistic license and go full gung ho into the arms of a serious top disco producer in France, Alec Constandinos. It's even acceptable to give it the utterly disco-flavored title of *Love Explosion* and have Tina smiling in her shiny vinyl jumpsuit (who could complain about that?), and who knows, it may have all worked as an end-of-the-decade experiment in the prevailing musical trend of the times. But of course, it didn't, not even with the familiarly themed "Fool for Your Love" on it.

It had minor success on both European and American charts, wasn't certified, and led to all her labels deciding to part ways from her in utter disappointment. It doesn't seem to have occurred to the corporate types (this was her last album for EMI and United Artists) that the problem wasn't so much Tina as it was their own decision to allow her to go on a blind date with synth-disco in the first place.

The two nondance tracks were promising soulful ballads, including a great one first done by Dusty Springfield ten years earlier, but the sandwiching of them with the thump thump of the disco vibe doomed the overall enterprise. Once again, massive innovations were afoot in the music industry when this sweet confection was unwrapped. One of them went on to become the most influential musical style of the late twentieth century: the arrival of rap and its consequential cousin, hip-hop, in the form of Sugarland Express and their 1979 breakthrough of "Rappers Delight." Things would never be the same.

As with her prior effort *Rough*, *Love Explosion* did not in fact either ignite or explode, and it is currently and thankfully out of print. *Love Explosion* anonymously fizzled in a slick dimension where the urgent grit of rap had yet to penetrate. The good news was that following this release and after a five-year hiatus for Tina, her resurrection was waiting in the wings, patiently ticking away like a nuclear fission detonation. Tina's musical shift away from rhythm and blues, soul, funk, and rock and toward pop was almost as massive in its industry impact as punk or rap but in a totally different direction altogether.

In retrospect, we all have some shared and some different perspectives on the incredibly wild ride that we call the 1980s, in many ways the polar opposite of the 1960s yet maybe an unexpected yet logical extension of that decade. For Aaron Cohen, these two decades were more than opposed extremes of liberation and repression; they were almost distorted funhouse mirror images. "I think the generally conservative 1980s needed a persona who, in many ways, was anything but. I'm also not sure what was happening with the women's movement at that time, but she would have been a strong voice for empowerment at a crucial time. She also had a stronger understanding of such media as video than many of her contemporaries from earlier decades."

In many ways, the 1980s was perhaps an even more perfect decade for Tina's special vibe than the 1960s had been, if that's even possible.

❊   ❊   ❊

From the perspective of the newly solo Tina Turner and from our perspective as a global audience about to witness her astonishing reincarnation, Roger Davies would be Karma Incorporated. For Davies and Kramer, their first San Francisco encounter with her post-Ike presence was a startling revelation as Davies described it to Kurt Loder in what I often refer to as her early testimonial. "We went into the Fairmont Hotel, the Venetian Room, this big room with chandeliers and people in tuxedos and I said, this can't be the right room. But then Tina came on and had so much energy, she blew me away. People were standing on tables, the chandeliers were shaking."

Kramer was equally bowled over, even though he thought he knew what to expect from the new her. Both he and Davies enthusiastically agreed to take her on, the main challenge being how to dramatically renovate her act and presentation in order to lift her out of what they accurately characterized as "cabaret purgatory." As usual with Turner, the sudden opportunity arose from a most unlikely direction: an offer for her performing services for a $150,000 deal to perform in South Africa, then still segregated, for a five-week tour.

This was naturally risky for an artist of color and one of considerable notoriety who had been raised in a segregated part of America herself, but she was assured that all the venues would be integrated, and yes, ever the optimist no matter what the odd circumstances, she firmly believed that she might be able to contribute to bridging some gulfs and help bring people closer together—that, plus, of course, it was a way out of the cabaret circuit. So she and her Tina band played Johannesburg, Durban, and Capetown. There was at that time no big Sun City, so she was fortunate enough to evade that sin and has since rejected all offers from it, though she still garnered considerable (and perhaps understandable) public criticism back then.

Following that questionable but financially necessary choice, she was clawing her way back from the darkness of cabaret exile and needed whatever help she could get, so they worked out favorable tours of Australia and Southeast Asia. Somewhere along the way, the ever-astute Roger Davies realized that she was drastically in need of a style makeover. This Tina was neither the young soul-shaking Tina we knew before with the Revue nor the elegant tough dame Tina we know now after her resurrection was finalized. Davies needed to alter the lounge-age image and the cabaret disco look and erase the Las Vegas glitz covered in what he saw as Bob Mackie–soaked Cher-ness (no offense to Cher lovers, she's great at what she does).

So they ditched her look, her band, her dancers, her stage design crew, everybody, and went back to the drawing board, literally. It was 1980, and things were changing. Music Television (MTV) was preparing to launch the following August, and they already had an insatiable appetite for new mini-movies to sell songs and albums. Davies had an early intuitive grasp of the importance of videos, and he also knew that record executives were frequently mired in the past, so he needed a way to give birth to a new Tina Turner who would utterly eradicate all memory (almost but not quite) of the old one. Music videos provided the perfect vehicle for him to launch his new Tina.

Her comeback practically happened live on television, twenty-four hours a day. And she largely had Roger Davies to thank for its skillful deployment. It was a medium simply made for Tina's flashy persona, and along with performers such as Michael Jackson and Madonna, she would both capitalize hugely on the technology and revolutionize it as an artistic form of expression. Her flashy videos, of which she made a relentless truckload, were veritable *National Geographic* documentaries of the passion she wore on her sleeve or, rather, on her skirt.

Totally perfect for the staccato visual language of videos and having often described her concerts themselves as "small movies," Tina Turner's first such short films appeared just in time to catch this new wave while it was in full early swing and also to define its parameters with her personal sense of style. More so even than in her supposedly straight acting roles in big-budget films, it is in her music videos that we see the tangible and tactile evidence for her charismatic appeal.

In addition, after artists have departed and independent of their fans' memories of seeing them live or hearing their albums, their videos are often the only historical archive remaining that one can consult in order to explore their theater craft. And hers were among the most visually seductive in the new medium.

Manager on a mission: the other, almost military technique Davies employed to promote his most gutsy client was more old fashioned but still effective, that is, to situate her strategically in selective live gigs. He brought her into the Ritz in New York City, a city she hadn't appeared in for at least ten years, and he made damn sure every celebrity on the planet, people who did have a long-term memory, packed the club to the rafters.

Davies then orchestrated a cover story in *People* magazine called "The Return of Tina Turner," and then, realizing that her old guardian angels the Rolling Stones, now the undisputed royalty of rock, were about to plunge into yet another U.S. tour winding up with a host of dates in New York, he choreographed a second stint at the Ritz.

Club owner Jerry Brandt agreed to have her back again, and the appearance brought her into the heady orbit of rock star Rod Stewart, who began almost competing with his fellow Brit rockers the Stones to see who could command as much of Tina's attention as possible. First out of the gate, the Stones had her all to themselves as the incendiary opening act for their tour.

After her tour with the Stones, the competitive Stewart was performing live in Inglewood at the Great Western Forum for a concert to be broadcast via satellite across the planet, and he invited both Kim Carnes and Tina to duet with him on his song "Stay with Me." He also included their finale together on the *Absolutely Live* album he released. By this time, Tina was clear what direction appealed to her: she wanted to be like the Rolling Stones and Rod Stewart and all the other big-guy acts out there that were packing the giant sport stadiums.

Rocker Rod had also appeared at her Ritz show along with record producer Richard Perry in tow and announced that he was about to appear on *Saturday Night Live* and perform his song "Hot Legs." How would the dame with the hottest legs in music like to join him for a duet? Really? She had a sudden audience of untold millions, once again as a result of a Brit rocker who had adored her for years.

Meanwhile, her old karmic buddies the Stones were by then appearing at the Forum and were delighted when Tina's aggressive and imaginative new manager Davies brought her backstage for a catch-up. They loved her work with Rod on *Saturday Night Live* and wondered why she wasn't touring with *them* once again. Coyly responding in her most purring voice that *they hadn't asked her*, the band on the spot booked her to open for them on their next stop, at the Brendan Byrne Arena, close to New York, a cozy little stadium offering 20,000 seats and also providing a massive venue attracting every music honcho and critic in the industry.

On top of that phenomenal coup, always the canny showman, Jagger himself requested that Tina might join him onstage to deliver a song duet of (what else?) "Honky Tonk Women." Needless to say, when the new new new Tina came loping onstage to meet with Mick, with shorter, spiky, wigless hair in her form-hugging black leather pants and saucy leopard-skin boots, virtual pandemonium erupted. People suddenly realized—or remembered—what she really meant to them.

They also realized what they meant to her: vindication, validation, liberation, not so much a comeback per se as much as the collective expression of a common feeling: that she was somehow beyond mere linear time and was a force of nature beyond anyone's control, maybe even her own. But here it's also instructive to consider how paradoxically the term "tumultuous" applies to her.

Aaron Cohen reminded me that even though she appeared to be out of control as a stage persona, in reality she was a consummate professional in total command of her game at all times. "While she came across as unbridled onstage, I think she also exhibited much control in that arena in terms of codirecting/leading her bands (as part of the Ike and Tina Revue, or on her own later). Similarly, her '80s success in film and other show business avenues wouldn't have happened so effectively if she didn't have a totally firm sense of self-control."

❀   ❀   ❀

Having seen Tina perform in Toronto in 1982, subsequent to her first two solo records and just prior to her bombastic third re-launch, John Corcelli had firsthand experience with what seemed to make that time, the early 1980s, just seem so right for her comeback as a solo pop performer. "Her voice and her sexuality. This was a woman who was now utterly comfortable in her own skin, and she wasn't afraid to show it. Our musical heroes often reflect who we want to be on a deeply personal level. But because we're afraid of failing, we live through them, vicariously.

"Turner has a strong moral compass and an uncompromising personality. You either dig it or you don't. Her strength of character is what distinguishes her from the rest of the pack." That seems like an accurate assessment of how we, as listeners, appeared ready to choose *this* particular storied feminine figure as an emblem of our own dreams and desires at *that* particular moment in musical history.

The time was right for some fresh positive karma again, and it was actually on its way in the form of yet another appearance at the Ritz in New York, this one with a special added attraction. Because David Bowie was in New York having a listening session for his latest album, *Let's Dance*, he was asked by a horde of record executives, promoters, critics, and general movers and shakers what he was doing later on after the session. He replied that he was going to catch a show by his favorite singer: Tina Turner. He had quipped that whenever Tina Turner was on a stage, that became the hottest place in the universe.

So, guess who happily tagged along on Bowie's little late-night out-ing to unwind with him? Only half of the most top-flight music industry luminaries on planet Earth. Naturally, they too all wanted to be sitting near the hottest place in the universe. After her stellar stint, which was even hotter than usual, a backstage crush included Bowie and Keith Richards, who both wanted to retire to Keith's Park Plaza apartment to listen to old music and drink champagne with Tina in tow. They hung out together, along with Ron Wood and others, listening to old records, singing, drinking, dancing, and laughing far into the next day.

Following her big Ritz gig, Capitol Records was suddenly interested in signing her up for new records, but the crafty and creative Davies also wanted to approach EMI in England, where she still had an already established base, so he booked time at Abbey Road studios to test out some material. They focused on an old Al Green song, "Let's Stay To-gether," from 1971, one of her banner years in another life.

She knocked this song out of the park and also took it away from Al Green completely; as usual, she now owned that song. Davies released it as a single and planned a big tour to coincide with a tune that had be-come a smash hit in Europe even though America's Capitol Records had declined to support it. They evidenced a lack of vision, which wasn't that surprising from a label brand that had often ruined great works by titans like the Beatles and the Beach Boys out of a stunning lack of creative sensitivity on their part.

Davies was swiftly on the move, and so was his top client (he was also doing double duty as manager for Olivia Newton-John at the same time). He booked a gig at a little club owned by Virgin Records called the Venue, where it was necessary to extend her run by more than a week to serve all the frenzied audience demand. She then appeared on *Top of the Pops*, and Davies hired that show's producer to shoot a video, a very basic piece of footage of her singing "Let's Stay Together," along with her dancers, Ann Behringer and Lejeune Richardson. It would be the first of the avalanche of music videos she would make.

By the time the end of 1983 rolled around, "Let's Stay Together" was a Top 5 hit in England and rising fast across all the rest of Europe. After some influential deejays played the tune on several famous black music radio stations, Capitol Records finally relented and rushed the single's release forward. Capitol, ever the vultures in suits, now suddenly also wanted an album to follow it up and support the wave it had created. Davies refused to return to America, however, having committed to a big tour through Britain, a place for which Tina felt a strong sense of loyalty and appreciation. Somehow he convinced Capitol to let them record the album they hungered for at an English studio instead.

While Tina took her band out on the road there, Davies stayed in London to try to find suitable material for an as-yet-nonexistent album. He had one song in mind already, one that both he and Tina enjoyed, written by Holly Knight for a group called Spider. It was called "Better Be Good to Me." Now he and Tina needed another armload of songs to round out the record, so he contacted an old Australian acquaintance, Terry Britten, who had cowritten a song with Graham Lyle called "What's Love Got to Do with It?" Davies wasn't so sure about this one. It was very pop oriented, albeit well-crafted pop, so he booked studio time to capture it and continued his search for other songs to accompany it.

Tina had some predictable responses at first to "What's Love?"—not her style, even calling it too "wimpy." But the writers and producers were willing to let her play around with it and change it into any key or tempo she desired. Also at this time and by pure chance, she came on an unfinished song that had been written by Mark Knopfler of the band Dire Straits, just a little track without a vocal put on it yet that had been left off their next album, *Love over Gold*. It had been deemed too "girly" for them.

Knopfler was a friendly and amenable kind of guy, not your average rock star really, and he offered to sing a vocal just to give them a sense of the melody, but he also gave them permission to rerecord the track with Tina's pipes on it any old way they liked. Meanwhile, Capitol was monitoring the progress from afar and dispatched producer John Carter over to ensure forward momentum. The band was missing its lead guitarist at this point, but an able-fingered guitarist happened to be available who was willing to play sessions on the song: none other than legendary rock superstar Jeff Beck.

They added another song by Ann Peebles from 1973, "I Can't Stand the Rain," as well as "Let's Stay Together"; a raunchy romp called "Steel Claw" by Paul Brady; and Bowie's "1984," in addition to what they'd already been able to squeeze together through some kind of strange alchemy. Rupert Hine, producer of the Fixx, agreed to produce the upcoming album. Davies was as pleased as he could be while also having utterly fried his nerves.

Capitol quickly released "What's Love Got to Do with It" in order to whet the public's appetite for the soon-to-be-released upcoming record. It swiftly became a Top 50 pop hit. Tina had morphed far away from her initial rhythm-and-blues roots, equally distant from her rock-and-roll spirit and light-years away from her rock vibe, and had arrived in a bright and shiny place. This was what pop can be when it works perfectly, like a well-oiled machine. With multiple producers and a shimmering technical quality associated with that decade, the album had a title now as well, a title that capitalized on that discarded little unfinished song that Knopfler had so generously let them have. It was a little ditty called "Private Dancer."

If the first half of her career was all about the Big Wheel Rolling, both together and apart, the second half would be about her remarkable skill at Reinventing the Wheel, as her comeback feverishly continued, with no sign of abating anytime soon. Indeed, it still hasn't. In her solo career, Tina Turner released nine spectacularly successful record albums (well, five great ones anyway), each one first approaching and then eclipsing the admittedly high-water marks she had achieved in her prior partnership.

She released two sound track records, six compilations records, three live concert albums, eighteen video albums, and forty-seven music videos, a medium that hadn't even existed yet when she was collaborating with her earlier bandleader. In addition, after her liberation, she also released sixty singles, only eight short of the number they had delivered together over the course of their sixteen-year collaboration.

How this evolution took place is still something of a mystery. The times changed of course, and she was smart enough to change right along with them. Even if there's some cosmic vibration that she tapped into through her chanting practice, as a means of both surviving her abuse and balancing her subsequent solitude, that still can't ever explain the unexpected return and phoenix-like rise again of this stalwart rock goddess or her morphing with such seeming smoothness into a mega pop star of such grandiose proportions.

Talk about your transformations! After already evolving from a scrappy young rhythm-and-blues singer with a penchant for a spectral and soulful blues holler into a state-of-the-art rocker chick with Stones-scale arena credentials, Tina Turner was about to mutate yet again, this time, most surprisingly, into a scintillating pop star of epic proportions. And it took only half a decade of being off the grid long enough to shed her skin in the most shocking midlife crisis ever recorded.

So what do you do if two years after leaving your abusive husband and after two albums that were less than warmly received with open arms by your legion of former fans you have some time on your hands to reflect? Well, perhaps you begin reflecting. The main impetus for all her actions, apart from clearing her personal slate emotionally before her comeback, also seemed to be finding a way to get people to stop asking her questions about her troubled marriage and musical partnership.

She must have been deeply pondering how she could ever bring to a halt the incessant curiosity about the struggles of her youth and her early creative career. How to stop the relentless memorializing of what she hoped would eventually fade away (in what decade? she had famously wondered). She privately harbored a hope, in perhaps a too-innocent expectation, of just being allowed to get on with her life and make new music.

Yet embedded in that dilemma also lies the key, she suddenly must have realized. Yes, make *new* music, she deduced, but not just new: music drastically different from anything and everything we've ever heard from her before. It's not rhythm and blues, it's certainly not soul or funk, it's not even rock and roll or even rock; it's kind of bluesy but not in any traditional way.

It has a slightly postmodern torch song feeling about it but only if you happen to subscribe to the technique so vividly described in that punchy Bowie song "Putting Out Fire with Gasoline." In the end, it can really be accurately described only as Tina goes pop!

PRIVATE DANCER (CAPITOL RECORDS)

Released May 29, 1984. Farmyard Studios, Mayfair, Wessex, Abbey Road, and CBS (London). Produced by Rupert Hine, Terry Britten, John Carter, Martin Ware, Greg Walsh, Joe Sample, Wilton Felder, Ndugu Chancler. Duration: 44:02.

I Might Have Been Queen (Jeanette Obstoi, Jamie West-Oram) 4:10 / What's Love Got to Do with It? (Terry Britten, Graham Lyle) 3:49 / Show Some Respect (Terry Britten, Sue Shifrin) 3:18 / I Can't Stand the Rain (Ann Peebles, Don Bryant, Bernard Miller) 3:41 / Better Be Good to Me (Mike Chapman, Holly Knight) 5:10 / 6) Let's Stay Together (Al Green, Al Jackson, Willie Mitchell) 5:16 / 1984 (David Bowie) 3:09) / Steel Claw (Paul Brady) 3:48 / Private Dancer (Mark Knopfler) 7:11 (The international pressing also included her version of the Beatles tune "Help!")

Some things in life are well worth waiting for. For a forty-five-year-old entertainer who had been in show business for almost thirty years, this was one of them. Her fifth solo studio album was the charmer. Recording sessions took place in one of her favorite places, England, engineered by no less than four different production teams of eight people and with material in almost as many different styles. It's fair to call it a radical departure from everything she'd been known for with the Revue and even everything else that came after Ike as well.

Up-tempo tunes mixed with sad ballads and a difficult-to-describe jazzy blues element, all expertly superimposed over her unique vocal talents, made it not only a blockbuster solo record but also one of the most successful crossover products in music history: a masterpiece of reinvention. It was rewarded with global success, garnered multiple platinum certifications, and reaped a commercial bonanza for Turner in her new identity, a spiky-haired vixen posed somewhere between Aunty Entity and the Acid Queen but also way beyond both.

Slick in its production values to the extreme but in a good way, it ideally captured the opulent essence of the mid-1980s and provided her with a long-range legacy: the creation of a landmark event in the evolution of not only pop rock but also pop pop. It was perfect pop, period. She would promote it vigorously with a dazzling stage show in a 177-date concert tour across the planet: the Private Dancer Tour. Several songs on this album would be such suitable embodiments of her ethos that they remain permanently etched in our memories, not only of her record but also of her challenging private life leading up to it.

"Better Be Good to Me," "Show Some Respect," "What's Love Got to Do with It," and of course the title track (weirdly written originally by Mark Knopfler for his Dire Straits band but held back by the hand of fate for Tina) all became massive single hits. The album remains the only Tina Turner record to have been reissued in a digitally remastered format.

Accolades of course poured in like rain. The *Los Angeles Times* review claimed that her voice "melts vinyl." *Rolling Stone* called it a consummate and powerful comeback, "rasping but strong, in a modern rock format neither detached nor fussy." Robert Christgau praised its ability to "deliver with honesty the middlebrow angst of professional songwriting, while remaining in control of an album with four different production teams to give it all seamless authority." *Allmusic* stated that it "was slicker than her r & b classics with the Revue but she was still able to sing with throaty passion to deliver her finest solo production yet."

Stephen Holden in the *New York Times* wrote that by using her English producers to soften her raw southern style, "discarding the blaring horns, frenzied percussion and gospel calls and responses, the album became a classic in the development of pop-soul music." Michael Lydon, in *1001 Albums You Must Hear before You Die*, said that the album's lyrical themes "embodied her persona as a tough, sexy woman in a tough world, one whose vocal delivery overcomes the slick production styles with her indomitable soul unifying the multiple disparate producers."

Slant Magazine listed the album on its list of best albums of the 1980s, saying that "both a personal liberation and sonic redemption, *Private Dancer* established Turner not only as a genuine diva, but a bone fide force of nature." I second that emotion, except for the diva part: she was always too down to earth to ever be described by that overused term. Strangely enough, it was also its multiple producers and manifold songwriting styles with varying emotional temperatures that made it a perfect pop record. In pop, perfection means it had something for everyone, of every taste, age, and style demographic, meaning also that it sold big and that Tina was back, big time.

Although the process of its planning, production, and release was very rushed and she wasn't entirely sure about the new high-tech pop musical material, she had learned by then to have faith in Roger Davies and his perhaps younger musical tastes. She was a clever enough showwoman to know that even if she could say these were not quite her kinds of songs, their backs were against the wall to get the album out. So she simply agreed to whatever formula was going to give them a hit record. And clearly her flexibility paid off.

One thing she especially liked about the record once she got used to the synthesizers and digital production was how hard it rocked yet also avoided certain rhythm-and-blues conventions that had always bugged her, things about its moaning and pleading attitude that were a downer for her. For quite a while before this outing, she had come to really prefer the straight-ahead energy of rock and roll and how *you wanna put it on to get you going*, as good a definition of rock as any.

No less a luminary than rock specialist Keith Richards, possibly her biggest fan, agreed with both her tastes and her motivations on this record, telling *Newsweek*, "She's probably even more energetic than she was twenty years ago!"—and that's saying something. No doubt it was partly her newly won freedom, her working only for herself and not for a music maestro anymore, and partly just the desire to have as much fun as possible in life in general from now on.

In *Off the Record*, she is referenced as saying that she felt better than ever about performing. "I'm a strong healthy person, it comes from being homeopathic and never abusing my body. I'm an unusual person, I could get onstage right *now* and do a show. Had I abused myself (with drugs or drink) in the early days, I would never have gotten as far as I did. I'm healthy and I'm in control."

As finishing touches were being put into place on the record, Tina, never being one to linger around patiently waiting for much of anything, went off on a four-month tour opening for Lionel Ritchie while *Private Dancer* was undergoing its arcane surgical production process. Much of the album harkened back to her own personal, professional, and private life, even though none of the songs was in any way about her per se, instead being a cleverly sculptured techno-dance record of distinctly different parts, but it just happened to catch the zeitgeist feeling of that moment in time. The literal meaning of the German word Zeitgeist, strikingly similar to Poltergeist (which means "noise ghost"), is "time ghost."

And that's what Tina Turner had in some exotic way proven herself to be—not necessarily timeless exactly (though she is some of that as well) but more in the sense of being displaced from one time and emerging into another, a person *out* of time entirely and definitely a person ahead of her time in many ways.

Listeners and critics alike also fell in love with both *Private Dancer* the album as well as the new Tina Turner behind it. She made appearances in every conceivable venue and for every imaginable show, all over radio and television, spinning endlessly on MTV and being extolled by magazines as the grittiest rock-and-roll singer in the world despite the fact that she was no longer exactly a rocker and instead was "something else." My contention is that she had already been a rock star for years, but *this* venture made her into a bona fide pop star, which by my definition is music so universally appealing that it is successful for vastly diverse audiences and crosses over every conceivable taste border.

By September 1984, *Private Dancer* had arrived at number 3 on the pop charts and stayed put for three months. The LP naturally also encouraged erstwhile Capitol to release yet more singles from it: "Better Be Good to Me," "Private Dancer," and a Euro hit, "I Can't Stand the Rain." The album stayed in the Top 100 for more than two years and eventually sold 19 million copies.

She ended 1984 by touring in a variety of American and Canadian concert dates that had already been planned prior to the release of her new record, which went full ballistic during its ascent. Returning to America on January 28, 1985, for the American Music Awards, she picked up several top prizes in female vocals and video performer slots before joining a small group of forty-two of her fellow musical superstars for a ten-hour recording session targeted as a charity record in support of African famine relief. It was an emotional, humanist anthem called "We Are the World."

❖   ❖   ❖

I asked James Porter how a historian of black rock like him might address the shift from harder to softer stylistic vibes in Tina's later music. "I think her solo records are 'lighter' but only in that they're not as bluesy as when Ike was around. The influence was still there—she covered a Tony Joe White song or two—but it was not as pervasive. I do however think the later records are just as serious musically as the earlier sides . . . but just in a different direction. You listen to songs like 'Private Dancer' now, and they might sound like an ironic dry run for a

INXS album, but then Tina's Voice of Experience comes in and sets the record straight." Indeed, setting the record straight was always what she was about, from start to finish.

At the Grammy Awards ceremony in February 1985, the reborn Tina Turner commanded the whole show with a performance of "What's Love Got to Do with It?," and she was bestowed a Grammy for best female pop vocal, best female rock vocal, and finally record of the year for "What's Love Got to Do with It?" When she soaked up the roaring love of the crowd, perhaps expressing their spirited admiration for her tenacious survival almost as much as her tremendous musical achievement, she intoned in that distinctive breathy rasp of hers, "We're looking forward to many more of these."

About this same time, her now extremely prescient manager Roger Davies shared with *Vogue* one of the things that bothered her to no end: people and the press continuing to refer to her as a victim in her earlier life. "She was so unhappy for so long, she can't stand it to get too dark, and she hates it when people feel sorry for her." As she herself succinctly told *GQ* magazine, "The *victim thing*, it's put in our heads, and I don't think it does anybody any good really." The only ones she considers real and actual victims are the innocent people suffering from starvation around the world, which is why she loaned her energies to the "We Are the World" charity single.

Maybe not so surprisingly, Hollywood was also calling yet again. She had often mused, mostly just fantasizing out loud really, that she would love to get another larger-than-life movie role, something even more over the top that *Tommy*'s Acid Queen part, something along the lines (so she mused) of the Grace Jones part in *Conan the Destroyer*. As part of the icing on her cake, back while she was playing the Ritz, Roger Davies had come to her hotel and told her he'd just received a call from director George Miller offering her a big part in his next *Mad Max* film. Suddenly, her life seemed to truly be an actual dream rather than the toxic nightmare it had been before.

In *Beyond Thunderdome*, Tina would be playing the wild role of Auntie Entity, a surreal kind of Amazon figure who is the matriarchal warlord of an outpost city called Bartertown. She loved the fact that for her second role in ten years, she'd be playing yet another Queen. Not only that, but she would also be performing two songs in the film: the iconic "We Don't Need Another Hero," a curious counterpart to one of her favorite Bowie lyrics about being heroes but "just for one day," as well as "One of the Living," which ended up in a massively visible position playing over the Maurice Jarre film titles. Naturally, it also meant the release of a sound track album.

MAD MAX BEYOND THUNDERDOME (CAPITOL RECORDS)

Released in 1985. Movie sound track recording produced by Terry Britten and Graham Lyle (who also wrote her hit "What's Love Got to Do with It"). Personnel: Tina Turner, vocals; Charlie Moran, drums; Kings School Choir; Nick Glennie-Smith, keyboards; Graham Bond, percussion; Tim Cappello, saxophone; Terry Britten, guitar; Holly Knight, keyboards; Gene Black, backing vocals; Charles McMahon, didgeridoo. Duration: 44:27.

We Don't Need Another Hero (Terry Britten, Graham Lyle) 6:05 / One of the Living (Holly Knight) 5:59 / Hero Instrumental (Terry Britten, Graham Lyle) 6:30 / Bartertown (Maurice Jarre) 8:28 / The Children (Maurice Jarre) 2:11 / Coming Home (Maurice Jarre)

The blockbuster sound track music from the film starring Mel Gibson and Tina Turner also featured twenty-six minutes of orchestral score composed by Maurice Jarre and performed by the Royal Philharmonic Orchestra. Most notable for fans, though, were Turner's U.S. number 2 and U.K. number 3 single "We Don't Need Another Hero," which played over the end titles of the movie. The single was released the year after Turner's *Private Dancer* album. The song received a Golden Globe nomination for best original song in 1986 and a 1986 Grammy nomination for best pop female vocal performance.

The second Turner track on the record was the film's opening title piece, produced by Mike Chapman and Holly Knight; the song won Turner a Grammy Award in 1985 for best rock female vocal performance. This sound track for the film sequel was a long way from the original and grittier Brian May (Queen) approach, but Jarre managed to pull it off with considerable aplomb in his own vernacular.

As *AllMusic*'s critic James Monger pointed out at the time, *Mad Max Beyond Thunderdome* divided critics and fans alike with its big-budget rendering of Gibson's iconic vigilante. "What sounded odd in theory came across much better on screen. Jarre conjured up an elegant storm of a score that remained reverent to May's brutish dissonance, while establishing a memorable melody—The Children—and introducing a tonal lushness that was absent from the first films."

Her over-the-top Aunty Entity role is actually utterly perfect for her. Like the singer, the character is very strong, a lady of power. Turner has never wanted to do sexy films and claims she's not funny, so she wanted to be dealing with some kind of war, with physical strength in a woman. It's her basic personality, it's how she's built. Amazingly, when asked to imagine future film roles, she told *Maclean's* magazine that "I want to do really heroic women things. I'd like to do a female version of Sylvester Stallone's *Rambo* character."

Apparently, her personal karma had kicked into action and was rocketing her forward at full throttle once again. It was as if not only she had become some kind of female archetype representing survival but also triumph had surfaced in our midst and part of the collective unconscious we all share consisting of monumental metaphors had arisen from wherever it resides. And right on cue, Stephen Spielberg would later call to offer her the starring role in his film adaptation of Alice Walker's story *The Color Purple*. But she decided, quite rightly I suspect, to turn that one down, as big a deal as it would have been, perhaps realizing that the narrative was just way too close to home, literally. "I've lived that story!" was how she put it at the time.

Given that attitude of her attachment to heroism and strength, it wasn't surprising to anyone that Spielberg had approached her to be the lead female star in his *Purple* adaptation, and also not surprising that she politely rejected the complimentary offer. Personally, she felt that black people can do better than that and also declined because it was too close to her personal life and it was far too soon to be reminded of it. Although she was excited and flattered to be asked by Spielberg to be in his movie, it was just the wrong role for her at that time.

Sticking close to her personal musical interests was also likely a smart move professionally. Acting had always been a bit of a sideline for her, apart from her main job description of acting the part of Tina Turner. In 1985, she joined another massive cross section of international stars for a global rock-and-roll *Live Aid* telecast, and of course the hits in the mid-1980s kept on rolling. The single release of "We Don't Need Another Hero" became number 3 in the United Kingdom; her video for "What's Love Got to Do with It?" won best female video at the second annual MTV Video Awards ceremony; that fall, the single for "One of the Living" (her second *Mad Max* song) was number 15 in America; and at the end of the year, she won an award for best actress from the National Association for the Advancement of Colored People for her role in *Mad Max Beyond Thunderdome*.

For her, the 1980s was an incredible time in an already incredible life, especially being able to perform for massive mixed-race audiences. Clubs and theaters had been left behind in the dust, and she was now an arena act of gargantuan proportions, right up there with Queen and Elton John. It's what made the notion of *Break Every Rule* so perfect for a new album motif. As she told *Vogue*, "When we're talking about those guys who can pack those football stadiums, we're talking about the men that all the girls love. So it's like breaking the rules for me to get a chance to be with them." Tina clearly loves first bending and then breaking every assumption that comes her way.

BREAK EVERY RULE (CAPITOL RECORDS)

Released in 1986. Produced by Terry Britten, Bryan Adams, Bob Clearmountain, Rupert Hine, Mark Knopfler, Neil Dorfsman. Personnel: Bryan Adams, guitar; Terry Britten, bass and vocals; Samantha Brown, vocals; Jack Bruno, drums; Tim Cappello, saxophone; Margo Buchanan, vocals; Richard Elen, sound designer; Mickey Feat, bass; Nick Glennie-Smith, keyboards; Gary Katell, percussion; Steve Winwood, synthesizer; Tina Turner, lead vocals. Duration: 50:13.

Typical Male (Terry Britten, Graham Lyle) 4:18 / What You Get Is What You See (Terry Britten, Graham Lyle) 4:31 / Two People (Terry

Britten, Graham Lyle) 4:11 / Till the Right Man Comes Along (Terry Britten, Graham Lyle) 4:11 / Afterglow (Terry Britten, Graham Lyle) 4:30 / Girls (David Bowie, Erdal Kizilcay) 4:56 / Back Where You Started (Bryan Adams, Jim Valance) 4:27 / Break Every Rule (Rupert Hine, Jeannette Obstoi) 4:02 / Paradise Is Here (Paul Brady) 5:35 / I'll Be Thunder (Rupert Hine, Jeanette Obstoi) 5:21

The A-side of the original vinyl version was produced by the award-winning team behind "What's Love Got to Do with It?," Terry Britten and Graham Lyle, with the B-side produced by Bryan Adams, Rupert Hine, and Mark Knopfler. Following this session, Tina also recorded a duet with Eric Clapton that was included in Phil Collins's 1986 album *August*. *Break Every Rule* was highly successful worldwide, reaching number 4 on the *Billboard* 200, number 2 on the U.K. Albums Chart, and number 1 in Germany and Switzerland.

The album went on to sell 12 million copies, was certified platinum, and continues to be popular to this day. Tina went on a massive world tour to promote it, including one filmed concert date in Rio de Janeiro, Brazil, during which she played for more than 180,000 people, and several other concerts that would be recorded for release two years later.

Her *Break Every Rule* album followed the pattern of *Private Dancer*, with some notable exceptions: no cover songs, all fresh material, a better focus, and packed with fellow megawatt stars to make it rock out the way she liked it. Brian Johnson saw the first show on a 1985 cross-continent tour in Canada and reveled in *Maclean's* magazine about the extent to which she shook up expectations: "For an hour and a half she shimmied, strutted and slithered her way into the hearts and libidos of about 5,000 fans packed into a hockey arena. At the age of forty six, Tina Turner has never been hotter."

In June of that year, her new single "Show Some Respect" hit number 37 on the charts during the same month her wild turn as an action heroine premiered in *Mad Max Beyond Thunderdome*. It's fair to say that she was definitely getting well-earned respect and that music fans definitely appeared to need another international heroine.

The year 1986 will also forever be remembered as the time she finally broke her public silence about her early traumatic years with Ike. Tina was once again baring her soul to the press, something she seemed quite comfortable doing actually. After the tidal wave of her first great come-back hit and literally only weeks after the release of her racy follow-up to it, *Break Every Rule*, she was more comfortable musing in her usual intimate manner about where she was in her life, how she got there, and where she was going.

She was even okay with *Rolling Stone* magazine's identifying her as the Queen of Rock and Roll, although for me, by 1986, she had clearly established herself as the Queen of Pop. She had further solidified her true achievements as a 1980s woman, not just as a recipient of vast suc-cess but also for the joys of liberation after surviving in a business known for the notorious exploitation of women. In addition to the adoration of countless fans—and perhaps almost as important to her—she became an emblem of sorts: a living symbol of sheer survival instincts.

She credits Roger Davies, the new manager who had masterminded her climb back to the top of the rock-and-roll world, for her longevity through the glittering pop gems of *Private Dancer* and *Break Every Rule*. The second album's title is also an apt one for Turner, clearly at a pivotal stage in her life where she barely recognizes the existence of rules let alone submitting to them.

And in some strange way, the notion that, as her new album sug-gested, she *breaks every rule* is perhaps unconsciously tethered to a self-deprecating attitude she still carried within her. The surprising thing is that someone who had achieved so much, both personally and professionally, could still feel herself lacking in some deep way that must obviously be attached to her childhood.

Her closest friends were aware that she was still searching for the re-spect she thought she deserved as well as for the recognition of a sense of classiness she had always craved. At this stage in her life, at age forty-six, she was also still hoping for the love of the kind of man she thought she deserved. Sure enough, not only was it coming, but Erwin Bach had already quietly entered her life by the side door—that very year in fact.

❖   ❖   ❖

In 1987, it was Grammy Award time again, which meant Tina time: she won for best female rock vocal performance for her song "Back Where You Started." But obviously, she was far, far away from where she started. In fact, she was now her own personal, real-life Rocket 88!

"I'm not looking for pity about my life with Ike," she told *Life* magazine at the time. "It was years ago. I'm done with it." And in 1993, the year the film version was released, she told *GQ* magazine about the challenge of revisiting the past. "I drank a lot of wine, but I did it. The world was shocked." We still are.

For Tina Turner, the year 1988 simply meant another new solo album release, one celebrating her mammoth concert tours to support both *Private Dancer* and *Break Every Rule*. And a live Tina record was at least as exciting as a live Ike and Tina album ever was, in some ways maybe more.

TINA LIVE IN EUROPE (EMI/CAPITOL RECORDS)

Released in 1988. Produced by John Hudson, Terry Britten. Personnel: Tina Turner, vocals; Jamie Ralston, guitar; Bob Feit, bass and vocals; Jack Bruno, drums; Stevie Scales, percussion; John Miles, keyboards; Ollie Marland, keyboards and vocals; Deric Dyer, saxophone and keyboards; Jamie West-Oram, guitar; Don Snow, keyboards; Tim Cappello, keyboards and saxophone; Alan Clark, keyboards; Kenny Moore, keyboards; Gary Barnacle, saxophone. Venues: Birmingham, Wembley, London, Camden, England; Westfallenhalle, Dortmund, West Germany; Issadion, Stockholm, Sweden. Duration: 121:54.

Disc 1: What You Get Is What You See (Terry Britten, Graham Lyle) 5:34 / Break Every Rule (Rupert Hine, Jeannette Obstoi) 4:28 / I Can't Stand the Rain (Ann Peebles) 3:25 / Two People (Terry Britten, Graham Lyle) 4:26 / Typical Male (Terry Britten, Graham Lyle) 3:59 / Better Be Good to Me (Holly Knight, Nicky Chinn, Mike Chapman) 6:29 / Addicted to Love (Robert Palmer) 5:22 / Private Dancer (Mark Knopfler) 5:37 / We Don't Need Another Hero (Terry Britten, Graham Lyle) 4:56 / What's Love Got to Do with It? (Terry Britten, Graham Lyle) 5:28 / Let's Stay Together (Al Green, Willie Mitchell, Al Jackson) 4:40 / Show Some Respect (Terry Britten, Sue Shirin) 3:05

Disc 2: Land of a Thousand Dances (Chris Kenner) 3:06 / In the Midnight Hour (Wilson Pickett, Steve Cropper) 3:32 / 634-5789 (Eddie

Floyd, Steve Cropper) 3:05 / A Change Is Gonna Come (Sam Cooke) 6:44 / River Deep, Mountain High (Phil Spector, Ellie Greenwich, Jeff Barry) 4:11 / Tearing Us Apart (Eric Clapton, Greg Phillinganes) 4:41 / Proud Mary (John Fogerty) 4:47 / Help! (John Lennon, Paul McCartney) 5:03 / Tonight (David Bowie, Iggy Pop) 4:15 / Let's Dance (David Bowie) 3:27 / Overnight Sensation (Mark Knopfler) 3:54 / It's Only Love (Bryan Adams) 4:15 / Nutbush City Limits (Tina Turner) 3:43 / Paradise Is Here (Paul Brady) 5:41

This is the first live solo record by Tina Turner, a compilation of concert performances made between 1985 and 1987, containing both dates from her Break Every Rule Tour and also her Private Dancer Tour in addition to live material from her HBO special in London. This concert record won a Grammy Award for best female rock performance in 1989. The public acclaim continued when the album reached number 8 in England as it passionately documented several of the most successful performances from her triumphant tour, and it's an ideal aural archive indeed.

Some of us were fortunate enough to see her perform live in concert, and some were not. For those of us who missed the opportunity, here was an album that at least captured some of the fire in her personal delivery and made us feel like part of the massive European audience writhing in pleasure as she bestowed the gift of her hits, both the old ones and the new ones.

She was always very generous with her fans when appearing live, well aware that they were paying top dollar to see her, and when they left the arenas or theaters, she had only one single objective: she wanted them to feel as blissed out as humanly possible. As listeners can attest to from hearing this double album set, she usually succeeded in that objective.

But her huge success—and her personal identification with both struggle and triumph—is still tempered by that now longtime spiritual equanimity that so many people find synonymous with her basic, everyday, down-to-earth character: huge but humble.

7

RE-LAUNCH

Firsthand Emotion

"Turner's voice is anthemic. Seething with anger yet whimpering as if wounded, it's not pretty, it's not feminine, at times it doesn't even sound human."

—Christian Wright, *Trouble Girls*, 1997

All along the way and to this day, Tina Turner has credited her early encounter with Buddhism for the dramatic turnaround in her life, with altering her old ingrained patterns of thought about who she was, what she was, and what she was capable of doing. Who can argue the point she makes? Because then, her outer reality started to reflect that positive inner attitude almost like a mirror, so much so that she's quite comfortable saying that someday, when she's finished with the entertainment industry, she feels a calling to engage in teaching some of what she's discovered about the spiritual life.

Until that time, however, and thank whatever gods exist for this, she's still actively with us in the sweaty carnal world, what George Harrison called living in the material world, because we need bold warrior women like her to keep us company amid the chaos. I've always found the way she expressed it in her testimonial quite moving: "My career is still in bloom. I'm not ripe enough to teach anybody. When I'm ready, I will devote all my time to this—I'll tell what I've learned. Many of you will listen, and some of you will hear."

You don't have to know a single thing about Buddhism to relate to what she's saying, and you don't have to have the slightest grasp of the alluring spiritual concept of actions and their consequences to appreciate what she's offering. Anybody anywhere can see that Miss Bullock was a veritable living example of both bad and good karma coming to fruition, of eventually getting exactly what she deserved. Everyone does, it seems, sooner or later, sit down to a banquet of consequences.

In a sense, the only other aspect of her life that might still be hoped for, wished for, and dreamt of was that of a deep romance and an intimate relationship with a good and kind partner, someone who knew who she really was. But that too was on the way. Her good karma was not finished with her quite yet. Not by a long shot.

Perhaps her then upcoming 1989 album title *Foreign Affair* actually had to do with something quite down to earth, something like a foreign affair? She had been singing her now signature song about what love had to do with it for three years. How often, one wonders, does someone have to question who needs a heart when our hearts can be broken before they look up and find a reason not only to have one but also to share it with another person? It had to be a challenge of course given her early experience with intimate bonds, but surely if anyone deserved to finally meet someone worth sharing her life with, it was Anna Mae Bullock.

Foreign, in name only perhaps, because, after all, it was in Europe where she got both her first acknowledgment as a star and her renewed acceptance as a reborn artist who was asking for a second chance. Europe had always embraced her with open arms, and it turns out that a European man, someone seventeen years younger than her, would be the one who won her heart and, she would say, fully embraced her soul. I don't want to overuse the word "karma," but what would you call it when you meet the man of your dreams by pure chance when he innocently happens to drop off a jeep for you to use while touring through Germany?

Call it fate, call it destiny, or, if the word "karma" makes you uneasy, call it serendipity—it hardly matters really, but that's the word Tina would naturally use in such a situation. She makes a pretty good case for actions and their consequences leading her to meet someone special enough to cope with her history, her energy, and her future, someone unique enough to click in an instant, even though it would take three years for their relationship to really get off the ground.

Also, this would be someone caring enough to weather her upcoming health challenges with her, to stand by her side through medical treatments for intestinal cancer, to donate one of his own kidneys in a transplant when needed, and even to cope with the trauma of his donated kidney being rejected and followed by seizures and strokes. This is what some people would call a mensch, a real person, and just such a man seems to be her current life partner, Erwin Bach, a German record executive. Initially meeting in 1985 during her Private Dancer Tour, they decided they didn't really need to officially marry, and only after a twenty-seven-year romance did they do so, in Switzerland in 2013.

Suddenly, by the 1980s, she was about as busy as she'd ever been in the 1960s, but it was a different kind of busy, a second blossoming, without the obvious strains attached to her first frenzied ride into fame and misfortune. She's admitted that it was seemingly a case of instant romance, that mythical at-first-sight experience we've all heard of. Indeed, it was definitely a heart-going-boom moment, but her natural caution in these matters caused her to wait for three years before finally committing to what her heart was telling her so clearly.

Subsequent to their literally just bumping into each other, she had been throwing a birthday party for a friend in West Hollywood at Wolfgang Puck's original Spago, and they all then retired to her home in Sherman Oaks. Bach was among them, again by chance. Many observers have noted that at that party, something magical started to happen. After their first chance encounter and openly interested in pursuing him further, she had then deliberately rented a house in Switzerland and invited him to a Christmas party there with mutual friends in 1988. The relationship just continued to blossom naturally and grow from there, having taken on a life of its own.

Now, in addition to her mature second career flowering, her love life seemed to be doing likewise. Against all odds, including being introduced to a family who may have been a little apprehensive about his new relationship with someone older than him (she was by then forty-eight, he was thirty-one), being an American black rock star to boot, and despite the fact that they may have harbored some secret desires that the woman of his dreams might be a German one (and a white one), they quickly fell in love with her too. Everyone seems to sooner or later.

Her busy career was still flying high, however, and that had to be attended to as well, especially in 1989. She performed before not only the biggest crowd of fans she'd ever had as an audience but also the largest audience ever recorded by anyone anywhere. In Rio de Janeiro, when headlining at the Maracana Arena during her Break Every Rule Tour, she drew more than a quarter of a million adoring people, which caused the *Guinness World Records* to make an official entry to that effect. She also continually broke all house records when the tour concluded in Osaka, Japan.

Things continued to speed up even faster. Shortly after visiting New York in January 1989 for the Rock and Roll Hall of Fame induction ceremony, where she inducted her old producer Phil Spector into the hallowed ranks of music legends, she attended the Grammy Awards, where she won her seventh trophy in the category of best rock vocal performance for her *Live in Europe* album. Then her aptly titled next album, *Foreign Affair*, was released to high acclaim, rising to number 1 in the United Kingdom and number 31 in America. The first single from that album would go on to become one of her signature tunes, "The Best."

On November 26, 1989, she celebrated her fiftieth birthday with close rock pals such as Mark Knopfler, Eric Clapton, and Bryan Adams, and even though it sounds like a long time, half a century was just beginning to feel like warming up to her. To say she'd hit her stride in the following decade of the 1990s would be a gross understatement, even for someone with legs like hers.

FOREIGN AFFAIR (EMI/CAPITOL RECORDS)

Released in 1989. Produced by Dan Hartman, Tina Turner, Rupert Hine, Roger Davies, Graham Lyle, Albert Hammond, Tony Joe White. Personnel: Tina Turner, vocals; Tony Joe White, guitar; Dan Hartman, acoustic guitar; Eddie Martinez, rhythm guitar; Neil Taylor, guitar; Mark Knopfler, guitar; Elliot Lewis and Nick Glennie-Smith, strings; Gary Barnacle, saxophones; Edgar Winter, saxophone; Phil Ashley, keyboards; Jeff Bova, synthesizers; Casey Young, keyboards; Carmine

Roja and Rupert Hine, bass; J. T. Lewis and Art Wood, drums; Albert Hammond, percussion; Lance Ellington, Sandy Stewart, and Tessa Niles, backing vocals; Roger Davies, Graham Lyle, and Holly Knight, additional vocals. Engineers and sound mixing: Chris Lord-Alge, Andrew Scarth, Mike Ging, Nick Froome, Tom Fritze. Overdubs done at Ezee, Mayfair, and Swanyard studios. Duration: 52:16.

Steamy Windows (Tony Joe White) 4:03 / The Best (Mike Chapman, Holly Knight) 5:30 / You Know Who (Tony Joe White) 3:45 / 4) Undercover Agent for the Blues (Tony Joe White, Leann White) 5:20 / Look Me in the Heart (Tom Kelly, Billy Steinberg) 3:46 / Be Tender with Me Baby (Albert Hammond, Holly Knight) 4:18 / Can't Stop Me Loving You (Albert Hammond, Holly Knight) 4:00 / Ask Me How I Feel (Albert Hammond, Holly Knight) 4:46 / Falling Like Rain (David Munday, Sandy Stewart) 4:03 / I Don't Wanna Lose You (Albert Hammond, Graham Lyle) 4:20 / Not Enough Romance (Dan Hartman) 4:04 / Foreign Affair (Tony Joe White) 4:27

Tina was in the midst of having a foreign affair of course, the one that would eventually lead to her second marriage. One consistent irony in Tina's career was also that she was always having a foreign affair with music lovers in Europe and the rest of the world, one that usually far outdistanced her American listeners. It was just an intriguing demographic to her backstory.

Her seventh solo studio album and the third release since her huge comeback hit six years earlier, this outing did not perform quite as well as *Private Dancer* or *Break Every Rule*, but it was still a gigantic hit in Europe and internationally. It reached number 1 on the U.K. Albums Chart and sold more than 6 million copies, also reaching number 1 in both Germany and Sweden as well as topping the overall European charts for more than a month.

In Europe, six of the record's twelve tracks became number 1 hit singles, with "Foreign Affair" and "The Best" going on to become stalwarts of her concert performances ever afterward. By this time, she was globally recognized as a pop star, and some younger listeners may not have even been very aware of her long earlier history as either a rhythm-and-blues torcher or a rock queen.

With her latest single "Steamy Windows" steaming up the charts, on April 27, she leapt into her international 121-date concert tour to promote *Foreign Affair*, ostensibly while still conducting said affair privately. Commencing in Antwerp, Belgium, and ending the roller-coaster ride in Rotterdam, Holland, during the course of the concert travel binge, she'd entertained more than 3 million joyous followers.

At about the same time, she was jubilantly, even exultantly, bringing pleasure to half the planet, her ex-husband was also making vague head-lines of his own albeit for the opposite kind of reasons. In his fourteen years of Tina-less life, he'd been arrested eleven times for a variety of crimes, and finally, in 1990, he was put in prison for cocaine violations, transporting drugs, and a few other miscellaneous bad lifestyle issues.

Meanwhile in October, on the brighter side of life, Tina's new al-bum, *Simply the Best*, a greatest-hits package, came out, with all her most popular tunes from the 1980s and featuring a brand-new version of "Nutbush" in addition to three new songs by her: "I Want You Near Me," "Way of the World," and "Love Thing."

SIMPLY THE BEST (EMI/CAPITOL RECORDS)

Released in 1991. Various producers, as per originals. Her first greatest-hits compilation, released on October 22, 1991, featured her most popular tracks recorded between 1973 and 1991 with an emphasis on her tracks since the big comeback in 1984. The collection is her biggest-selling record in the United Kingdom, with sales in excess of 2.4 million copies, certified 8x platinum, and staying on their hit charts for more than 140 weeks straight with worldwide sales of more than 7 million.

The Australian special edition featured five new bonus tracks, includ-ing a rerecording of "The Best" as a duet with Jimmy Barnes retitled "Simply (The Best)," released as a single, as well as a new song, "I'm a Lady," released as a single and B-side to "Love Thing." Personnel as per original recordings. (Understandably, perhaps, no songs were included from either her *Rough* or *Love Explosion* albums.)

The Best (Mike Chapman, Holly Knight) 4:10 / What's Love Got to Do with It (Terry Britten, Graham Lyle) 3:50 / I Can't Stand the Rain (Ann

Peebles, Bryant Miller) 3:44 / I Don't Wanna Lose You (Albert Hammond, Graham Lyle) 4:18) / Nutbush City Limits (Tina Turner) 3:44 / Let's Stay Together (Al Green, Al Jackson, Willie Michell) 3:39 / Private Dancer (Mark Knopfler) 4:01 / We Don't Need Another Hero (Terry Britten, Graham Lyle) 4:14 / Better Be Good to Me (Holly Knight, Mike Chapman) 3:40 / River Deep, Mountain High (Jeff Barry, Phil Spector, Ellie Greenwich) 3:37 / Steamy Windows (Tony White) 4:02 / Typical Male (Terry Britten, Graham Lyle) 4:14 / It Takes Two (Sylvia Moy, William Stevenson) 4:13 / Addicted to Love (Robert Palmer) 5:10 / Be Tender with Me Baby (Holly Knight, Albert Hammond) 4:17 / I Want You Near Me (Terry Britten, Graham Lyle) 3:53 / Way of the World (Albert Hammond, Graham Lyle) 4:19 / Love Thing (Holly Knight, Albert Hammond) 4:28

Simply the Best shot up to number 2 in Britain, and on her fifty-second birthday in 1991, she was also awarded a Quintuple Platinum Award to commemorate sales of 1.5 million copies of *Foreign Affair*. She rounded out the middle of 1992 by celebrating the completion of her longtime Capitol Records contract in July and signing a fresh new deal with a spanking-new company, Virgin Records, thus offering a new lease on her creative life as well. Life was good, and the future looked brighter and brighter.

The past, however, is never really dead; in fact, as William Faulkner once rued, it isn't even past. And the long shadow of her ex-husband continued to interrupt her activities—not disrupt them so much but definitely sour them slightly. He would work on penning his own wonky "side" of the story, *Takin' Back My Name: The Confessions of Ike Turner*, written with the assistance of Nigel Cawthorne and released in 1999, in which he grumbled publicly about his ex-wife's open reportage of events surrounding their life together.

By this stage in her life, she always spoke haltingly about her ex-husband in general (if at all), but in my opinion, she still managed to express considerable compassion for someone who treated her the way he did. Friends knew well that her newfound peace of mind included never feeling any vengeance or animosity. It just wasn't her Buddhist way, so instead, she later demonstrated authentic happiness for him when he was eventually released from prison, perhaps conscious that he might even return to making his own music, which was always a primary cause for any happiness he ever experienced in his rough-and-tumble life.

I suspect most readers might agree with my sense that this deep feeling that Tina shared was being expressed by a person of extremely strong character indeed—and one with considerable compassion under the circumstances. By then, at the awkward time of his heavily skewed book's attempt at name rehabilitation (or rewriting history), Tina had already moved permanently to Europe, and she no longer wanted to memorialize that earlier part of her life.

She left America mainly because her biggest success was always in another country, and Europe had always been so supportive of her music. Besides, her new boyfriend lived there, in addition to which she openly admitted that after trying England for a couple of years, then her new partner's home of Cologne, Germany, they settled comfortably in Switzerland. Although obviously American to the bone, she still felt like she had never known her *real* home until she moved to Europe.

❁ ❁ ❁

It's one thing to escape from your life, even your country, but it's quite another to escape from your history. The first two are achievable if you're brave enough; the third is more stubbornly persistent and requires an even more steely spirit to withstand. Tina Turner had turned a corner in terms of music, career, and love, but she still had to deal with the fallout from her own earliest sorrowful life experiences. She'd been popular before of course, but now she was a mega pop star, so naturally an even greater number of newfound fans wanted to know her personal backstory.

Her ex-husband's ongoing illegal shenanigans always spawned a whole new raft of news stories and interviews, as had her 1986 testimonial book that morphed into that huge Hollywood biopic in 1993. That film seems to have pushed Ike right over the edge that he was already teetering on. Fortunately for her, the induction of Ike and Tina Turner into the Rock and Roll Hall of Fame in 1991 took place *before* his release from prison, so she at least didn't have to contend with the regrettable episode of either accepting a hugely important award with him near her or else not attending one of the most crucial events in her career.

She lucked out and was inducted along with LaVern Baker, John Lee Hooker, the Impressions, Jimmy Reed, and the great Wilson Pickett, soaking up the adulation of a massive audience of both attendees and viewers around the world, some of whom were only old enough to know her since her triumphant return in 1984. At that stage, during her Hall of Fame induction, Ike could only watch the official induction of his namesake Revue partnership from the comfort of his jail cell. But *everyone* on the planet seemed to now be aware of her harrowing youthful ordeal once the movie based on her life hit the big screen. It was déjà vu all over again.

Disney Corporation and Touchstone Films had purchased the rights to make the film based on her testimonial, *I, Tina*, for which they also paid her ex-husband a large enough sum that he would agree to accept the portrayal without recourse to lawsuits if dissatisfied. They knew of course he would be miffed given how he was being depicted for public consumption.

He would later claim that he signed the deal only because he was still under the influence of drugs and didn't realize what he was doing.

In a *GQ* magazine profile during the time of its release, she admitted that the film was both true but also narratively contoured to fit the dramatic format, as always happens during the shift from story to screen. "I've got to admit that they took the idea of my life and sort of wrote *around* it." She definitely felt that much was left out of the story, such as the quite valid parts of the creative process of making music in the early days before they went off the rails and also her positive family life with her children.

But she understood their cinematic decisions to not only take certain liberties with facts but also focus mostly on her meeting, singing, and recording with, marrying, battling abuse from, and later on escaping from her maniacal husband. It's not that what they showed wasn't true, except for certain "poetic liberties" taken with chronology or events for the purposes of dramatic compression into two hours. She just wished they had showed more of the occasional good times and interpersonal relationships that made it all at least bearable—and eventually maybe survivable.

Some of the narrative differences she detected were of course very noticeable to most people who had followed her life and music: Ike did not sing or play guitar on his early song "Rocket 88" as depicted, instead writing the song and playing piano; the song Anna Mae first performs onstage with Ike, "You Know I Love You" by BB King, was actually a much slower down-tempo blues ballad than depicted; the first song Anna Mae records, called "Tina's Wish" in the film's story line, was actually a 1973 track written by her on 1973's *Nutbush City Limits*.

In the film, a theater marquee announcing a 1960 show starring Otis Redding, Martha and the Vandellas, and Ike and Tina Turner is shown, but in reality, Martha's group was known as the Del-Phis until 1961, and Otis did not become a solo act until 1962; in the film, Anna Mae learns of her name change to Tina Turner after a song is played on the radio where she has just given birth, but in reality, Tina had already seen a vinyl copy of the song that showcased Ike and Tina Turner. She reported that her first physical argument with Ike occurred after she expressed her concerns about the name change and he hit her with a shoe stretcher.

The film suggests or implies that Tina's firstborn son, Craig, was Ike's biological child, but in reality, Craig was the son of Ike's saxophone player Raymond Hill, with whom Tina was briefly allied; the film shows the couple getting married after Ike and his gang sneak Tina out of the hospital, but in reality, Ike was not present for the birth of their son, and Tina checked herself out of the hospital when she discovered that Ike had hired a prostitute to impersonate her while she was recuperating; they married in 1962, two years after the birth of their son, for the purposes of preventing a former spouse of Ike's (probably his earlier singer and piano player Anna Mae Wilson) from demanding property rights.

The film showed a reenactment clip of an interview the couple did in 1964 rather than in 1971, when the real-life pair were in a similar context (Tina speaking throughout the interview with Ike remaining silent with his back to Tina and smoking a cigarette); in a scene dated 1968 in the film, the couple opened for the Rolling Stones, performing "Proud Mary," but in reality, they didn't perform that song until after it was released by Creedence Clearwater Revival in 1969, and the Rolling Stones did not have any concerts in 1968, with Ike and Tina opening for them only in 1966 and 1969.

Most perilously, the film depicts Tina's suicide attempt in 1974 (for reasons that are unclear) when it actually occurred in 1968; during the time that Tina is planning her comeback in the early 1980s, in the film, a reenactment of an interview features her rehearsing her song "I Might Have Been Queen," but that song wasn't recorded until her album *Private Dancer* was produced; and in the film, before performing "What's Love Got to Do with It?" at the Ritz in New York, the emcee announces that it was her first appearance, although she had actually first appeared there in 1981. Her 1983 appearance there occurred before the recording of her signature song and led to Capitol Records signing its recording contract with her.

Some details needed correcting, and Tina was never proud of the way the film portrayed her as a "victim" when her own actual take on her narrative was considerably more complex and nuanced. But, hey folks, it's Hollywood, and movies are magic lanterns selling both dreams and nightmares. Directed by Brian Gibson and produced by Doug Chapin and Barry Krost, the screenplay was adapted by Kate Lanier, with the film grossing about $40 million and $20 million in rentals, while in the United Kingdom, ever her supreme fan base, it grossed £10 million alone.

Angela Bassett won a Golden Globe Award, Laurence Fishburne was nominated for an Oscar, and the film also received an American Choreography Award for some of its dance sequences. Fishburne had to be offered the role five times and turned it down before relenting, apparently concerned that it did not really explore the root causes of her ex-husband's behavior or explore why a person like Tina would stay with him for sixteen years. Ironically, many of Tina's more graphic accounts of his abuse were not actually included in the film. According to the liner notes of the original film sound track on Virgin Records, Tina was rather surprised that the film even got made, accurate or otherwise.

When the Disney Company bought the film rights to her story, she never really believed it would make it to the screen. It also surprised her to hear how well some of the songs had withstood the test of time. She recorded three new songs for the sound track and was out on the road again previewing a few of the new songs when she went to Monaco in May and was honored at the World Music Awards with a trophy for outstanding contribution to the music industry, singing the appropriately titled "I Don't Want to Fight" at the ceremony.

Also that May, she was a guest on the *Tonight Show* and also sang the song again for the BBC show *Top of the Pops*. In June, she launched her first North American concert tour in six years, starting out in Reno, Nevada, and being opened by Fleetwood Mac star Lindsey Buckingham, later replaced for the second part of the tour by Chris Isaak. While she was on the road doing what she does best, the film opened as a gigantic box office hit, bringing even more attention to her tumultuous history. She had to be wondering just when in her life she wouldn't have to talk about Ike Turner anymore, having already managed to create an Ike-less future for herself.

As always, she shared with friends who knew the backstory that it was a challenge not only to see the story of her life filmed that way but also to cope with the resurgence of primal energies associated with her relationship, which is why I believe she has been so adroitly managing posttraumatic stress for years. She felt that getting it out of her system would be tantamount to not suppressing the pain anymore, to letting the world know her by letting them into her true story. At first, it felt like no one really understood her choices, but slowly, it became clear that they, we, were starting to.

She had always felt that what actually ruined him was that Ike had this peculiar way of believing he controlled people through sex, but that was naturally not what kept her in the traumatic relationship. Rather, it was her deep sense of loyalty. One more deep regret she has is that the movie didn't really show her whole complex story, the creative early career growth, or her family connections. In fact, given how terrible her personal narrative was, the Disney company actually felt that audiences would never have believed that there were some (many actually) good moments as well.

As she expressed her dilemma to Hirshey for her history of soul music book, "What else was I supposed to do? I had to work. So I've worked." Essentially, in a very real way, the film is the story of a woman trapped in a nightmare relationship who nonetheless has to be both a mother and a professional, meeting as many commitments as she can all at once. The film was a blockbuster and garnered mostly positive responses: the *Los Angeles Times*, *Entertainment Weekly*, and the *Chicago Sun-Times* all agreed it was one of that year's top ten movies.

Roger Ebert of the *Sun-Times* said it "ranked as one of the most harrowing, uncompromising showbiz biographies I've ever seen. It has a lot of terrific music in it, but it's not a typical showbiz musical. It's a story of pain and courage, uncommonly honest and unflinching, and the next time I hear Tina Turner singing I will listen to the song in a whole new way." Most of us will too. Rita Kempley of the *Washington Post* observed, "What's love got to do with it? Not much I'm afraid. It's a sketchy but brutal biopic with a weft of beatings and a warp of rhythm and blues. One minute she's belting out 'Proud Mary,' the next minute Ike's belting her. The film, like the couple's co-dependent relationship, is fiercely acted out and ablaze with flashy production numbers." Once again, it also garnered another new album.

WHAT'S LOVE GOT TO DO WITH IT? (PARLOPHONE-VIRGIN RECORDS)

Released in 1993. Produced by Chris Lord, Rupert Hine, Bryan Adams, Terry Britten, Robert "Mutt" Lange. Personnel: Tina Turner, vocals; Laurence Fishburne, spoken vocal on "It's Gonna Work Out Fine"; James Ralston, guitar and vocals; Gene Black and Keith Scott, guitar; Tommy Cappello, saxophones; Lee Thornburg, trumpet; David Paitch, piano; C. J. Vanston, keyboards; Rupert Hine, keyboards; Bob Feit, bass; Robbie King, Hammond organ; Trevor Morais, drums; Simon Morton, percussion; Tuck Back Twins, vocals. Engineers: Chris Lord-Alge, Steve McNamara, John Hudson, Doug Sax. Duration: 51:52.

Her eighth studio album was the sound track for the film of the same name, released by Touchstone Pictures. This venture found Turner rerecording many of her songs from her earlier Ike and Tina Turner period, including their first single together, "A Fool in Love." It also included a vampy version of the Trammps disco classic hit "Disco Inferno," one of her favorite songs to perform live in the late 1970s. Two tracks were also included from her *Private Dancer* album.

This album rose to number 1 in the United Kingdom (as usual with Tina) and was certified platinum in various countries. Note: Tina's version of "You Know I Love You" was not the same tune as the BB King song she famously first sang with Ike while still a teenager; hers is a slightly different more rock version written with her bandmates for this sound track, though she still credits that title to BB King.

I Don't Wanna Fight (Lulu, Billy Lawrie, Steve DuBerry) 6:06 / Rock Me Baby 93 Version (Riley King, Joe Josea) 3:57 / Disco Inferno (Leroy Green, Ron Kersey) 4:03 / Why Must We Wait until Tonight (Bryan Adams, Robert Lange) 5:53 / Stay Awhile (Terry Britten, Graham Lyle) 4:50 / Nutbush City Limits, 1993 Version (Tina Turner) 3:19 / Darlin You Know I Love You, 1993 Version (Riley King, Jules Taub) 4:27 / Proud Mary, 1993 Version (John Fogerty) 5:25 / A Fool in Love, 1993 Version (Ike Turner) 2:54 / It's Gonna Work Out Fine, 1993 Version (Sylvia McKinney, Rose McCoy) 2:49 / Shake a Tail Feather, 1993 Version (Verlie Rice, Otis Hayes, Andre Williams) 2:32 / I Might Have Been Queen, 1993 Version (Jeannette Obstoi, Rupert Hine) 4:20 / What's Love Got to Do with It (Terry Britten, Graham Lyle) 3:49 / Tina's Wish, 1993 Version (Tina Turner) 3:08

✿　✿　✿

Less carefully scrutinized in 1993 of course was Tina's brief appearance as a town mayor in Schwarzenegger's *Last Action Hero*. That role was a lark, a bit of fun for her. But at least the biopic film on her earlier life, as challenging as it was for her to participate in and watch, did inaugurate yet another huge hit record, with the movie sound track booming up to number 1 in England and number 17 in America. It also crowned the singles charts in France, Germany, and Switzerland, the last of these soon to be her new home. She completed the final concert date in her then current U.S. tour in August in Miami before shifting gears and performing in Australia, while during December, Fox Television aired a special called *What's Love? Live*, with fragments from the whole tour.

After a hectic and soul-stirring opening to the 1990s and after the end of the tours, films, accolades, and acclaim associated with her recently documented history in the 1960s, she decided to do something she had never in her life actually experienced: go on vacation. She took off three whole years for the first time in her busy life, from 1993 to 1996. It had always been a grind, year after year, album after album, touring and then starting an album again. But what would a dynamo like her do on vacation? She coyly claims that it was a lot of nothing really, just experiencing what it's like to do nothing for a change.

But of course, it wasn't exactly all *nothing*; it never is. She decorated a new house, and in 1994, she moved with her new young paramour Erwin

Bach from his home of Cologne to their new home of Zurich, Switzerland, where he had been transferred to run that branch of his music company. She told Sarah Mower of *Harper's Bazaar* that she "lived the first half of my life in America, the second half I'll live in Europe. I don't believe I'll ever go back to America to live. What I don't like in America is having the press down my throat about all the old stuff. Too much of the past, I don't dwell. That's me—I don't go back again."

But of course, even though she may have been out of the public spotlight, her music wasn't. The *Simply the Best* album stayed in the U.K. Top 50 charts for a rather amazing 154 consecutive weeks, impressive even by her standards. Then in 1994, her label, Capitol Records, as usual seeking the most capital from its artists, released a three-CD boxed set called *Tina Turner: The Collected Recordings*, accompanied by an eighty-four-page color book and extensive notes by Paul Grein. And to make her vacation of *doing nothing* even more paradoxical, in 1995, she went into the studio with the group U2 to sing the theme song for the then new James Bond film *GoldenEye*, with the single from it becoming an instant hit in the United Kingdom, as usual for her. You know you're still on top when they want you to sing the title song from a new Bond movie.

TINA TURNER: THE COLLECTED RECORDINGS, SIXTIES TO NINETIES (EMI/CAPITOL RECORDS)

Released in 1994. Various producers. Executive producer Roger Davies. Digital remastering by Larry Walsh. Recorded between 1960 and 1993. Personnel, as per originals. Duration: 194:48.

In November 1994, Capitol released a unique boxed set of thirty years of Tina Turner's recordings, digitally remastered in a sixteen-bit three-disc set and covering everything from the first one, 1960's "A Fool in Love," up to 1993's film sound track, "What's Love Got to Do with It?" This set is, in my opinion, the most perfect vehicle for any listener/reader who wants to know what all the fuss has been about over the past three decades. It also quite rightly gets to be considered a truly genre-bending and border-breaking spectrum of her talents. It's a transformative sequence of stylistic growth development, approximated perhaps only by Madonna (as she so ably demonstrated with the 2019 release and tour for her *Madame X* at age sixty-two).

At this stage in the mid-1990s, Tina is no longer only a rhythm-and-blues singer, southern soul goddess, rock-and-roll chick, or rock queen but has become, just as Madonna did in her own way, a planetary superstar who encompasses and erases all those categories in one fell swoop. Disc 1 focuses on Turner's early career with the Revue, disc 2 contains the sweep from her first solo albums through to her blockbuster comeback, and disc 3 consists of fifteen of her most memorable hits subsequent to the *Private Dancer* bonanza. Once again, for what I believe are sound creative reasons, *Rough* (1978) and *Love Explosion* (1979) were omitted from this ongoing curated mix. Also missing in action (but for different reasons) was "One of the Living," a song used for the title sequence of the film *Mad Max Beyond Thunderdome*.

Disc 1: A Fool in Love (Ike Turner) from *The Soul of Ike and Tina Turner*, 1963, 2:53 / It's Gonna Work Out Fine (Rose Marie McCoy, Sylvia McKinney) from *Dynamite!*, 1963, 3:03 / I Idolize You (Ike Tuner) from *The Soul of Ike and Tina Turner*, 1963, 2:52 / Poor Fool (Ike Turner) from *Dynamite!*, 1963, 2:33 / A Letter from Tina (Ike Turner) from *The Soul of Ike and Tina Turner*, 1963, 2:34 / Finger Poppin (Ike Turner) from *Live! The Ike and Tina Turner Show*, 1964, 2:47 / River Deep, Mountain High (Phil Spector, Jeff Berry, Ellie Greenwich) from *River Deep, Mountain High*, 1966, 3:39 / Crazy bout You Baby (Sonny Boy Williamson) from *Outta Season*, 1968, 3:26 / I've Been Loving You Too Long (Otis Redding, Jerry Butler) from *Outta Season*, 1968, 3:54 / Bold Soul Sister (Ike and Tina Turner) from *The Hunter*, 1969, 2:36 / I Want to Take You Higher (Sly Stone) from *Come Together*, 1970, 2:54 / Come Together (John Lennon, Paul McCartney) from *Come Together*, 1970, 3:42 / Honky Tonk Women (Mick Jagger, Keith Richards) from *Come Together*, 1970, 3:10 / Proud Mary (John Fogerty) from *Workin Together*, 1971, 4:51 / Nutbush City Limits (Tina Turner) from *Nutbush City Limits*, 1973, 3:33 / Sexy Ida, Parts One and Two (Tina Turner) singles from 1974, 5:31 / It Aint Right (Ike Turner) from *Come Together*, 1970, 2:30

Disc 2: Acid Queen (Pete Townshend), sound track version, from *Tommy*, 1975, 3:48 / Whole Lotta Love (Willie Dixon) from *Acid Queen*, 1975, 4:43 / Ball of Confusion (Norman Whitfield) from *Music of Quality Vol. 1*, 1982, 4:11 / A Change Is Gonna Come (Same Cooke) from *Music of Quality Vol. 2*, 1991, 4:45 / Johnny and Mary (Robert Palmer) from *Summer Lovers*, 1982, 4:11 / Games (Andrea Farber, Vince Melamed), previously unreleased 1983 demo, 4:16 / When I Was Young (Eric Burdon) from *Better Be Good to Me* single, 1984, 3:12 / Total Control (Martha Davis, Jeff Jourard) from *We Are the World*, 1985, 6:28 / Let's Pretend We're Married (Prince) from *I Can't Stand the Rain* single, 1985, 4:16 / It's Only Love (Bryan Adams) from *Reckless*, 1984, 3:15 / Don't Turn Around (Albert Hammond, Diane Warren) from *Typical Male* single, 1986, 4:17) / Legs (Billy Gibbons), previously unreleased, 4:59 / Addicted to Love (Robert Palmer) from *Tina in Europe*, 1988, 5:24 / Tearing Us Apart (Eric Clapton) from *August*, 1986, 4:17 / It Takes Two (Sylvia Moy, William Stevenson) from *Vagabond Heart*, 1991, 4:12

Disc 3: Let's Stay Together (Al Green) from *Private Dancer*, 1984, 5:17 / What's Love Got to Do with It? (Terry Britten, Graham Lyle) from *Private Dancer*, 1984, 3:46 / Better Be Good to Me (Mike Chapman, Holly Knight, Nicky Chinn) from *Private Dancer*, 1984, 5:10 /Private Dancer (Mark Knopfler) from *Private Dancer*, 1984, 7:11 / I Can't Stand the Rain (Ann Peebles) from *Private Dancer*, 1984, 3:43 / Help! (John Lennon, Paul McCartney) from *Private Dancer*, 1984, 4:30 / We Don't Need Another Hero (Terry Britten, Graham Lyle) from the sound track *Mad Max Thunderdome*, 1985, 4:15 / Typical Male (Terry Britten, Graham Lyle) from *Break Every Rule*, 1986, 4:15 / What You Get Is What You See (Terry Britten, Graham Lyle) from *Break Every Rule*, 1986, 4:27 / Paradise Is Here (Paul Brady) from *Break Every Rule*, 1986, 5:29 / Back Where You Started (Bryan Adams) from *Break Every Rule*, 1986, 4:27 / The Best (Mike Chapman, Holly Knight) from *Foreign Affair*, 1989, 5:29 / Steamy Windows (Tony Joe White) from *Foreign Affair*, 1986, 4:04 / Foreign Affair (Tony Joe White) from *Foreign Affair*, 1986, 4:28 / I Don't Wanna Fight (Lulu, Steve DuBerry) from *What's Love Got to Do with It?*, 1993, 6:05

After her slight breather, in October 1995 Turner was ready to choose material and begin recording sessions for her new album, the first in five years, to be produced by the prodigious hit king Trevor Horn and featuring a raft of young artists, such as Pet Shop Boys and Sheryl Crow, who would all kill to work with her. Once they had crafted the new disc, *Wildest Dreams*, she naturally had to turn up the heat with yet another world tour, this one covering almost every huge stadium in Europe.

Finally, in April 1996, *Wildest Dreams* was released everywhere in the world, except for America, and it became a respectable seller, followed by the release of *GoldenEye* as a single. Not before whetting the appetite of the United States by making them watch and hear about the stir she was causing abroad, she then released *Wildest Dreams* in September 1996, where it leapt to number 61 on *Billboard*.

WILDEST DREAMS (PARLOPHONE/VIRGIN RECORDS)

Released in 1996. Produced by Trevor Horn, Terry Britten, Chris Porter. Personnel: Tina Turner, vocals; Sting, Barry White, Sheryl Crow, Antonio Bandaras, vocals; Anne Dudley, orchestral arrangements; John Altman, strings; Terry Britten, guitar; Chris Olins, piano; Neil Tennant, keyboards; Reggie Hamilton, bass; Keith Le Blanc, drums; Trevor Horn, backing vocals; Durham Cathedral Choir. Duration: 47:00.

Do What You Do (Terry Britten, Graham Lyle) 4:23 / Whatever You Want (Arthur Baker) 4:52 / Missing You (Mark Leonard) 4:36 / On Silent Wings (Tony Joe White, James Ralston) 6:12 / Thief of Hearts (Jud Friedman) 4:05 / In Your Wildest Dreams (Mike Chapman, Holly Knight) 5:33 / Goldeneye (Bono, the Edge) 3:27 / Confidential (Chris Low, Neil Tennant) 4:39 / Something Beautiful Remains (Terry Britten, Graham Lyle) 4:20 / All Kinds of People (Sheryl Crow) 4:43 / Unfinished Sympathy (Robert Naja) 4:30 / Dancing in My Dreams (Mark Cowley) 12:05 / Love Is a Beautiful Thing (Seth Swirsky) 3:45

Suddenly, with her ninth solo album, she was designated as "soft rock" officially on the charts. It's been a long, strange trip indeed, but now we also have strings, an orchestral arranger, and a large vocal choir on hand to provide even more lush environments for her own voice to writhe around in. Gone is the grit, and embraced is the glitter, although it is still well-done glitter.

This is a long-distance-running performer who is still at the top of her game, even if the rules of that game have changed drastically. This outing also finds her collaborating with a wide range of other notable artists, namely, Sting, U2, Barry White, and Neil Tennant, all along for the soft ride. It naturally went double platinum in the United Kingdom and Europe, where her fan base was still unbreakable. Another tour of course, the second to last, would further embed her in the hearts of fans who had faithfully followed her twists and turns for nearly forty years.

Perhaps even more impressive was the stamina she evidenced during her Wildest Dream Concert Tour, her biggest tour to date at that time, performing more than 250 dates in Europe, North America, and Australia, surpassing even her Break Every Rule Tour from 1987. It lasted nearly sixteen months and was estimated to have grossed more than $100 million, with an audience attendance of some 700,000 worshipful fans.

As Turner herself expressed it to *Jet Magazine*, "It could be my best tour ever in America. When I walk on stage, there's such a feeling of faces looking back at me with love and admiration. It turns into a togetherness, it's really about a desire from the people. The last tour I actually announced to the audience that I would be back. It was only because of that feeling, because that's the kind of audience I have."

Onward with the tour. She stopped briefly in August 1997 when the tragedy occurred with the loss of Princess Diana and almost every big music star on the planet convened for a charity recording to raise funds for the Princess of Wales Memorial Fund. *Diana—A Tribute* was a double album with, as the old MGM movie studio used to say, more stars than there are in heaven.

Among her peers were Aretha Franklin, Queen, Annie Lennox, Paul McCartney, Whitney Houston, Lesley Garrett, Bryan Ferry, Eric Clapton, and others—and of course, the Queen of Rock and Roll herself. Turner donated her version of the song "Love Is a Beautiful Thing" to the double tribute album, the only place it was ever featured on any recording.

Perhaps it was the sad loss of another globally revered woman, Princess Diana, in 1997, that prompted Turner to reflect on the public process of aging. Or perhaps it was only the endless references to her spookily permanent youthful appearance and energy and exuberance that caused her to tell a friend that she sometimes felt like Mother Teresa. Over the course of fifty years, both Anna Mae Bullock and Tina Turner have admirably demonstrated that perpetual *change* was the real name of the game from the start—up to and including the solemn fact (recently) that your life will eventually have to end. But until that end came, this consummate entertainer would still have only one thing on her mind: she was from the beginning on a mission—to give people a good time because that's what life is all about for her. She's never claimed once to have a message of any kind. It's all been about a lot of laughter and a little bit of dancing. Paradoxically, though, perhaps that *was* her message all along.

8

BETTER THAN ALL THE REST

We Need Another Heroine

"I love quiet. If I want to have music, I make it. But who wants music when they can hear silence."

—Tina Turner, *Harper's*, 1996

One of the best ways to examine the social and cultural impact of a musical artist, apart from putting on headphones and listening to the recorded artifacts they left behind, is to explore the visual archive of videos they bestowed in order to both document and promote their songs. This is especially so in the case of so photogenic and dynamic a performer as Tina Turner, whose coming of age for the second time just happened to coincide with the birth and explosion of televised music videos at just the right historical moment for them to fully capture and capitalize on her style and substance.

It was a medium simply made for Tina's flashy persona, and along with many other large-scale performers, she would benefit hugely from this technology as well as revolutionize it as an artistic form of expression. Her dazzling videos, of which she made a nearly relentless truckload, were veritable *National Geographic* documentaries of the passion she wore on her sleeve or, rather, on her skirt. Her voice, her face, and even her legs were ideally suited to the vibrant strut that videos celebrate so viscerally.

Totally perfect for this visual narrative and having often described her concerts themselves as "small movies," Tina Turner's first videos appeared just in time to catch this new wave while it was in full early swing and also to define its future parameters with her personal sense of style.

More so even than in her supposedly straight acting roles in big-budget films, it is in her music videos that we see the tangible and tactile evidence for her charismatic appeal. They are scopophilia writ large.

Apart from certain celestials such as Madonna, Cher, or Michael Jackson, few music stars corraled the sheer raw theatrical power of Turner on film despite the surprising fact that her videos used no special effects or bombastic production gimmicks. She was her own personal special effect. They were deceptively simple and basic: just Tina standing or, more often, strolling and delivering the song in a straightforward manner. Her videos often feel like private diary entries being shared in an arrestingly intimate manner.

After artists have departed, taking their magical aura with them and independent of their fans' memories of seeing them live or hearing their albums, their videos are often the only historical archive remaining that one can consult in order to explore their theater craft. The best way to approach this exercise in appreciation, from my perspective, is for the reader, listener, and viewer to consider this brief curated selection.

To begin with a sense of her raw power, start out by watching those *accidental* videos that predate the medium, such as the easily available classic 1970–1971 performances Tina did with the Revue on the *Ed Sullivan Show* delivering "River Deep, Mountain High" and "Proud Mary." Then shift gears slightly and get a feel for her depth by watching what she was capable of later on in the videos she produced after she had become a lauded solo artist and consummate pop star. Notable among these mini-melodramas are several videos that reveal glimpses of some of her unique performing tactics, her strategy of appearing to be seemingly effortless after decades of hard practice.

Here is a brief appetizer. But just who *is* the person we're watching in all these videos? Apart from obviously being some kind of otherworldly creature, she's also a performer who doesn't need much phony or glitzy dazzle to turn us on. Her approach is so simple that it's almost shocking: sing the song—and sing it so realistically that we often barely register the fact that she's lip-synching the tune out in the middle of city streets. Who is she? An enigma for sure, to this day.

But it occurs to me that she is *confessing* her feelings in these songs and their videos. Even more surprising perhaps, she is still *testifying*, in the classical sense of that term, but she is also doing so in a *gospel-funk* manner: she's not worshipping at any altar anymore—she has *become* the altar.

It now seems fairly clear, at least in retrospect, that she was using an extraordinary survival mechanism through her work as a performer. She was bearing her life by baring her soul. Another one of her performance secrets also seems plain enough to me as well. She reminds me of one of the stage teachings of our own Swiftian satirist George Burns and the sage advice he gave to performers everywhere: the most important thing you need to have is authenticity; if you can fake that, you've got it made. She also was so authentic that you couldn't detect even a glimmer of the profound artifice that just had to be there. And it's in her music videos that her lack of guile most obviously celebrates itself. Turner appeared in a flock of fine ones, but some of her best are almost classically intimate self-portraits.

"BALL OF CONFUSION," 1982, DIRECTED BY DAVID MALLET: 3:50

Originally a soul song and hit single from the Temptations, it was covered by Tina Turner for volume 1 of the *Music for Quality and Distinction* series in 1982, using a very early modern synthesizer background. Charting surprisingly well in Europe, it was reissued on CD in 1991 in a remixed version and also in her boxed set of collected recordings, but the single was not issued in America. This would be the very first single with a music video from Turner, filmed as a live performance onstage with her female dancers and musicians; however, the music came from a tape with Tina lip-synching the lyrics. Mallet, who would go on to direct several of her biggest videos, also used special effects, such as stop-action animation and slow motion. Tina made history on this video as one of the first black artists to appear on MTV when the evolving network added it to its programming schedule. It was never officially released to home video.

"WHAT'S LOVE GOT TO DO WITH IT?," 1983, DIRECTED BY MARK ROBINSON: 3:47

Tina's first number one hit in America and the single released to promote the album *Private Dancer*, the song would win two Grammy Awards in 1985. Two video versions exist. The first, produced by John Caldwell, is black and white and somewhat melancholy, showing Tina close up with bare shoulders as several couples behind her are having troubled interactions. At the end, she goes up a spiral staircase in a leather dress, and her eyes are revealed in extreme close-up, leaving an overall impression of sadness, which perhaps explains the fact that it was rarely shown on television.

The second version, produced by Bud Schaetzle, is dramatically different in visual tone and emotional mood, with Tina filmed live in New York City wearing a jean jacket and black miniskirt. While looking at the East River, later emerging from a subway station, walking down busy public streets, and interacting with people, the song unfolds until the end, where she stops at a graffiti chalk drawing of the *Private Dancer* album cover image. The video won an MTV Music Award and is also available on *Simply the Best* on DVD.

"BETTER BE GOOD TO ME," 1983, DIRECTED BY BRIAN GRANT: 4:03

This fourth single from *Private Dancer* was a rock song originally done by the U.S. band Spider and won Turner her third solo Grammy Award for vocal performance in 1985. The music video, produced by Adrian Irving, was filmed at the Beverley Theater in Los Angeles in 1984 while Tina was taking a break from her concert tour with Lionel Ritchie. The theater was filled with fans who had been drawn from ads and her shows in order to stage a concert specifically for the filming, in which she wore racy trousers and a leather jacket with her band, including the guitarist from the British rock band Fixx, Jamie West-Oram. Cy Curnin is seen dancing the part of Turner's treacherous lover in a betrayal scene choreographed by Toni Basil.

A shorter version of this clip was first released on the *Private Dancer* EP, while a longer version also shows more of Curnin's guest appearance. The American music magazine *Cashbox* reported in July 1984 that an additional video was filmed at the same venue for "I Might Have Been Queen," though that song was never released as a single. In their assessment, they referenced her inimitable rough sassiness that illustrates her uncontested stature as rock's first lady. "'Better Be Good to Me' grinds with a menacing beat that rolls and charges forward with the energized Turner vocal"—not to mention her amazingly tight shiny black leather pants.

"PRIVATE DANCER," 1983, DIRECTED BY BRIAN GRANT: 5:25

Produced by Pam Grant, the title track and fifth single from *Private Dancer* is staged as a pop ballad of considerable heft. This is the song that Turner claims she never knew was actually about a high-class prostitute. Because company advertising isn't allowed in the United Kingdom, the lyric referencing the American Express company was altered to mention the British currency of pounds sterling, whereas all other commercial releases include the actual line about American Express.

The video was filmed in the London suburb of Lewisham at the Rialto Theater, revealing Turner as a "hostess" looking somewhat tired and pale as she is dancing with a man in a dance hall until she starts to dream. She experiences several different fantasy scenes, looking rather splendid in a sparkly sequined dress, until she wakes up and realizes her sad reality, turning away from her dance partner and running out of the room. A longer version, with an extended introduction and expanded instrumental section, was also produced.

✿   ✿   ✿

Sometimes it feels like her entire comeback decade was captured live on video. In fact, sometimes it seems like the entire 1980s era happened only on television. The question of why the time of the mid-1980s just seemed so right for Tina's resurgence was pondered by James Porter with his usual clarity. "Everybody loves a good hard-luck story. Even better, everybody loves to see a person bounce back from all that hard luck. During 1984–85, Tina was the Comeback Queen. I remember reading articles about older performers from the early rock & roll era, and they'd always be sure to throw in a reference to Tina, almost as if to say *if Tina Turner can do it, then I can too!* Even better, her comeback had permanence."

Porter also extolled Tina's virtues to me as a visionary trendsetter. "Tina has often claimed that the shift into a rockish sensibility was her idea. This is borne out by the fact that since her solo career started, she moved in that direction. Looking at her string of comeback hits in the eighties, she wasn't trying to assume parity with Anita Baker, Shirley Murdock, Whitney Houston, Gwen Guthrie, or fellow veteran Patti La-Belle. Listening to those songs now, she sounds like a high-tech ancestor to Melissa Etheridge or Sheryl Crow, only less acoustic. While Tina's status as an R&B institution shouldn't be taken away from her, she does deserve the status of being one of the earliest black female rockers, pre-dating everyone from Betty Davis to Nikki Hill.

"When most performers return from nowhere, they're seemingly around for a year, then disappear again. In Tina's case, she stayed in the spotlight with a whole new era of hits. It's hard to say why the time was so *right* for her. During the so-called Cosby decade, in the wake of Michael Jackson's success, there was a brief window of time when white America was open to black performers who had just enough of a pop sheen: Lionel Richie comes to mind, and to a lesser extent Billy Ocean.

"Tina Turner, survivor of a disastrous marriage and a career that almost went with it, might have been caught up in this wave. The difference was, Tina, along with Prince, had an overtly rock image, something not seen in mainstream black performers during the mid-80s. Lionel Richie was more pop, gunning straight for the middle-of-the-road with preppy clothing and a nice-guy image. Tina, even with sophisticated U.K. production, never let go of her hot rock mama persona. And she could pull it off with exquisite taste."

Similarly, I asked Aaron Cohen if he thought something in her character made her a special kind of heroine, one highly suited to the specific qualities of our time and culture, especially back in the 1980s. "Her willingness to take chances, her seemingly open perspective and her sheer endurance would make her a heroine for *any* time and culture." Indeed, and for me, a big part of her heroism was about her ability to share all of herself with us, especially the most vulnerable parts.

Always willing to bare her soul and be intimate about her feelings, Tina Turner has openly admitted that when she was experiencing her freedom for the first time after liberating herself from her cultish first marriage, back when she had no money to speak of and plenty of time to kill, she made her fair share of mistakes with men—none as big a mistake as her first huge one of course and probably no different from anyone else who was searching, experimenting, and maybe even playing around for the first time in her life. I'm pretty sure that her initial freedom also involved some degree of therapy, whether it was self-applied via her chanting or professional in nature, as in a talking cure.

Perhaps her preparation for the blockbuster biographical film on her life and music had, in a sense, also been a kind of talking cure, maybe one designed to contribute to the deprogramming necessary when someone escapes from a cult. But then, along came Erwin Bach, a sort of human remedy, it appeared. By all accounts a self-assured but shy and retiring individual who was accomplished in his own right, he didn't crave any attention or spotlight for himself; he even avoided it like the plague, it seems, and he was quite happy to let all the cameras be focused on his lady. Erwin seemed quite content to let her be adored in public while he adored her in private.

"I finally got involved with a man who cared about me," she told *Harper's*, "I even had a problem getting a relationship out of him, because he didn't want a high-profile life. He's beginning to accept this lifestyle now." One of her unique skills, one she seems to share with Bach, was how their separation of business life (especially his) and professional life (especially hers) and personal life (especially theirs) was a sound strategy. Their relationship has nothing to do with work, a sound choice given the well-known dangers of having tried it the other way.

One obviously valuable life lesson learned from her early experiences was never to mingle the business and private sides of her activities again the way she had when her husband was also her manager, her musical partner, her producer, and her spouse, especially since her new love was already a music executive with EMI at the commencement of their romantic alliance together. That way lies madness, she knew.

She also still has little time for the concept of retirement, although her highly publicized health issues have clearly curtailed much of her public barnstorming. She might entertain the *idea* of retirement quite often, as a vague, abstract concept perhaps, and she did actually make a halfhearted attempt once or twice, but the notion never really seemed suited to her temperament.

On April 13, 1999, VH1 invited the then mostly calm and peaceful pop star to take another break from listening to silence in order to star on its second-annual *Divas Live* TV special—and not only to star but also to open the whole extravaganza as the show's headline act. The other so-called divas (a word, remember, originally meaning *goddess* or divine creature much more than merely a prima donna) were Faith Hill, Cher, Chaka Khan, Mary J. Blige, and Whitney Houston. Perhaps Diana Ross and Barbra Streisand were unavailable for some reason.

In addition, a couple of young diva students were invited, Brandy and Leanne Rimes, and a special kind of diva all his own, Elton John, was also invited to represent a kind of reverse distaff side for the special event. That's a lot of diva energy in one place at one time. On March 23, Polygram Records had just released Elton's most recent outing, his personal take on the famous opera *Aida*, on which Tina had sung a song called "Easy as Life." In addition, they were also involved in discussions about a new project they'd both work on together later in the year.

All seemed ready steady go until during a full rehearsal the two divas clashed in an very vocal argument, emotional enough of a difference of diva opinion for Elton to run from the stage to his dressing trailer, followed by Tina, where they engaged in another mysterious scream-fest before Elton returned to the rehearsal and apologized to Turner in front of all the other musicians. The proposed concert tour together that year was abruptly shelved and eventually canned.

Despite this little bump in their path, the *Divas Live* show was an enormous televised hit concert event, with the two of them doing that ironic duet together on his quirky song "The Bitch Is Back." After wowing the crowd, Tina chortled, "Wow, divas and bitches, my goodness." Their follow-up number was an even more raucous barnstormer,

"Proud Mary," a song Tina introduced as being about the oldest diva of them all. In the middle of the song, they were joined by another star with equivalent diva-wattage, Cher, and the three of them rode the tune home in an exquisite vehicle of divine ham at its finest.

But of course 1999, like most years in this star's wild life, was a strange mixture of pleasure and pain, triumph and tragedy. In October of that year, her mother, Zelma, the person who never showed her an ounce of love and who abandoned her as soon as she could, passed away at age eighty-one (the same age Tina is at the time of this writing). The perhaps irreconcilable issues in their complicated relationship would remain forever unresolved, and though I'm no psychologist, I sense that Tina's own traumas of being abandoned contributed to her inability to ever abandon her first husband despite everything he did to her. She had somehow been hardwired, so to speak, to remain loyal long beyond the point at which it was in her own best interest.

She had tried to bridge the chasm between herself and Zelma, knowing that her mother had obviously benefited from the global success of her boisterous daughter, but without much maternal success. As she told *People* magazine, "She ended up living in a very nice big house, being very respected and recognized as 'Tina Turner's mother' and her last days were her best. My mother never really knew me—and my success she always attributed to Ike. She never thought it was me, so there was a gap between us."

It just seemed impossible for Tina's mother or her elder sister Alline (who passed away at age seventy-three in 2010) to ever really respect her for her obvious talent, with Tina telling *Us* magazine that "we were two separate people but Ike took all the credit, they thought he did everything. They weren't even smart enough to see that I mattered. Eventually I brought Ma to Paris, London, Switzerland and New York, to show her what the world was like, and she *still* didn't believe I had done everything for myself."

Tina chose not to attend her mother's funeral in order to avoid taking all the attention away from her on that special day. Besides, Ike was there, having been released from prison and signing autographs from his car window, and she wasn't about to share space with him again. So, fresh from that grief moment, Tina did the thing she always did best in order to sublimate her suffering, once again going back to work.

Throughout 1999, she'd been working on her next album, *Twenty Four Seven*, as well as the inevitable world tour that would follow. The record was her classic merging of pop and harder rock, with ample contributions from fellow stars who by now had all become stalwart collaborators: Terry Britten, the Gibb brothers, and Bryan Adams, among others.

TWENTY FOUR SEVEN (VIRGIN RECORDS)

Released in 1999. Produced by Johnny Douglas, Terry Britten, Brian Rawling, Mark Taylor. Personnel: Tina Turner, vocals; Bryan Adams, vocals; Pete Lincoln, acoustic guitar; Pino Palladino, bass; Peter Hope-Evans, harmonica; Duncan Mackay, Mike Stevens, Nichol Thompson, horns; Mark Taylor, keyboards; London Musicians Orchestra, strings; Steve Sidwell, trumpet. Engineers: Mark Lane, Ren Swan, Paul Wright. Mastering: Doug Stax. Duration: 47:09.

Whatever You Need (Harriet Roberts) 4:49 / All the Woman (Paul Wilson) 4:03 / When the Heartache Is Over (Graham Stack) 3:44 / Absolutely Nothing's Changed (Terry Britten, John O'Kane) 3:43 / Talk to My Heart (Johnny Douglas, Graham Lyle) 5:08 / Don't Leave Me This Way (Paul Barry) 4:19 / Go Ahead (James House, Anthony Little) 4:20 / Without You (Paul Wilson, Andy Watkins) 4:06 / Falling (Tim Fraser, Sol Connell) 4:21 / I Will Be There (Barry Gibb, Robin Gibb, Maurice Gibb) 4:37 / Twenty Four Seven (Terry Britten, Charlie Dore) 3:47

True to her words spoken to an audience at one of her last *Wildest Dreams* shows, she *was* back again three years later with this her tenth studio album as well as being the last record and last concert tour before her first of several *announced* retirements. This final record was produced by the same team behind Cher's *Believe* blockbuster among others. Another parallel, following the same kind of arrival at a similarly lofty pop peak shared by both Cher and Madonna, this time the album cover needed only her single, first name to identify the star: Tina.

For Jane Stevenson of the *Toronto Sun*, "*Twenty Four Seven* found Turner in an upbeat, adult, contemporary kind of mood. This collection came together after Turner and Cher's knockout performances at last

year's *VH 1 Divas* show, in which they both wiped the floor with Elton
John, Brandy and Whitney Houston." They both had also not joined the
all-cast finale version of Houston's epic "I'm Every Woman" for reasons
that have often been speculated about but never clearly defined.

Paul Elliot of *Q* magazine wrote of the record, "Gone is the grit of the
music she made with former husband Ike. . . . Tina Turner remains a
genuine superstar fifteen years after staging the most unlikely comeback
of the 80's. These eleven tracks of grown up pop should keep business
ticking over smoothly." It did, indeed, keep on ticking.

The last year of the twentieth century also provided another landmark
for Tina Turner, her sixtieth birthday (it's hard to believe as I write these
words that she turned eighty in 2019), and naturally enough, the best
way she could think of to celebrate her sixty years on earth was to stage
a gala concert in London.

It was, of course, also captured on film and released in a DVD titled
The Best of Tina Turner: Celebrate! And, just as naturally, she performed a mixture of her biggest hits—"River Deep" and "What's Love"
of course—mingled with tracks from her newest album, *Twenty Four
Seven*, tunes such as "When the Heartache Is Over," "Whatever You
Need," and the touching ballad "Talk to My Heart," dedicated to her
late lamented mother.

When asked by *People* magazine about the impact of her sixtieth
year, she responded that "it's just mental." And then she moved on to
shortly celebrate the upcoming millennium with a giant concert show
in Las Vegas, immediately following up with the release in January of
her new record in America, and on January 30, she performed both
"Proud Mary," by then for her a kind of private anthem, and "When the
Heartache Is Over," by then a kind of secular hymn, at the Super Bowl
pregame show in Atlanta, Georgia.

Once her album was in stores globally, she launched yet another tour
of 116 concert dates starting in Minneapolis and ending in Anaheim in
the middle of which she announced that this really *was* to be her *final*
tour, causing tickets to vanish in a feeding frenzy. This is one smart lady.
Commenting on how she managed to maintain the energy to be a rock-
and-roll dynamo at her age, she told *Rolling Stone*, "I've never worked
out at all. I'm a country girl and I lived a full country life, and it made
me strong I think."

Twenty Four Seven would be the last recording released by Turner apart from *All the Best* in 2004, *Tina: The Platinum Collection* in 2008, *Love Songs* in 2014, and *The Greatest Hits* in 2018, all compilations of past songs. There were, however, still some surprises in store for fans: a series of non-pop albums with a Buddhist and interfaith content that showed her shifting gears once again. Just as she had promised a few years earlier, eventually she was going to give up pop and rock music and concentrate on spiritual pursuits and teachings. Until then, though, her party train kept on rolling.

On December 6, 2000, she played the last stop on her farewell tour to a humungous sold-out crowd of 18,000 squirming and screaming fans, who may as well have been attending a Beatles concert, at the Arrowhead Auditorium in Anaheim near downtown Los Angeles. The entertainment industry bible *Hollywood Reporter* stated that "Tina Turner, 61, took in $80 million in ticket sales for 95 concerts," and according to *Pollster*, was the highest grossing concert attraction of the entire first year of the 21st Century.

Her absolutely mind-boggling concert at Wembley Stadium in London had been captured on film and released as *One Last Time in Concert*, and you really have to witness how she dazzled the crowd next to her backup dancers (her flowers), each of whom was about a third of her age. She is simply beyond belief.

✿   ✿   ✿

Sure enough—and like clockwork—after four years, Hollywood came buzzing around her once again like a bee around a flower, this time potentially in an even more exotic and over-the-top role than her *Mad Max* Aunty Entity turn. The Associated Press reported in 2004 that Tina Turner was in discussions with Merchant Ivory Productions to play the lead role in a film called *The Goddess* about the Indian deity Kali/Shakti, a female deity of destruction, fertility, and renewal. "Famous for power-packed musical performances in high heels and leather miniskirts, the 64-year-old singer would star as the Hindu symbol for female power and energy in a film being planned by Ismail Merchant and James Ivory, the Indian-Anglo duo best known for their series of lavish period pieces."

The announcement set off an immediate backlash in the orthodox Hindu community, feeling that her participation was an "outrage" and complaining in mass protests that her reputation as a "sex icon" disqualified her from the role—somewhat ironic considering that Shakti also symbolizes creative energy and specifically feminine sexuality in keeping with the dualist principles at play in the Hindu philosophy.

Ismail Merchant posted a response in the *Times of India* stating that the protests by religious groups were based on "misconceptions about the film," one that was actually being made in a "spirit of reverence." He said that "Tina Turner is one of the great artists of our time and has also been a practicing Buddhist for the last twenty years, an artist of such international stature should be welcomed."

It's hard not to resort to an apt pun for this film, perhaps likening it to *Doom with a View*, given how vociferous the backlash was, but Merchant seemed to have his heart set on it despite the apparent obstacles. He tried to clarify his and her positions by pointing out that they had traveled together to India in preparation for the collaborative project, seeking to experience some of the many cultural and spiritual wonders found there. Their story, he further tried to explain to the anxious religious community, was to be based in part on a tale in the Kathasaritasagara, a huge archive of folktales, and it would take place in ancient India.

"Contrary to the accusations of the objectors," Merchant expressed in a Merchant Ivory press statement designed to quell the commotion, "nobody is going to sing and dance on the back of a tiger, the Goddess is not going to be half-naked, or a sex symbol. She is not meant to be a specific representation of a single deity, whether Kail, Laxmi or Druga. She is instead Shakti, the universal feminine energy which is manifest in Kali, Druga, Mother Mary, Wicca, and each and every woman on the planet."

Merchant made a valiant if hopeless effort to state that no one has the right to dictate how one should worship the Goddess or to discriminate against an artist who seeks to portray Her. "The Goddess spreads her compassion and her wisdom to all people, whether Hindu, Muslim, or Christian, or even atheist. A true devotee should join us in celebrating a film that will spread the life-affirming message of Devi all over the world." He further expressed his hope that the majority would not be swayed by a few extremists who are attempting to create a crisis where there is none. "I am encouraged in this hope knowing that all Hindus recognize its central message: all creation is one family."

Meanwhile, the *Independent* reported on Turner's typically optimistic viewpoint when it came to all her potential projects: "The cosmic energy of Shakti attracted me to this film and attracted the film to me. It signifies new beginnings." Alas, many were indeed swayed by the minority view, and further complicating the planned collaboration may have been a few health issues that began to emerge in Turner's life at the time. To this day, there has been no sign of the challenging and intriguing film about communal sharing being manifested in the real world.

One other powerful aspect of Turner's life, however, did appear to concretely manifest in her life later on. She would assume the role of goddess after all—but in her own way as usual. It was part of her private romantic life and was also something she once adamantly claimed would *never* happen again: she was going to take a new husband into her ongoing story. Marriage was asserting itself again in a most unusual way and after a long period of waiting on the part of the groom: her companion, lover, friend, and partner of many years, Erwin Bach.

Bach, a German music producer, actor, and managing director of EMI Music in Switzerland, was born on January 24, 1956, at more or less the time when sixteen-year-old Anna Mae Bullock started going with her elder sister Alline to the Club Manhattan in East St. Louis to secretly watch the Kings of Rhythm perform their sizzling boogie-blues music. There is some confusion about how Bach and Turner met.

According to most sources, they officially met at an EMI record label party in 1985, roughly nine years after the divorce filing from her first husband. She was still vulnerable enough to have her insecurities about any future love affairs. But she was also brave enough to share them as well. No one could ever convey them as accurately or as candidly as she did herself in her memories of late but true romance, something she would share in her Davis-curated memories she called *My Love Story*.

"The wig is a critical part of the Tina Turner look. If I walked on-stage with natural hair, the audience wouldn't recognize me, they'd say 'where's Tina?' I've always considered it an extension of myself. I will never stop wearing the wig. I always ran the risk of meeting a man who might object: a man who would have a problem becoming romantically involved with *Tina*, with her bountiful hair and glamorous trimmings, but waking up with unadorned Anna Mae. What if he was disappointed by the real me? I was always a bit nervous about taking that chance."

At least that was what she told herself until that fateful day when she and manager Roger Davies flew into Cologne to prepare for a busy set of shows in the Private Dancer Tour during 1984–1985. As they walked in, a youngish man stepped out from behind some columns to greet them. At first, she thought it was just some fan, but Roger recognized him right away and warmly greeted him with "Hello Erwin." He stretched his arms out and said, "Hello." As she did not know who he was, she took a few steps back. Then the formal introductions were made, and Turner found herself to be overwhelmingly attracted to this "unusually handsome" man.

She has since stated that as they got into the car together, her heart was beating rapidly. But naturally, as she relates, that dilemma wasn't ever a really big concern since she was so busy with the tour back then that she never really had time for a boyfriend no matter how handsome. Touring had become a way of life for the fabulously popular entertainer, who from her youth had always been a perpetual energy performer on the road, but this time she was actually enjoying it, although it did leave little to no time for much of a personal life to speak of.

But the real surprise for her wasn't the special Mercedes jeep he had brought for her to use but rather the man himself. "Apparently, the keys this charismatic stranger held in his hand were to my heart, which suddenly started to loudly beat and drown out all other sounds. All I could think of was 'oh my God, I am not ready for this!' It didn't matter that he was younger, or that he lived in Europe. I think I needed love. I was a free woman, free to choose. And I chose Erwin."

Further, in keeping with her Buddhist faith, in her *Love Story* she confided that she was certain they had been together before in another life and has also repeatedly addressed the obvious elephant in the room from the public's point of view: the age difference. She admitted that though the world thought of him as "Tina's younger man," in reality she felt like he was sixty and *she* was sixteen. "It was time for me to take care of *me*."

And much to her surprise and joy, a big part of taking care of herself in that way also ended up including letting Erwin take care of her too (once she became vulnerable enough with her health concerns to let him do so) to express the true extent of his fondness for her. Apparently, he charmed her into letting him do that too, just as he had charmed her sister and stern mother when they finally met him. As the world now knows, he even went so far as to eventually charm her into accepting his generous donation of one of his own kidneys when it was proven necessary for her survival later on.

Yes, this clearly was a genuine case of love at first sight. He took a bit more convincing, however, but soon enough, they were dating; in fact, they dated over the course of the next twenty-seven years. As the years went by, the relationship only strengthened. He helped her with her children and was a source of constant support. In the ensuing years, Bach proposed to Turner at least two times before they finally got married in July 2013 in Zurich, where they currently reside.

Turner has often referred to him as a man who made her feel dizzy when she first laid eyes on him. The first time he actually proposed to her was in 1989, three years after they'd already been together as life partners. At the time, she was fifty, and he was thirty-one; she knew how she felt about him but had been understandably cautious about marriage for years. Her response was a gentle admission that she didn't have an answer yet to the question. So, a patient man by all accounts, he waited a couple of decades and proposed again, next time while on board a friend's yacht sailing around the Mediterranean.

This time, she accepted; she was seventy-three years old, and in her young mind, she was getting married for the first time since the initial attempt as a twenty-one-year-old had not exactly been what it appeared to be at the time. Besides, her first husband took her to a brothel on their wedding night as the commencement of a long nightmare. This one, almost as if in some kind of fateful compensation for everything she'd been through, was more of a fairy tale, one unfolding in a floating castle, the Chateau Algonquin just outside of Zurich, where Bach had been working for the past fifteen years.

When they pulled up to the wedding site in a black Rolls-Royce convertible, they did so to the sound of what Tina must have considered a kind of theme song for her: Frank Sinatra's "My Way" ("The record shows, I took the blows and did it my way"). The walking-down-the-aisle music was provided by her musical friend and frequent album collaborator Bryan Adams, crooning his ballad "All for Love" ("Let's make it all for one and all for love").

She felt that magic was in the air, including the perfectly silly but romantically perfect performance staged by Bach and about fifteen of his friends dressed in Mexican sombreros serenading the crowd with surreal mariachi music. She was having the time of her life after working supernaturally hard during seriously hard times, all on her own without help from anyone. She can certainly be allowed to think in that moment that her life was blessed and even expressed her basically Buddhist notion: this must be my nirvana.

But 2013 was anything but a rosy nirvana-rama time. Three months later, she woke up suddenly with excruciating pains in her head and legs, barely able to call out to her new husband for help, caught helplessly in the midst of a serious stroke. The next thing she knew (or at least knew for sure) was that she was connected up to a lifesaving dialysis machine in the hospital in Zollikon, not far from where she lives, with only 20 percent kidney function and the need to become physically strong enough to accept a vitally needed surgical transplant.

Years of high blood pressure, possibly either misdiagnosed or ignored, had compromised her kidneys, now being further complicated by her stroke. Preciously guarding their privacy for several years, Bach had tended to his wife's treatments and kept everything on track during her sessions to have her blood "washed." Undergoing these rigors of course prompted Turner to do two things: look at every day through the clarifying lens of impermanence, to which her Buddhism already inclined her, and also to reflect on her good fortune in meeting the true love of her life.

The image of Tina Turner actually being photographed smiling while connected to her lifesaving medical machine and shared with the world is quite an eye-opener. Only the down-to-earth but usually terrifically glamorous Tina would have the gumption or honesty to share with so many people who care about her what she was going through at this stage in a life already incredible by anyone's standards. The lady's got guts, no doubt about it.

✿   ✿   ✿

Once she officially *retired* after her triumphant new millennium tours, she was often amused when people asked her "what do you do now that you're retired?" because she always imagined that that was the whole idea: you don't *do* anything anymore, you just live. But when people who loom so large on the public stage drop away into private relaxation, their admirers start to imagine they've already passed away, a notion that she put to rest by emerging from her seclusion in 2005 to be honored along with Cher and Tony Bennett at the Kennedy Center Awards for contributions to American culture. She even got the distinct pleasure not only of being seen and worshipped again but also of seeing Beyoncé do a spirit-lifting rendition of her signature song (or one of them anyway), "Proud Mary," knowing full well that it was great dames like herself who made artists like Beyoncé even possible.

Her so-called seclusion was, of course, anything but lonely or immobile, first and foremost because she was traveling the world with her erstwhile Erwin and indulging in one of her favorite hobbies: decorating her houses with art and design treasures. She had spent the last couple of years peacefully planning, organizing, and preparing, confidently orchestrating the reasons for her retirement, her downsizing, and her dedication to focusing on what was truly important. She was taking full control of her own life once again. Do you know the wonderful expression, if you want to make God laugh, just tell him your plans? That was her wistful way of viewing it.

In retrospect, that's what she must have felt she heard, the creator's laughter, because "control" definitely wasn't a word that could be applied to her current circumstances. One answer to that public question about what you do when you're retired might just as well be that, sometimes, survival itself is a full-time job, just like being righteous is. Brought into the hospital in a wheelchair, in itself a shock for someone used to strutting so magnificently, she was gripped with the primal fear that comes with immobility.

Especially overwhelming for someone so used to commanding her stallion-like frame to do her bidding was the bizarre idea that Tina Turner could ever be paralyzed. Her physician Dr. Vetter explained how the stroke had affected her so powerfully. Her whole right side was numb, and she'd have to get physiotherapy to learn to walk again, forget about strutting.

She remained hospitalized for about ten days, during which time she did what we might expect Tina Turner to do: talk herself into believing that she would fight her way back to health.

One powerful concern was how the news and its attendant public gossip would become fodder for whisperings across the globe: Tina Turner has mystery illness, Tina Turner recovering from stroke, is Tina Turner still alive, and so on. She tried to eliminate all such thoughts and focus on her recovery, a long struggle involving acupuncture, traditional Chinese medicine, meditation, and chanting, her own personal form of prayer.

The physical effects of the stroke lingered for a long time. Even in 2018, five years later, she still had trouble with facial muscles, getting up, walking, and even signing her signature. That's when her doctor told his despondent patient that her high blood pressure, perhaps causing the stroke or perhaps just latent for years, was impacting kidney function, now only risen to a still-low 35 percent. She was sent to a specialist, Dr. Jorg Bleisch, a nephrologist who needed to monitor her frequently and who also began prescribing intensive blood pressure medication.

Then the severe vertigo set in, and she was sent to Dominick Straumann, a neurologist at an acclaimed Swiss research facility who provided treatments to rectify her otoconia, a loosening of crystals in the ear canal causing the dizziness. The procedures, more physically and mentally taxing than anything she had ever experienced, were taking effect slowly but surely. As she put it in her *Love Story* recollections, "How did I go from being the picture of health, a cover girl and a bride, for God's sake, to being *Job*?," referencing the biblical figure who was forced to endure so many grueling tests and threatening trials sent his way.

Then, in a drastic case of just one damn thing after another, her kidneys began to totally fail her, unable to do their job of eliminating waste from the body and endangering their host, the person they ostensibly "belong" to. In this case, someone else's kidney may have to be found for a renal transplant, where at least one fully functioning kidney can more or less do the job of two. Historically, kidney transplant recipients live much longer than those who remain on the dialysis scrubbing regimen as well as generally have much better quality of life while doing so.

Then—yes, yet another *then*—in January 2016 while getting used to the idea of recuperation, therapy, and transplants, and being forced to embrace, to some degree, the limits of being an invalid, Turner was stunned by the news that she had been diagnosed with intestinal cancer. She had a carcinoma with several malignant polyps, requiring a whole range of surgical interventions and further treatments. This was one of those last-straw situations it appeared, one that forced even the ebullient Tina to become despondent enough to ask her beloved Erwin if he were sorry now that he had married an *old woman*.

But one thing she could be fully grateful for, apart from meeting him in the first place, was the fact, as she was discovering more and more, that this was not a normal man. His optimism and love of life and his love for her seemed to shine through and lift her up and over these occasional dark times, including her surgery only a month after the diagnosis, during which part of her intestine was removed and it was hoped that the cellular growth had been arrested. But the aggression against her immune system from the cancer and the surgery was also simultaneously further weakening her renal system and her already compromised kidneys.

She was refusing her doctors' attempts to persuade her to continue with dialysis. Being a woman then in her seventies, one with cancer, and one who had a certain strength of character, to say the least, she was also one who rejected out of hand the idea of living forever connected to a machine. Instead, she began valiantly investigating end-of-life possibilities, such as assisted dying and supportive suicide, and even joined an organization called Exit just in case. Another Swiss group called Dignitas was also available to her should she need to undertake final steps.

But it was then that her partner Erwin declared that he would give her one of his own kidneys. She tried to get him to consider his own future, given his younger age, but he announced that their future *was* his future, and by doing so he once more gave her the hope she so desperately needed to carry on with the full-time job of survival. His perspective, which was certainly not lost on the part of his Buddhist wife, was that giving was also a gift to the giver. If you give, he believed, you receive. There's that surprising concept of karma rearing its hopeful head in her life one more time.

So for the next nine months, the clinic's dialysis chair would become the center of not only her life but also pretty much of their universe. Their shared kidney transplant was scheduled for April 7, 2017. She whiled away the hours with memories, with reading her favorite spiritual books, with homeopathic remedies, and with meditation and chanting, but mostly she spent her time being three people at once: Anna Mae Bullock, Tina Turner, and Mrs. Erwin Bach.

Subsequent to what appeared, medically at least, to be a quite successful transplant, her husband also kept her busy, knowing that the best way to help his wife would be to help her continue being Tina Turner, the woman he'd fallen in love with almost thirty years before. One day, he brought about ten people into their home to discuss a creative project they had all been developing: a Broadway musical theater production called *Tina: The Tina Turner Musical*, the story of her life in song and dance and drama live onstage.

After some coaxing and cajoling, she must have realized that this theatrical extravaganza was something meant to be, so with her usual resignation in the face of fate (*her* fate, that is), she agreed to give it her blessing. Her strategy was to become healthy enough to join the theater group for the official announcement of the show's creation on October 18, 2017, at which they would also present the talented young actress chosen to portray Tina: Adrienne Warren.

Six months after her major organ transplant surgery, her body seemed to be already threatening to reject Erwin's gifted kidney by this stage, and she wondered if she'd be in good enough shape to do what she eventually did do, as if by sheer force of willpower: dress up as Tina Turner once again and join young Adrienne onstage at the launch reception to sing "Proud Mary" together. She was apparently still the living embodiment of a key existential principle: I can't go on, I'll go on.

The official grand-opening show of the *Tina Turner Musical* took place six months later in April 2018 at the Aldwych, one of London's oldest operating theaters. Once the show kicked off with its opening number, "Nutbush City Limits," she realized she was in for a truly surreal experience. Both Warren and the actor chosen to play her first husband, Kogna Holdbrook-Smith, turned in inspired performances, even if it was spooky and unsettling to see someone who so captured Ike's appearance and essence in performance.

Her closing remarks to the audience that opening night, after a hugely successful show mounted in her honor, were as wise as they were revealing. They encapsulated everything she had learned in her whole life, a life of harrowing hellish trauma and yet also a life of blissful blessings beyond her wildest dreams. She remembered an old Buddhist expression: *it is possible for us to transform poison into medicine.*

Sometimes it seems like that might be the entire story of her whole life right there, hiding in that one deeply spiritual sentence. Next up? The Broadway stage premiere of *Tina: The Musical* in New York for the fall of 2019. And like her other favorite Sinatra song once said, if she can make it there, she'll make it anywhere. And, once again, she did just that.

HEAVY WEATHER IN A DRESS

The Legacy of Tina Turner

"What you've heard about me is all true. I change the rules, to do what *I* wanna do."

—Tina Turner, *Rolling Stone*, 1984

Apart from my own personal interpretations and lengthy listening to her whole musical arc and after speaking to so many fans, critics, journalists, and historians of both the soul and the rock styles, it becomes abundantly clear that Tina Turner is exactly as Winston Churchill once described the inscrutable East: she is "a riddle, wrapped in a mystery, inside an enigma." Most crucially and often overlooked, however, was his follow-up observation: perhaps there is a key. So many different perspectives on the same public persona: shy but raunchy, humble but haughty, meditative but maniacal.

Tina Turner was obviously so prismatic a personality and character that she was almost a self-fulfilling prophecy—but of the good kind. She was also that rare breed of being about whom all commentary and observation, even the ones that are totally divergent or drastically opposed to each other, are still absolutely accurate. She was, in other words, a figure whose creative shadow was so huge that almost everything contradictory one could say about her was equally true. Is there indeed a key?

Much more than a mere survivor, Tina Turner was actually a sort of alchemist, and she seemed to specialize in transformation. To paraphrase Victor Bockris, biographer of the beat writer William Burroughs, Turner's career is counted out in transformations. There is no one single Turner. And since there's clearly more than one of her, there must therefore logically be more than one legacy. John Corcelli expressed to me a twofold appreciation of her inherent legacy: "Her ability to embrace her own pain and to cultivate an ever expanding audience. Tina Turner should be remembered as a much beloved entertainer whose loyal audience was absolutely always rewarded with a great performance."

Totally true, after all, we've already witnessed about four of five Turners, and who knows, more of them may be on their way. And that too is also a big part of her legacy: everything she ever touched seemed to turn to gold. She turned Ike Turner into gold and then proceeded to turn her own solo music into gold.

Legacy can be such a loaded word. It sometimes sounds so imperious. And yet in the case of someone as imperial as Tina Turner, it also seems ideally appropriate. Her legacy in a nutshell? Tenacity—apart from the music itself and the presence of the person who gave it to us all as a collective gift: her refusal to be repressed, suppressed, or depressed and her inability to ever give up. She didn't give up in her difficult childhood, not in her challenging private relationship, not in the creative drought subsequent to her split, and not even in the life-threatening illness that eventually even someone as strong as she could not fully combat. But through it all and in her own words, "I stayed on course."

Her legacy of tenacity is something lasting not only in the way it affected her many fans but also in the impact it had on the entire music industry and her fellow artists. In *The Guardian* in mid-2018, Daphne Brooks examined the making of a rock-and-roll revolutionary when she previewed the new live musical stage production about the sixty-year career of a singer who crossed racial lines and overcame violent oppression to revolutionize music. "With singularity, Turner merged sound and movement at a turning point in rock history, navigating and reflecting back the technological innovations of a new pop-music era in the late 60's and early 70's.

"She catapulted herself to the forefront of a musical revolution that had long marginalized and overlooked the pioneering contributions of

African-American women, then she remade herself again when most pop musicians were hitting the oldies circuit. Turner's character has always been a charged combination of mystery as well as light, melancholy mixed with a ferocious vitality that often flirted with danger. Perfect, for a big budget musical."

Brooks also put Turner's long artistic shadow into context very well by name checking the people who probably wouldn't even exist without her influence, reminding us that way beyond Beyoncé, Turner's legacy remain rich and varied in the diverse worlds of pop. From the dark soul of a Meshell Ndegocello to the white funk vocalist Nikka Costa and every time Rhianna takes to the stage and even rapper Cardi B, they all owe Turner a huge debt of in-your-face female funk. Sisters, as the catchy feminist song had suggested, are doing it for themselves.

I've always liked the way Lucy O'Brien put it in her definitive history of women in rock, pop, and soul, *She Bop*, when studying the "natural woman" that Tina Turner so powerfully exemplifies. "A female assertion of identity within a male-dominated sphere is arguably an act of protest in itself, from Madonna's populist attack on Catholicism to Tina Turner strutting her survivalist ethic in stadiums throughout the world."

What's appealing about that assessment is that it suggests that she is a protesting folksinger of sorts, even without realizing it, just by being herself. And as O'Brien tellingly quoted Turner from her own feminist perspective, "People like me not just because I have big hair, lips and legs. I've got credibility!" She does indeed, holding out for her own independence and freedom, refusing to go backward. "It wasn't until British designer/pop producer Heaven 17 persuaded her into the studio to record a cover version of 'Ball of Confusion' for their 1981 nostalgia compilation album that she realized she could make the move away from oldies soul (on her cabaret circuit) to a more commercial sound, wrapping her raunch and emotional vocal style around such anthems as 'What's Love Got to Do with It?' and 'We Don't Need Another Hero.'"

In a great section of her book about soul and funk queens, O'Brien refers to Tina Turner as a kind of feminist pharaoh, a Hatshepsut (an Egyptian queen) taking her throne. "Turner has several weapons at her disposal; the constitution of a horse, good legs, and a solid background in raunchy r & b. Allied to this is a penchant for a lion's mane and outrageously red lipstick. Turner knows that she's a ham, and that this is show business. It's a strand of r & b that went deeper than the girl-group sound, it was the gospel-derived dynamics of deep southern soul, a grainy gutsy genre spearheaded by Stax-label artists such as Carla Thomas and Mavis Staples. These artists, together with the blues belter Etta James, paved the way for full-throated stars like Tina Turner."

I've long felt that Christian Wright's take on her vocal chords in *Trouble Girls* captured her essence. "She has that voice, completely unique, organic but unnamed, as if it were left off the table of the elements. She's an accident of fate. Her voice still sounds like freedom." Turner knows her voice doesn't sound conventionally "pretty" or sometimes even good. She can sound lovely when she wants to but long ago learned that people don't want that from her: they actually want her sounding as raspy as possible. She had obviously also discovered very early on that she could be a sexy rock chick at the same time as being a free and emancipated woman.

Another angle of approach, to give her a context in the women's movement that prevailed during her middle years, was ably provided by Ellen Willis in her insightful preface to *Women in Rock*, a great assessor of the politics of that social liberation wave that still demanded the right to rock. Answering the question posed by Karen Durbin in *Ms.* magazine of whether a feminist can love the world's greatest rock-and-roll band, Willis wryly observed astutely, "I try to explain that love didn't preclude tension and conflict. My own personal subject was the bloody crossroads where rock and feminism meet: a sense of entitlement to seize the world, uninhibited by that old feminine commandment, thou shalt not offend."

That sensibility aligns perfectly with what Turner may have been demanding for herself, again without entirely being fully conscious of the social side of her innate and often hidden feminism. "Music that boldly and aggressively laid out what the singer wanted, loved, hated—as good rock and roll did—challenged us to do the same, encouraged my struggle for liberation. Where women's liberation and musical liberation intersect: rock and roll as a catalyst for utopian inspiration, when you live in a world that *could* be."

These observations (and a few others) will help us situate Turner's legacy on the radically redrawn map of 1980s music in general and women's role in it in particular. They help us revisualize how powerfully she must have appeared to be coming into her own, just at the time when the rest of society was finally there to fully support her kind of heavy-duty assertion of female self. It's also an angle that Christian Wright touched on well in the book *Trouble Girls*, which was mostly a chronicle of the distaff side in heavy rock and even punk circles.

"She definitely blazed a trail," Wright asserted, "but her voice echoes way beyond genre: *Private Dancer*, the 1984 hit-filled album that marked her renaissance, contained flashes of rock and roll, but it's really a perfect pop record made with synthesizers and various producers. With Turner though, songs almost aren't the point. In anyone else's hands, 'What's Love Got to Do with It?' would sound like the manufactured pop conceit it is instead of the anthem of sexual liberation it became."

However, one proviso I would again add is that pop *should* be taken seriously, that it's a dark mirror, and that the best pop on earth (think of the Brian Wilson album *Pet Sounds* or the Beatles' *Revolver* from 1966) is an ideal reflecting lens of the times and also a great work of art.

"Never mind that she was forty-five years old when she made her comeback," Wright continued, "and that she competed in the pop marketplace with newcomers such as Madonna and Sade, for whom she'd opened the door—she was already legendary. She'd become an icon for black people because she'd crossed over in segregated times; for women because she'd succeeded in the predominantly male world of music; and for herself because she'd made it through all of it alive."

By now, it's pretty much an accepted truism that Tina Turner is a feminist icon. But it was not always thus. Like many of you who either saw it live or watched later footage, I can still vividly recall Tina appearing with her entire strutting Revue and the ominously swaying Ike on Ed Sullivan's Sunday-night variety show. I can also recall pondering what Gloria Steinem thought about this spectacle: you've come a long way baby—or not.

There was Tina, in her tiny micro-miniskirt squirming all over the stage and on occasion even doing a reprise of her notorious microphone massage trick. She was a paradox for sure, one that Laurie Stras correctly nominated as a "Bold Soul Trickster" in her *She's So Fine* study. Her chapter title on Tina was of course a play on the title of one of her singles from 1969, "Bold Soul Sister," from the album *The Hunter*. I also recall thinking how stunning it must have been for largely white middle-class audiences to be exposed to that much black woman-ness all at once, in one fell swoop. I'm still stunned, in fact.

Her "Bold Soul Sister" wasn't especially one of their better outings, really mostly a channeling of the basic James Brown ethos pumped up with enough estrogen to suit her special vibe, but Stras's name change in her study of rock femininity is a telling indicator of two things for me: Tina's ironic status as a combination of conflicting images, both a hot rock chick turning on crowds *and* a towering feminist metaphor for surviving oppression. I've always believed that she was indeed a trickster since, as I've suggested, I feel that she was largely a female impersonator (I don't mean that in a mean way) who was masquerading as a character quite at odds with her actual shy and retiring nature, as hard a notion as that might be to accept.

She would really become a feminist icon only later on after her private life had become glaringly public and when she finally left Ike. From my perspective, though, she really assumed the true mantle of female icon only once she had also left behind the label of rhythm-and-blues singer (she was never ever really a soul singer anyway) and when she also even left behind the label of rock singer. I think she accidentally ascended to the throne of feminist icon largely when she had become a certified pop star transcending every racial and gender line altogether— a planetary-style citizen.

After all, in her last great concert at England's Wembley Stadium in 2000, she was still flanked by a new assortment of her song and dance girls, all roughly a third of her age, and *still* slithering while step dancing across the stage. But something had changed in her, irrevocably altered in her own essence since she had first done that exact same act (more or less) in her earliest show business days forty years ago. Then it was at the behest and direction of her boss man, but now, she was and still is (as the feminist anthemic pop song from Aretha and Annie has it) a sister doing it for herself.

Laurie Stras ruminated very incisively about femininity in pop and rock music, and she dissected how the male maestro needed to make ever more behind-the-scenes claims of credit and control in order to co-opt or diminish the role of *embodied voices* on stage or in the recording studio. "This was evidenced by the innovative sounds and performances for which the Revue became increasingly acclaimed but which were often downplayed as the result of *his* supposed creative brilliance rather than Tina's obvious significance. Thus Ike's control over Tina and the Ikettes was always a familiar story, that of continuing to dilute women's agency."

As Jacqueline Warwick has pointed out in *Girl Groups, Girl Culture*, the majority of women who succeed in music have to contend with the tacit assumption that it is the men in their lives who are the actual architects of their success. Warwick has approached the issue from an angle that allows her to position the bodies producing the music at the center rather than in the outskirts of this dynamic equation. That insight is crucial to understanding the age-old Svengali scenario, the conceit that it was *he* who created her look and movements (apart from the obvious ability he had in recognizing her innate skills as a young woman), but, as that author so ably stressed, "It is Tina who *materialized* these extraordinary elements of her performances."

She also clarified that it was Tina's "embodied voice, her physical presence on the stage, her costumed moving body to which the eye, heart and soul are drawn. Perhaps that's exactly why," she concluded, "that despite his desire to control the show, Ike was so profoundly frustrated with her." Warwick has clearly identified Tina as a *signifier*, a symbol that conveys meaning through her actions, stating that "this gives her tremendous agency and control over her career (real or imagined) since no matter what material she is given to sing, no matter what musicians she works with, it is that very materiality of her voice that defines her work."

It is also always the inherent hard but aching quality of Tina's voice that identified her with the mostly male-modeled rock and roll she always signified: a bigness, a rawness, and a hard-edged assertiveness that is aggressive and demanding but still always feminine too, if slightly strained and choked. In that very contradiction resides her power.

So much so, in my opinion, that it was in her later post-Ike rock and pop material that she eventually and ironically assumed that feminist crown, even though she still wore it while also wearing her exploding red wigs and miniskirts teetering perilously on dangerously sexy stilettos. True, she still remains today what she was back then: an *embodied meaning*.

❖   ❖   ❖

For me, the other word that most aptly applies to Tina Turner is "serendipity," the operation of meaningful coincidence in our lives that the psychologist Carl Jung referred to as synchronicity. Of course someone with the philosophical or spiritual inclinations of a Buddhist Tina would also call it by its more colloquial name: karma. Let's stick simply with serendipity, though, since it sounds slightly less ominous and perhaps a little more lighthearted.

It was serendipity that caused her broken-up family to move to St. Louis and serendipity for her to follow shortly thereafter and by chance to enter the field of a certain nightclub with a hot rhythm-and-blues band performing. It was serendipity for her to get up and sing along without the slightest bit of formal training and also serendipity for her to be driven by violence forcefully into an independent career she may never even have had if her musical partner had simply been a nicer guy. It was also an ultra chance encounter with someone who passed on to her the Buddhist spiritual practice that she credits with saving her life back then. That feels like supersized serendipity to me.

It was even an exotic brand of serendipity that she ended up making her final solo album at all and going on a blockbuster final tour: the mysterious argument with Elton John that scuttled a planned joint concert tour together. Initially, it was her intention to go on the road with Elton at that point, and a shared project was in the works, but then came their ill-fated encounter at that *Divas Live* show. During a rehearsal with the whole band, Tina stopped the music and went over to tell Elton how she thought a certain passage should be played. Boom.

It didn't take long to realize that she had made a mistake when she thought she needed to show him how to play "Proud Mary." The mistake was that you don't show Elton John how to play his piano. He just went into a rage, and he said it was wrong. It was. The combined tour plans were jettisoned, and instead Turner went directly into the studio to record her final album, which might never have been made without the infraction that caused their fight. Ironically, the supposed trouble she got into at that moment was caused by what? By wanting the piano music to sound right for the song she was singing?

A bit of sour serendipity there perhaps, but nonetheless it manifested a whole unexpected album and a huge unplanned final tour that might otherwise never have happened. Meanwhile, while practically on her way into the studio to record her final *Twenty Four Seven* album, she took a few moments to perform "Proud Mary" live at the Super Bowl pregame show. Just to limber up. Guts galore.

About her perception of what performing meant to her in general and what she thought would be her final concerts felt like personally, she had an awareness that has been with her from the start. She knows that it's all a play, an act. For that single moment in time, she's acting in a small movie so to speak. That's why all the action and interplay between her and her girls always felt so natural to us as observers. It's real life onstage for those two hours. And even though she had been playing that part for almost half a century—and maybe even herself suspecting that she should hang up her dancing shoes—because she realizes she is at heart a living embodiment of rock and roll, she was happy to do it all one more time. She wanted people to see her at her best.

But since we're talking about Tina Turner here, she naturally had quite a different definition for the word "retirement" than most other normal people might. As usual, she didn't so much break the rules as refuse to admit that any rules even existed to break. Her eventual retreat from public life would be as slow and steady as her return to it had been. When *Vanity Fair* magazine asked her what her motto in life was and how she kept on going, she responded, "I put my right foot forward."

In a way, approaching her swan song phase, it must have been the case that one part of her was looking forward to simply being Anna Mae Bullock again and not having to impersonate Tina any longer—or, as she herself put it, to play that role in a small movie onstage almost every night. Then again, another part of her had already become Tina permanently, and that's the part that would always naturally prevail, as we'd all witness soon enough over and over again—until it was over for good, until the encores ended.

Becoming the private person Anna Mae Bullock again naturally did not mean going home to Nutbush in the literal sense of course, though as I've suggested, since Nutbush has no city limits, she never really left it at all; rather, she brought it with her wherever she went. Meanwhile, in 2002, Tennessee State Route 19, that little escape route highway between Brownsville and Nutbush, was officially renamed "Tina Turner Highway," maybe just to inspire any other citizen with similarly big dreams to hit the road.

Other legacy honors would be quick to follow, among them her previously mentioned Kennedy Center Honor, at which her close friend Oprah Winfrey lauded her with this touching introduction: "We don't need another hero, but we do need more heroines like you, Tina. You make me proud to spell my name w-o-m-a-n!"

In 2007, she became involved with a Swiss-based nonprofit interfaith spiritual group called the Beyond Foundation, founded to support causes that unite cultures in the world through music in order to create mutual religious respect and spiritual understanding. Their mandate was to plant seeds for inspiring a compassionate world through projects, proposals, events, concerts, mentoring, and tools for personal growth. She continues to devote her time and energy today to this social and cultural cause that is so very close to her heart.

Also in 2007, *River: The Joni Letters*, an album by Herbie Hancock, appeared, featuring Turner along with Leonard Cohen, Norah Jones, Corinne Bailey Rae, Lucian Souza, and Joni Mitchell. Her vocal contribution was "Edith and the Kingpin," a song by Joni Mitchell from the folksinger's experimental album *The Hissing of Summer Lawns* (1975).

The year 2008 saw a Grammy Award for album of the year for *River: The Joni Letters*, with Tina happily sharing honors as a featured artist. And perhaps to no reader's surprise, given all the hints I've dropped about the déjà vu nature of her retirement, 2008 saw the incredible arrival of a special series of concerts: *Tina! The 50th Anniversary Tour*, a suitably bombastic and super-successful celebration that also, not surprisingly, was accompanied by an equally celebratory album, *Tina!*, a compilation record of past hits. This would descend on the world in October of that year to cement the legacy of the superstar's fifty incredible years in show business.

Its origins also owed much to yet more serendipity. This was eight years *after Twenty Four Seven*, her supposedly final album and last tour, and while happily "retired" from both recording and touring. By that time, she was even absent from much of a public life to speak of, at least by her former spotlit standards. I guess you could say that history had caught up with her, and friends and peers alike began to murmur about the fact that she'd been an entertainer for half a century, literally, since first joining Ike in St. Louis and then finally putting away her dancing shoes for a well-deserved period of reflection.

But that pause didn't last very long of course, and she soon enough announced yet another milestone tour, claiming that the inspiration to launch herself out on the road again came during a fashion show in Milan where she was seated next to Sophia Loren, another long-term goddess like herself. Apparently, Loren balked when Tina told her she was taking a break, declaring that break time was over because people wanted to see her—needed to see her. So it was time to go back to work at the only job she ever really had: making people smile. She called her agent then and there and declared that it was time to work again.

Originally conceived as *Tina Live in Concert*, she quickly decided, after the overwhelming response to her Grammy appearance, to use the event to commemorate the official history of her career, dating from her first official appearance at the Club Imperial with the Kings of Rhythm in 1958. She also said she wanted the tour, announced in May 2008, to kick off in Missouri since that was where it all began for her. Tickets sold out in a matter of minutes, and the show itself would be filmed for a DVD movie called *Tina Live*.

The stage show for *Tina Live* was a very elaborate one and comprised theatrical design elements from many of her earlier notable concerts. It commenced with "Steamy Windows" and ended with an encore finale of "Nutbush City Limits" (after "Proud Mary" had completed the full set list naturally). Critics and fans alike raved. The *Washington Post* judged her still a force to be reckoned with, and *Rolling Stone* called it slick and soulful but in the old-fashioned way: nice and rough.

Tom Horan of the *Sunday Telegraph* opined that "Turner showed why she is still considered a Goddess in Europe. If you have to say what the feeling is you're left with Turner, it's a feeling of triumph: I've come this far, I've done it, I'm still standing." Most important perhaps, Ian

Gittins of *The Guardian* pointed out that "crucially, her voice has not been in the least bit damaged by her long layoff," while *The Observer's* Euan Ferguson exuded, "It was a moment of perfect triumph: for the grit and the feathers of her voice, for its still being there and for her, not just still being alive, but for doing *this!*" To which he added a special caveat: "What's age got to do with it? Absolutely nothing."

But perhaps Jonathan Cohen of *Billboard* said what we all were imagining. "The point is this: this woman defies so much conventional wisdom that being in her presence for two-plus hours is a bit of a head trip!"

While in post-tour and album release mode "resting up" in 2009, the Beyond Foundation she had formed with like-minded spiritual friends released the first of several CDs, albums of interfaith music, chants, and songs featuring Turner; Dechen Shak-Dagsay, a Tibetan Buddhist; and Regula Curti, a Christian singer. Thus began Tina Turner's utterly surprising post-pop phase.

2010: *BEYOND: BUDDHIST AND CHRISTIAN PRAYERS*

Produced by the Beyond Foundation and featuring Tina Turner, Regula Curti, and Dechen Shak-Dagsay. Duration: 90:00. Based on interfaith contemplative and prayer practices and the mystical poetry of the Persian poet Rumi, it merged Tibetan Tara mantras and lyrics from the medieval abbess Hildegard of Bingen. All the founding members of the Beyond Foundation were inspired by attending a ceremony on interreligious dialogue hosted in 2005 by the Dalai Lama and Martin Werlen, head of the Benedictine monastery Einsiedeln Abbey in Einsiedeln, Switzerland.

2011: *BEYOND: CHILDREN/CHORAL* MEDITATIVE WORKS

The second music release of the Beyond Foundation features the founders with more than thirty children from different cultures across the globe. Duration: 60:00.

2014: *BEYOND: LOVE WITHIN/BUDDHIST, CHRISTIAN, AND HINDU PRAYERS*

The Beyond Foundation's third release added an additional singer, Sawani Shende-Sathaye, and expanded their shared repertoire to include Hindu chants and songs. Their music "invites listeners to go beyond hatred, fear and revenge, singing takes you beyond . . . underneath the negative emotions you find yourself in a field where love and peace prevails." Duration: 60:00.

2017: *BEYOND: AWAKENING*

Produced and composed by Kareem Roustom (iGroove). The fourth album in the series from Tina's Beyond Foundation includes six different singers from six cultures. Featuring lyrics, prayers, and lullabies sung by Rugula Curti (Switzerland), Ani Choying (Nepal), Dimi Orsho (Syria, United States), Sawani Shende Sathaye (India), and More Karbasi (Israel). Turner narrates the spiritual message of unity. The sound track was performed by the London Philharmonic Orchestra and recorded at the historic Abbey Road Studios. Duration: 140:00.

Not exactly your average pop rock superstar's retirement life, is it?

Sometimes, dealing with someone as uniquely changeable as Tina Turner can feel like what the poet Richard Brautigan once cryptically described as "loading mercury with a pitchfork." Madame Mercury has said, "She's not only different from so many other artists of her era(s), she's also different from herself at various stages of her own career, and is constantly morphing into her next slippery incarnation."

Readers occasionally inquire as to how I have engaged with so many distinctly different and diverse female singers and songwriters, artists who, on the surface at least, may not appear to have that much in common. A good question—and one I often ask myself as well. Having written books about Amy Winehouse, Sharon Jones, and Tina Turner as well as chapters in my other books on Marianne Faithfull, Stevie Nicks, and Joni Mitchell, it occurs to me that they all *do* have something very strongly in common.

However, it might be something perhaps subterranean but shared in all their characters and in their work. For one thing, they all strike me as being powerful *empaths*: creatures who are able to perceive emotions at an intense level: to receive and transmit feelings through their own personas and to project them back outward to the world at large. In a very real sense, because of this shared trait, they also seem to be able to *channel* deeply universal feelings, so deep that we often believe they are speaking directly to or about *us*, almost as if they were mediums—because that's what they are.

Such a power also renders the empath quite fragile and vulnerable in a way despite their outward appearance of invincibility. And yes, Tina Turner, despite her obvious ferocity as a survivor, is just as fragile and vulnerable at a personal level as most other empaths. She just manages to either navigate or compensate through that fragility, to rise above it time and time again, to give voice to all the rest of us who feel either fragile or even wounded. By doing so, her music became a kind of remedial elixir, both for her and for all of us.

✿   ✿   ✿

As always, Tina Turner's professional and personal life were both an embarrassment of triumphant riches and a painful cauldron of mixed blessings: in January 2018, it was announced that Turner would receive a Grammy Lifetime Achievement Award, and in October of the same year the musical *Tina* opened to positive responses in England, followed the next year by the bright lights of Broadway, where the lamb lies down. Yet nothing ever seemed to come nice and easy to her, that's for sure, whether blessings or struggles: also in July 2018, her first son, Craig (fathered by her boyfriend Raymond Hill but later adopted by Ike Turner), was found dead by suicide from a self-inflicted gunshot wound.

But just as she had faced her own debilitating illness with flair and aplomb, she also faced the tragedy of losing her son with the same kind of grace. Just as Turner had refused to be depressed after getting up from her hospital bed and falling flat on her face to the floor and instead decided she would somehow fix her situation, she faced the loss of Craig in a similar deeply philosophical manner. In a lifetime of chronic violence and chaos, which she had long ago accepted as her karma in this life but not necessarily her life story, she made it an act of sheer will to finish her narrative on her own terms. This included wondering if something in her son's own life, that life of chaos they both shared with her first husband, had followed him like shadow, weighing on him until he just couldn't handle it anymore.

She even bravely decided that her son was now probably in a better place, a good place, a place where he was meant to be. And in keeping with the volatile energy and spirit that had guided her to where she was, and even then, despite all her health and wellness challenges of late, so was Tina Turner. Despite all that she's been through in a life full of ups and downs and ups, she still believes fervently that she's exactly in the place she's meant to be.

Sounds like a rare kind of equanimity and unique contentment. But imagine the paradox. She has accepted both the fact of her great achievements and that of own mortality, accepting even her own son's prior departure and that she herself has fewer days ahead than the ones behind. And yet then, a full fifty-three years after she first famously sang Phil Spector's rather strange song about a little rag doll, while sitting by her placid Lake Zurich, she heard it sung again on the radio in February 2018 in a new single release by Adrienne Warren from the cast album of the musical extravaganza based on her extraordinary life.

And suddenly it all came flooding back again back into her present, as if caught in a time warp. All or many of her dreams have already come true, even if it was a long, slow journey to fulfillment, yet she still had to relive many of the more difficult passages of her story when it was performed on Broadway in late 2019, and so, yes, it's déjà vu all over again. But it must have felt like *jamais vu* ("never seen") instead. The two key dreams she had—being recognized as the true talent behind the Ike and Tina Turner Revue that was launched so boisterously in 1960 and finding her true love with a kind and generous partner in Erwin Bach—came true.

Yet the funny thing about dreamers is that they don't stop dreaming; for them, it's as natural as breathing. And I'm reminded of the phrase used by the great American poet Delmore Schwartz as one of his titles: in dreams begin responsibilities. That's what Tina Turner has been able to remind all of us by her contributions to our collective dream: that what we can dream and that we also have a responsibility to make happen—that to gamble with life is to give it value and that even if the true meaning of life is that it ends and is found in its impermanence, the true purpose of life is somehow to make that very impermanence itself meaningful.

So even Turner herself seemed to accept the need for her culture to celebrate her once again in a live musical biography with the same equanimity and contentment she accepted in the rest of her saga. Okay, if you say so, fine with me because all of us are, in a way, now admiring her saga together and sharing our collective love for an iconic woman. Altering those Spector lyrics only slightly, we're able to say, "Our love has grown, and it gets stronger in every way, and it gets deeper, and it gets higher, day by day."

Yet still, it must be strange for her hearing "River Deep, Mountain High" again, ringing from the rafters of a Broadway theater, with another young singer, Adrienne Warren, attempting to channel her own inner Tina in order to do that majestic song proper justice. By all accounts, Turner was pleased with the theatrical results, as reported by the editors of *Qweerist*: "Tali Pelman, Producer of *Tina: The Musical* commented that 'River Deep, Mountain High' is a pivotal moment in our show. It demands not only an extraordinary talent but also an immense passion and fearlessness."

Speaking to them about that significant 1966 track, Tina Turner said, "At that very difficult time in my life, recording this song opened my eyes to many possibilities. I felt liberated, excited, ready to challenge myself vocally. It introduced me to the way I wanted to really sing. I am thrilled that Adrienne has picked up the mantle and not only risen to the challenge but also made this moment one of my favorites in the musical. It is just so right that this is the first single to be released from our new cast album."

As usual, Turner was being inordinately kind and generous since the Warren version, as earnest and genuinely evocative as it is, doesn't even approximate the power of the original—and for one ironic reason: Warren has a polished and normal-sounding voice. As usual, it's barely even possible to find the right words to describe the dry, gritty howl that came out of Tina's quivering mouth fifty-three years ago. But still, the musical was definitely a final and lasting tribute to a force of nature, a legacy of sheer love.

Directed by Phyllida Lloyd, written by Katroi Hall with Frank Kete-
laar and Kees Prins, it was choreographed by Anthony van Laast, with
set and costume design by Mark Thompson and musical supervision by
Nicholas Skilbeck, lighting by Bruno Poet, sound by Nevin Steinberg,
projection by Jeff Sugg, and orchestrations by Ethan Popp. The cast
album of the show was released in October 2019 by Ghostlight Records.

As the Tony-nominated (for *Shuffle Along* and *Bring It On*) lead actress Adrienne Warren told Greg Evans of *Deadline*, "Working on this
show has been a life-changing experience for me. Tina's unshakeable
courage, grace and determination have been a constant inspiration, and
I am honored to have had the opportunity to be part of telling her story.
This show is a dream come true." So, we have another young dreamer
who fits the overall vibe of our Tina narrative rather well. P.S.: She's also
got the legs for the job!

Michael Billington's April 2018 *Guardian* piece also captures some
of Tina's tumult nicely, calling it a whirlwind Turner tribute that leaves
you breathless in a heady celebration of triumph over adversity with an
astonishing turn by the young singer. Especially impressive is the fact
that the show rests entirely on the shoulders of Warren, who is rarely
offstage and is simply astonishing. "Above all, she captures the fact
that there is not one but several Tina Turners, how she develops and
changes, and how, in moving to rock stardom, she retains her ferocious
energy while introducing occasional notes of pungent melancholy. Warren conveys Tina's growth from stoic victim into a woman of defiant
confidence. As bio-musicals go, this is as good as it gets."

Indeed, Tina Turner's own famous brand of optimistic hopefulness
is also as good as it gets. But her characteristic optimism still had an
occasional shaky side, as she shared with such frankness in *My Love
Story*, admitting that she sometimes felt that death was tapping her on
the shoulder and announcing its arrival. And the flip side of that eerie
sensation of course is the ability, maybe learned over the course of a rich
and fruitful life, to look at everything through the lens of mortality. She's
able to skillfully reflect on the past, gratefully think about what it means
to be in the present, and wonder hopefully about the future.

Yet despite that profound sense of awareness that life is not only
temporary and impermanent but also shockingly fleeting, whenever she

is asked (as she often is) if there was anything more in life that she still wanted, she always confirms what we always suspected: that she has everything. She sits by Lake Zurich in her dream home with her dream husband and can't help but let serenity be the rule of the day. Yes, she's had a very hard life, but at no time during her long and rich life did she ever put the blame on anything or anyone. She has enough compassion it seems, and maybe that's the Buddhist core she upholds, to live her life on her own terms. She got through it all. And she is obviously a very content human being.

Having accomplished absolutely everything she set out to do in her life, she certainly has earned the right to want to do absolutely nothing, which makes her autumn encounter with *New York Times* reporter Amanda Hess all the more charming. In her profile piece, Hess characterized Turner's current status as "Tina Turner is Having the Time of her Life: a Swiss chateau, a Broadway musical all about her, and absolutely nothing she has to do." A big portion of the charming part was the metal plaque on the gate to Turner's estate that says, "Vor 12.00 Uhr nicht lauten, keine Lieferungen," which Hess interpreted as "Do not even think about bothering Tina Turner before noon." One detects the watchful tone of her German hubby Erwin Bach in that gentle admonition.

Hess captured the moment very accurately. "She was the symbol of rock and roll stamina for 50 years. She became a star with Ike Tuner in her 20's, escaped his abuse in her 30's, fought her way up the pop charts in her 40's, toured the world through her 60's, and now she would like to sleep in late." That's her legacy in a nutshell right there. Having been retired for ten years, she is, as Hess put it, "basking in all of the nothing she has to do."

Yes, Turner is relishing her well-earned retirement, declaring that she was simply just tired of singing and making everyone else happy, which is exactly all she's done in her entire life. But though she may not be singing much these days, there's still a whole squad of Tinas performing around the world on her behalf. The *Tina Turner Musical* brought a Tina to London, a Tina to Hamburg, and another Tina to Broadway. And when asked if it was strange watching all these other women pretending to be her, her response was that she had spent her whole career watching other women pretend to be her. In fact, when she would audition girls to be in the Revue as Ikettes a lifetime ago, she would often observe of this or that anxious hopeful that *she'd make a good Tina*.

Ironically, in fact, Hess remarked that when Turner got tired of talking about herself, something she's also spent a lifetime doing, the journalist left her for a while, and when she returned the following afternoon, she found the star transformed: wig styled, lips painted red, eyes sparkling. "That was Anna Mae yesterday," she told Hess. "Here's Tina today." She also surprised Hess by expressing the fact that after being a symbol of so many things—sex appeal, resilience, and empowerment—the idea of connecting her life to the feminist movement or recasting it through the current MeToo activism feels somewhat alien to her. She identified only with her own life since while everyone else was busy making her into a symbol, she was just busy living it. But still, she's got legacy written all over her.

Somewhere along the line, Anna Mae Bullock seemed to have figured out something that the playwright G. B. Shaw once characterized in the most salient way possible: "Life is not about finding yourself, it's not about finding anything at all, it's only about creating yourself." She'd been doing that right from the beginning, and she has succeeded in her chosen life by continuing to create and re-create Tina Turner. And even after all her ups and downs and ups, she also finally created a truly happy version of Anna Mae Bullock.

DISCOGRAPHY

IKE AND TINA TURNER'S SIXTEEN-YEAR RECORDING CAREER TOGETHER

1961

The Soul of Ike and Tina Turner (Sue Records) Produced by Ike Turner

1962

Dance with Ike and Tina Turner's Kings of Rhythm (Sue Records) Produced by Ike Turner

1963

Dynamite! (Sue Records) Produced by Ike Turner

It's Gonna Work Out Fine (Sue Records) Produced by Ike Turner

Don't Play Me Cheap (Sue Records) Produced by Ike Turner

1964

Live: Ike and Tina Turner Revue Live (Kent Records) Produced by Ike Turner

Live: Ike and Tina Turner Show Vol 2 (Loma Records) Produced by Ike Turner

Get It! (Cenco Records) Produced by Ike Turner

1965

Live: The Ike and Tina Turner Show Vol. 2 (Warner Bros. Records) Produced by Ike Turner

Ike and Tina Turner Greatest Hits (Sue Records) Produced by Ike Turner

1966

River Deep, Mountain High (A&M Records) Produced by Phil Spector and Ike Turner

The Soul of Ike and Tina Turner (Kent Records) Produced by Ike Turner

1967

Festival of Live Performances (Kent Records) Produced by Ike Turner

1968

Ike and Tina Turner (London Records) Produced by Ike Turner

So Fine (Pompeii Records) Produced by Ike Tuner

1969

Cussin', Cryin' and Carryin' On (Pompeii Records) Produced by Ike Turner

Get It Get It (Cenco Records) Produced by Ike Turner

Her Man, His Woman (Capitol Records) Produced by Ike Turner

Outta Season (Blue Thumb Records) Produced by Ike Turner

Ike and Tina Turner and the Ikettes—In Person (Minit Records) Produced by Ike Turner

The Fantastic Ike and Tina Turner (Sunset Records) Produced by Ike Turner

Get It Together (Pompeii Records) Produced by Ike Turner

The Hunter (Blue Thumb Records) Produced by Bob Krasnow

1970

Come Together (Liberty Records) Produced by Ike Turner

Live: On Stage in Paris (Liberty Records) Produced by Ike Turner

1971

Workin' Together (Liberty Records) Produced by Ike Turner

Live at Carnegie Hall: What You Hear Is What You Get (United Artists Records) Produced by Ike Turner

Live: Something's Gotta Hold on Me (Harmony Records) Produced by Ike Turner

1972

Nuff Said (United Artists Records) Produced by Ike Turner

Feel Good (United Artists Records) Produced by Ike Turner

1973

Nutbush City Limits (United Artists Records) Produced by Ike Turner

Live: The World of Ike and Tina Turner (United Artists Records) Produced by Ike Turner

Let Me Touch Your Mind (United Artists Records) Produced by Ike Turner

Ike and Tina Turner's Greatest Hits (United Artists Records) Produced by Ike Turner

The Best of Ike and Tina Turner (Blue Thumb Records) Produced by Ike Turner

1974

Strange Fruit: Featuring The Family Vibe (United Artists Records) Produced by Ike Turner

Sweet Rhode Island Red (United Artists Records) Produced by Ike Turner

The Gospel according to Ike and Tina Turner (United Artists Records) Produced by Ike Turner

1977

Delilah's Power (United Artists Records) Produced by Ike Turner

1978

Airwaves (United Artists/Capitol Records) Produced by Ike Turner

1979

Soul Sellers (United Artists Records) Produced by Ike Tuner

Mississippi Rolling Stone (Spartan Records) Produced by Ike Turner

1980

The Edge (Fantasy Records) Produced by Ike Turner

TINA TURNER'S SOLO ALBUMS

1974

Tina Turns the Country On! (United Artists Records) Produced by Tom Thacker

1975

Acid Queen (United Artists Records) Produced by Denny Diante, Spencer Proffer

1978

Rough (United Artists Records) Produced by Bob Monaco

1979

Love Explosion (Liberty Records) Produced by Alec Constandinos

1984

Private Dancer (Capitol Records) Produced by Rupert Hine, Terry Britten, John Carter, Martin Ware, Greg Walsh, Joe Sample, Wilton Felder, Ndugu Chancler

1986
> *Break Every Rule* (Capitol Records) Produced by Terry Britten, Bryan Adams, Bob Clearmountain, Rupert Hine, Mark Knopfler, Neil Dorfsman

1988
> *Tina Live in Europe* (EMI/Capitol Records) Produced by John Hudson, Terry Britten

1989
> *Foreign Affair* (EMI/Capitol Records) Produced by Dan Hartman, Tina Turner, Rupert Hine, Roger Davies, Graham Lyle, Albert Hammond, Tony Joe White

1991
> *Simply the Best* (EMI/Capitol Records) Various producers

1993
> *What's Love Got to Do with It?* (Virgin Records) Produced by Chris Lord, Rupert Hine, Bryan Adams, Terry Britten, Robert "Mutt" Lange

1994
> *Tina Turner, Collected Works Box* (EMI/Capitol Records) Various producers

1996
> *Wildest Dreams* (Virgin Records) Produced by Trevor Horn, Terry Britten, Chris Porter

1999
> *Twenty Four Seven* (Virgin Records) Produced by Johnny Douglas, Terry Britten, Brian Rawling, Mark Taylor

SOUND TRACK RECORDINGS

1985
> *Mad Max Beyond Thunderdome* (Capitol Records)

1993
> *What's Love Got to Do with It?* (Virgin Parlophone)

LIVE ALBUMS

1999
> *Divas Live '99* (VH1)

2009

Tina Live (Parlophone Records)

SPIRITUAL ALBUMS

2010

Beyond: Buddhist and Christian Prayers (Beyond Foundation Records)

2011

Beyond: Children (choral works, Beyond Foundation Records)

2014

Beyond: Love Within (Buddhist, Christian, and Hindu prayers, Beyond Foundation Records)

2017

Beyond: Awakening (vocals/London Philharmonic, iGroove Records)

THEATER

2019

Tina: The Musical: Live Broadway Cast Recording (Ghostlight Records)

BIBLIOGRAPHY

Agee, Phil, *Tina Pie*, Yale University, 1968

Ali, Loraine, Ike's Peak, *GQ*, June 2001

Ann-Margaret, My Story, *Putnam's*, 1994

Arrington, Carl, Tina Turner Interview, *Us*, November 13, 1989

Barker/Schremp, *St. Louis Post-Dispatch*, 2019

Bego, Mark, *Break Every Rule*, Taylor Trade, 2005

Billington, Michael, *The Guardian*, April 2018

Brooks, Daphne, *The Guardian*, March 2018

Cohen, Aaron, *Move On Up*, University of Chicago Press, 2019

Cohen, Jonathan, *Billboard*, 2008

Collins, Nancy, The Queen, *Rolling Stone*, October 23, 1986

Daily Herald staff reporters, Hometown Remains the Same, March 8, 2015

Dimery, Robert, editor, 1001 Albums to Hear before You Die, Universe Publishing, 2005.

Dougherty, Steve, Soul Star on Ice, *People*, September 30, 1990

Elliott, Paul, Review, *Q*, 1997

Evans, Greg, Broadway Finds Its Tina Turner, IMDb, February 5, 2019

Ferguson, Euan, *The Observer*, 2008

Fong-Torres, Ben, Ike and Tina Turner, *Rolling Stone*, October 1971

Fox, Ted, *Showtime at the Apollo*, Da Capo, 1993

Gaar, Gillian, *She's a Rebel: History of Women in Rock and Roll*, Seal Press, 1992

Gardner, Elysa, *Rolling Stone*, 1998

Harper's, Twenty Four Seven, 1997

Hasted, Nick, Story behind the Song, *Classic Rock*, February 9, 2018

Hess, Amanda, *New York Times*, September 9, 2019

Hirshey, Gerri, *Nowhere to Run: The Story of Soul Music*, DaCapo Press, 1994 / Women in Rock, *Rolling Stone*, November 1997 / Woman Warrior, *GQ*, 1993

Hollywood Reporter, December 2000

Horan, Tom, *Sunday Telegraph*, 2008

Hughes, Charles, *Country Soul: Making Music and Making Race*, University of North Carolina Press, 2017

Irwin, Colin, *The Mojo Collection*, Canongate, 2000

Jet, 1984, 1997

Johnson, Brian, Comeback Queen, *Maclean's*, 1985

Kempley, Rita, *Washington Post*, June 1993

King, Gayle, *CBS Sunday Morning*, October 14, 2018

Kirschling, Gregory, *Entertainment Weekly*, 2003

Kureshi, Hanif, *The Faber Book of Pop*, Faber, 1995

Lee, Minerva, www.lotus-happiness.com, 2018

Levin, Matthew, *TransLove Airways* podcast, 2019

Loder, Kurt, Heroes of Thunderdome, *Rolling Stone*, August 29, 1985

Maultsby, Portia, *African American Music*, Routledge, 2005

McGuigan, Cathleen, Rock's New Women, *Newsweek*, March 4, 1985

Memphis Music Recording Service, www.706unionavenue.nl

Miller, Debbie, Tina Turner Returns, *Rolling Stone*, August 1984

Miserandino, Dominick, Ike Turner, Hall of Famer, *Celebrity Café*, 2000

Moore, Lucinda, *Smithsonian*, November 2010

Mower, Sarah, Private Tina, *Harper's Bazaar*, December 1996

Norment, Lynn, Sizzling at 45, *Ebony*, May 1985

O'Brien, Lucy, *She-Bop: Women in Rock Pop and Soul*, Penguin, 1995

O'Dair, Barbara, *Trouble-Girls: Rolling Stone Book of Women in Rock*, Random House, 1997

Orth, Maureen, Tina, *Vogue*, 1985 / *Vanity Fair*, 1993

Palmer, Robert, *Rock Begins*, Rolling Stone Press, 1976

Palmer, Robert, *Church of the Sonic Guitar*, Duke University Press, 1997

Porter, James, *Wild in the Streets: Tales from Rock and Roll's Negro Leagues*, forthcoming from Northwestern University Press

Qweerist.com, March 2019

Ribowsky, Mark, *He's a Rebel: Rock n Roll's Legendary Producer*, Cooper Square Press, 1989

Seabrook, John, *Inside the Song-Machine: Inside the Hit Factory*, Norton, 2015

Sigerson, Davitt, Tine Repeats, *Rolling Stone*, November 1986

Smith, Joe, *Off the Record*, Warner Books, 1988

Smith, Suzanne, *Dancing in the Street*, Harvard University Press, 2001

Stevenson, Jane, Tina Turns It On, *Toronto Sun*, January 2000

Stras, Laurie, *She's So Fine: Reflections on Femininity and Class in 1960's Music*, Ashgate, 2010

The Independent, Merchant Ivory, 2004

Time, 1975

Turner, Tina (with Kurt Loder), *I Tina*, William Morrow, 1986

Turner, Tina (with Deborah Davis and Dominick Wichmann), *My Love Story*, Simon and Schuster, 2018.

Udovitch, Mimi, Hardest Working Legs, *Rolling Stone*, December 2000

Us, Twenty Four Seven, March 2000

Van Biema, David, *People*, 1984

Wallace, David, Tina Turner, Success Story, *McCall's*, 1985

Wendeler, Robert, Tina Turner New Acid Queen, *People*, May 5, 1975

Wenner, Jan, *Rolling Stone*, 1967/1997

Whitburn, Joel, Billboard *Top 40 Albums*, Record Research Inc., 1995

Wild, David, *Rolling Stone*, 2008

Winfrey, Oprah, *O, The Oprah Magazine*, November 2018

INDEX